Parsi Food & Customs

The Essential Parsi Cookbook

Bhicoo J. Manekshaw

Illustrations by
Bindia Thapar

PENGUIN BOOKS

An imprint of Penguin Random House

PENGUIN BOOKS

USA | Canada | UK | Ireland | Australia
New Zealand | India | South Africa | China | Singapore

Penguin Books is part of the Penguin Random House group of companies
whose addresses can be found at global.penguinrandomhouse.com

Published by Penguin Random House India Pvt. Ltd
4th Floor, Capital Tower 1, MG Road,
Gurugram 122 002, Haryana, India

Penguin
Random House
India

First published by Penguin Books India 1996

13 12 11 10 9 8 7

ISBN 9780140257595

Typeset in New Baskerville by Digital Technologies and Printing Solutions,
NewDelhi

Printed at Manipal Technologies Limited, India

www.penguin.co.in

FSC
www.fsc.org

MIX
Paper | Supporting
responsible forestry
FSC® C043100

This is a legitimate digitally printed version of the book and therefore might not
have certain extra finishing on the cover.

PENGUIN BOOKS
PARSI FOOD & CUSTOMS

Born in 1922, Bhicoo Manekshaw grew up in Mumbai. Her fondness for good food and cooking began at the early age of five, in her grandmother's kitchen.

In 1963, she became the first Indian to gain admission to the Advanced Course at the famed Cordon Bleu School of Cookery in London.

In a long career as expert chef and catering consultant, she has worked with the Taj Mahal Hotel, Mumbai and with the Spencer Group of Hotels, the India International Centre in Delhi and the Delhi Golf Club. She was also the catering consultant at Raj Bhavan in Bangalore during the tenure of Governor Dharma Vira.

For over a decade, she worked with Chef Air and Air India, where she was responsible for catering for all VIP flights, including those during the NAM and CHOGM conferences.

Bhicoo Manekshaw has also taught at the Delhi Polytechnic for Women and given numerous demonstrations of Indian and Continental cuisine in India and abroad.

She is the author of *Traditional Recipes of India* and has contributed recipes and articles to several books and magazines.

Bhicoo Manekshaw lives in New Delhi with her little dachshund, Oscar and works for the famous restaurant, *Basil & Thyme*.

Praise for Bhicoo J. Manekshaw

'Each page is a delight, full of information and unfussy writing . . . this book will be especially helpful to the modern generation who are invariably at a loss as to what exactly should be done for each ritual, occasion and ceremony.' —*Hamazor*

'The book market may be flooded with titles on cookery and even customs, but none can hold a spittering candle to Bhicoo's intelligent, eminently readable and thoroughly entertaining *The Essential Parsi Cookbook*.' —*Sunday*

'For those of you who're fans of Godiwala's wedding and Navjot dinners, *The Essential Parsi Cookbook* goes to and beyond the dinner table of a gentle and much-loved community.' —*Epicure*

To Indira Gandhi
who loved Parsi cuisine
and
to my community

I am proud of my country India, for having produced the splendid Zoroastrian stock, in numbers beneath contempt, but in charity and philanthropy perhaps unequalled, certainly unsurpassed.

Mahatma Gandhi

Contents

Acknowledgements		ix
CUSTOMS AND RELIGION		1
From the Land of Airyana Vaejah		3
1.	Torans and Chalk	15
2.	A Birth in the Family	28
3.	The Navjote	36
4.	Lagan	43
5.	Journey's End	64
6.	Navroz	79
7.	Jashan, Ghambars and Faresta	83
RECIPES		87
Prelude to the Recipes		89
8.	Pots and Pans	104
9.	Beverages	110
10.	Eggs	121
11.	Vegetables	150
12.	Fish	184
13.	Meat and Poultry	219

14. Lentils   269
15. Rice   286
16. Breads   301
17. Tea-time Snacks   309
18. Sweets   340
19. Achars, Chutneys, Murumbas   367
20. Kitchen Medicine   393
21. Chalo Jamva Avoji   398

Glossary   403
Index   413
List of References   435

Acknowledgements

I owe a deep debt to Vada Dasturji Meherji Rana K. Dastur for the support he has given me throughout the preparation of this book.

To Mehroo Meherji Rana K. Dastur I owe special thanks for her help in getting me the recipes from Navsari.

Among others who helped me in the preparation of this book I owe a great debt to:

Dr Vijay Pillai, a gourmand in his own right, for going through the present manuscript.

Eric Gonsalves and Premila Ghosh for going through the first manuscript, thus making the writing of this one easier.

Jer Kutar, Nellie Wadia and Dhun Bagli who have given unflinchingly of their help and advice.

My elder son-in-law Keki Wadia, who never once complained that his wife was never in the house, but out typing recipes.

My younger son-in-law Sunil Chandra, who has spared his computer at all times to get the manuscript typed.

My publishers David Davidar and especially Renuka Chatterjee who have been nothing but patience and encouragement and extremely helpful throughout.

K.K. Laskar for his photograph on the cover.

Bindia Thapar who has made the book come alive with her excellent sketches.

Ratty Kapadia and Mahaparvez Dhatigara who accompanied me to Gujarat, for their moral support.

Anand Bhardwaj who made our stay in Gujarat so comfortable.

The President Dr Sam Bhacca and members of the Parsi Panchayat, Surat.

The President Dara K. Deboo and members of the Parsi Panchayat, Navsari.

The late President Erach M. Kapadia, members of the Parsi Panchayat Bharuch and Mr and Mrs Khushru Cama.

Keki P. Shroff ad Mrs Aloo R. Shroff for all their kindness and help while in Valsad.

My husband Jimmy for his patience and acceptance of the long hours I spent at work instead of with him.

Last but by no means least I owe a deep and somehow a very proud debt, and something more than gratitude to my daughter Sherna Wadia, who has helped me in every way to complete this manuscript. She has brought some form and discipline into it and it would not have been possible to prepare this book without her help.

Customs and Religion

From the Land of Airyana Vaejah

The history of the Parsis goes back to the dawn of civilization. The followers of Zarathushtra, they claim Airyana Vaejah (the cradle of the Aryans) as their first primitive home.

Fire, their sacred symbol, was discovered by one of their earliest known kings, Haoshyangha of the Pishdadian period.

During the reign of King Yima or Jamshed, the population of this community had increased to such an extent that they began to migrate. They moved southwards, towards the sun, and eventually settled in the land they called Iran, after Airyana.

It is said that King Yima selected the vernal equinox as the beginning of the New Year. This day, 21 March, is called Navroz (new day) and is celebrated not only by the Parsi and Iranian Zoroastrians, but by the Muslims of Iran and Afghanistan and also the Kashmiris, irrespective of religion.

Tradition also points to King Yima as the discoverer of wine, liquor and hoama, corresponding to soama of the Vedic Aryans. It is difficult to say when the final split into two groups took place—those who settled in Iran and those who migrated to India. Common references from Iranian and Indian books suggest Afghanistan as the probable last stage of the southern journey when the Aryans camped together. The Iranian group established itself in Bactria and watched their kinsmen leave them, migrating further south until they disappeared beyond the mighty mountains of the Hindu Kush.

Next came the Kianian period which gave us Sam, Rustam and Sohrab immortalized by Firdausi in the *Shah Namah*. It also gave us Zarathushtra, the first prophet who taught of one God. It was he who converted Vishtaspa, the king of Bactria, and Zoroastrianism became the official religion of Iran.

Bactria became the seat of power during this period and Iranian influence—Avestan literature, art, architecture, dress and the calendar, spread to adjoining lands.

The Median period followed and lasted for about 150 years. The Medes were of Aryan descent. They came from the north-west and travelled southwards until they reached Iran.

Next came the famous Achaemenian period of Cyrus the Great and Darius. They came from the province of Pars (Perse or Persepolis in Greek). The empire stretched from the Aegean Sea to the Punjab and from the Black Sea to Egypt. The magnificent city of Persepolis famed for its library was built during this period.

Philosophers from all over the world visited Iran and it became the meeting point of East and West. The Iranian influence in thought, culture and literature was felt all over the then civilized world, and Zoroastrianism has enriched and influenced the great religions of Judaism, Christianity and Islam.

Food habits such as the use of rose essence and nuts, preparation of preserved fruits, dolmas, grilled food and sweets like baklava spread far and wide.

It was at Persepolis that Alexander of Macedonia completed his conquest of Persia and the Achaemenian

Aferghaniyu

Empire came to an end. The city was looted and vandalized and a heritage of beauty and culture was destroyed. Even the library, with its priceless storehouse of knowledge on subjects such as art, science, astrology, medicine and religion, was not spared. It is said that Alexander was beseeched not to destroy this magnificent treasure which had now become his property, but to no avail.

Alexander's successors could not hold on to Iran for long, nor could they Hellenize it. The Parthians soon overran the country. They came from the north-east, from near the Caspian Sea, and were influenced by Iranian culture and religion. The Iranians were allowed to lead their lives without interference, and not very much is known of this period.

With the Sassanian dynasty (founded by Artakshir

Papakan) came the rebirth of the Zoroastrian religion. The empire brought us the great names of Khusru, Parviz, Ardeshir, Noshirvan, Behram and Shapur. There was a gradual change in language from the Avestan and old Persian of the Kianians and Achaemenians to Pahlavi. There was greater sophistication in food with different flavours coming in from all over the empire. In time, with prosperity, decadence set in. The Arab hordes, with their zeal and vigour had no trouble overrunning Iran and the end came at the battle of Nahavand in 642 A.D.

In reality, Iran has remained Iran, except for the change in religion. Just like our own great country, India, Iran too has had many conquests, but the spirit of the people and their way of life absorbed all, and their own culture lives on.

When the Islamic wave spread to Iran many fled the religious persecutions that followed. Rather than accept conversion, they left their homes and went to the mountains of Khorasan where they stayed until the persecutions followed them. They then fled to the island of Ormuz and set sail for India, where they first landed at Diu and later decided to sail to the western coast of India.

It is said that a storm arose and drove them to Sanjan in Gujarat. Three elderly dasturs (priests) were sent to approach Jaidi Rana, the ruler of Sanjan. When he saw these tall, fair, well built men, the Rana tried to turn them away. Using typical inborn Indian politeness, he did not do so directly, but showed them a bowl full to the brim with milk to indicate that there was no space in the land. The senior dastur is said to have sprinkled some sugar into the milk and replied that the milk had been sweetened, but it had not overflowed! Thus the Parsis were allowed to land and practice their religion on certain conditions. For instance the women had to wear saris; the men could not bear arms; they should speak the local language, Gujarati; marriages should take place after sunset, which is still being done (but the author, a rebel, got married in the morning when the sun is at its most beneficial—between 10 a.m. and 11 a.m.)

The Parsis accepted all the conditions and were given land where they lived undisturbed. They later migrated to other places like Navsari, Udvada, Bharuch, Valsad, Tarapore, and Billimora, and later still to Surat and Bombay, to trade with the British.

This minuscule community has contributed tremendously to the development of the country and many of the great names in industry, commerce, law, medicine and the arts are Parsi.

The Zoroastrian religion is a 'happy' religion, believing in good living, hard work, enjoyment of life and charity—irrespective of race or creed. Its motto is humata, hukhta, havarshta (good thoughts, good words and good deeds). Sacrifices and martyrdom are discouraged. Priests and laity are encouraged to marry and have children and the childless are encouraged to adopt. There is no pressure to do tapas or distance oneself from family and life. In fact life is to be lived to the full—enjoying the good things, fighting wrongs, and overcoming temptations and hardships.

There are very few food taboos, and those that exist are more for health reasons. There are four days of parhezi (abstinence) in the month, when Parsis are expected to abstain from meat—Bahman, Mohar, Ghosh and Ram roj. Meat is not to be eaten during the eleventh month of the year, presumably because this is the lambing season and Bahman is the protector of cattle. However, fish and eggs are permitted on such days, and some, like my mother consider birds (pankheru) acceptable on parhezi. As I was told, a chicken is not a four-footed animal! Meat is also not eaten for three days after the death of a near one, as bereavement affects the digestion. The period of abstinence is broken on the fourth day with dhan sakh which is why this dish is never prepared on an auspicious occasion.

The cockerel heralds the sun and is the bird sacred to

Sarosh, the guardian angel of all our urvan (souls), and is not knowingly eaten. As the cow is venerated in India many Parsis abstain from beef.

Wine and alcohol, drunk in moderation are acceptable, and were used to toast the king in ancient times. The exhilarating drink hoama made by pounding the twigs of the Ephedra plant and extracting the juice was a consecrated drink and used in the yasna ceremony. Wine was given to a woman after the birth of a stillborn child to give her strength. A kutli or small container of wine is a part of the satum and jashan ceremonies which will be described later.

During the 1300 years that the Parsis have lived in India, they have assimilated the various influences with which they have come into contact to develop their own distinctive cuisine. Parsi curry is a typical example of the combination of the influences of Iran (nuts), and Gujarat and Maharashtra (coconut and spices). Trade ties with the British introduced them to Western cuisine from which they have adopted many dishes and made them typically their own.

The coconut, fish and rice as symbols of plenty are taken from India and no Parsi feast is considered complete without these items. The pomegranate as a symbol of fertility (the fruit is likened to the womb of nature containing hundreds of seeds), and the date symbolizing the tree of life are remnants of the Iranian influence on Parsi ceremonies and eating habits. The pomegranate leaf is eaten by a person having the nahn or religious bath.

Parsis are basically meat eaters and no meal is complete without a meat, fish or chicken dish. Their food has no predominant flavour arising from the use of any specific oil or spice. Chillies and spices are used in moderation and the cuisine takes care to preserve the subtle flavours of the different dishes. Its distinctive taste has universal appeal.

The Iranian influence is seen in the meat and chicken dishes cooked with vegetables—potatoes, okra, spinach and green peas being the most popular; in the use of nuts and rose-water; and the preparation of pulao, biryani and Mughlai dishes.

Dhan sakh, the best known of Parsi dishes has probably evolved from the Iranian khoreste esfannaj, a dish cooked with meat, lentils and spinach. As tastes changed, spices were added to the dish to make dhan sakh what it is today. The flavour of rose-water in most Parsi sweets—ravo, sev, falooda, and in their murambas and sherbets, has its origin in Iran. The halvas and murambas made in India, the Middle East, Turkey and Greece have all been influenced by Iran.

The Parsi love for eggs has created many egg dishes which are unique to their cuisine. Most are cooked on precooked vegetables. When I was a novice cook, I gained admission to the prestigious Cordon Blue School of Cookery in London by demonstrating kera per eeda (eggs cooked on bananas)!

Many pickles and chutneys are adapted from the western coast of India. Exceptions which are typically Parsi are lagan nu achar, meva nu achar, gorkeri nu achar, gharab nu achar, bafenu, and the tomato and mango chutneys. The rotli and poori made from wheat flour, millet or milo are adapted from Gujarat, as also most of the tea-time snacks such as bhajias, patrel, the famous bhel poori, sev and choora. However dishes like bhakra (a type of doughnut), and sadhna (steamed rice pancakes), both made with toddy are typically Parsi. The dals and vegetable preparations are also Gujarati or Maharashtrian based.

Most fish dishes are typically Parsi, except perhaps for the masala ni tareli machhi. The famed patra ni machhi uses a delightful adaptation of the coconut chutney of this region. The sas ni machhi is the creation of the Parsi housewife—the origin is the bechemel sauce of the West. The different fish patias (thick sweet and sour curries) were created in the different regions and towns of Gujarat. The famous Tarapori patio made with sookha boomla (Bombay duck) is the speciality of the Parsis of Tarapore.

The quaint and pretty towns of Gujarat have given the world the most delectable dishes. The historic town of Bharuch, overlooking the Narmada estuary, has given us wonderful and distinctive sea food. Bhoojelo Bharuchi bhing made with the bhing fish (hilsa, palla or shad) caught in the estuary is a classic! Unfortunately, this prize dish has been forgotten or is not often made because of the little extra effort involved.

The city of Navsari is especially famous amongst the Parsis for its pickles, chutneys, murambas and vinegars.

Valsad is renowned for its masalas. The dhan sakh made by the Parsis of this town is unparalleled. I once visited Valsad with some friends. We had decided to find our roots and hunt out the original recipes of the Parsi towns of Gujarat. We were introduced to the brother of the president of the Parsi Anjuman. We asked him what the specialities of the town were and he promptly replied that they were Parsi curry and dhan sakh. Conversationally, I told him that I too had an excellent recipe for dhan sakh given to me by my mamaiji, and was taken aback when he replied that it must be rubbish. The situation was saved by his sister-in-law, who hastily explained the purpose of our visit. The gentleman relented and indeed proved to be a mine of information throughout our visit. When I did taste the dhan sakh, he was proved right. I had to admit that my grandmother's recipe was, if not rubbish, certainly a poor comparison.

The ancient city of Surat is famous for its textiles. Through the Parsis it has given the world the Surti ghat (a type of satin) and tanchoi (woven silk brocade), so called because it was brought to India by three (tan) brothers who learnt the art in China (choi). Foodwise, it is renowned for its different varieties of biscuits—Surti biscot, pur nee biscot (a biscuit like puff pastry—an influence of Iran), and buglu, which is so light that if it is put under a fan the top layers fly away! Buglu means cygnet in Gujarati, and the fine thin layers of the pastry are supposed to resemble the fine down of this bird. Today there is only one man left in Surat who makes this pastry and he will neither teach it to anyone nor part with the recipe! Malai na khaja, another delightful rich sweet is also made of puff pastry, using rice flour. It is filled with sweet cream, lightly flavoured with rose essence.

This city is also known for its Surti topli na paneer (light cream cheese made in baskets). No other cream cheese in the world, not even the Ricotta of Italy can compare with this cheese. I still recall the paneerwallas from my youth, coming down our road, bringing this manna from heaven in large mutkas (earthen pots), to sell to us, calling out *'Surti paneer! Khara mora paneer!'* (Cheese from Surat! Cheese with salt and without salt).

Another delightful street cry of my childhood was of the seller of the ice fruit of the tar palm—*'Targole, tazé, tazé targole.'* (Targole, fresh, fresh targole). The fruit is covered with a fine yellow skin which has to be carefully peeled before eating and it must be bitten carefully too, lest the delicious juice inside flows out. On the tree three of these fruit are contained in a small coconut like shell which is generally removed before they are sold. Targole, eaten chilled, is an experience not easily forgotten.

In the early and mid-twentieth century, most affluent Parsi homes had Goan cooks, butlers and ayahs. Goa fish curry was a household name, as the staff prepared it for themselves almost every day. The curry was eaten with ookra chaval (parboiled rice), sometimes with the addition of fried Bombay duck or bhangra. The food for the domestic staff would be ready by 11.30 a.m., so that they could come and eat as and when they found time. The ayahs would give the children little mouthfuls to taste and as this generation grew up, it developed a taste for this superlative curry. It has now become as much a part of

Parsi cuisine as it is of Goan cuisine.

The cuisine was further influenced by the British, when the Parsis came into contact with them. Slow assimilation of English dishes started taking place and the results were sas (sauce), custer (custard), estew (stew), and dhai and masala roasts (offshoot of the English roast beef).

Vivid Vani, a Parsi cookery book written in the early twentieth century by Mrs Meherbai Jamshedji Naswanji Wadia (the equivalent of Mrs Beeton of British cookery) has about 700 English recipes out of a total of 2050. It includes recipes for Tipsy cake, soups, fritters, puddings, ices, stews. Typically British puddings like bread and butter pudding, vermicelli pudding, blancmanges, and ice creams were prepared in my grandmother's days, and I remember custard apple fool—quite delicious, being one of my favourites.

Parsis celebrate all the festivals of India, the most popular being Diwali, Christmas and Id, with all the traditional food that goes with them.

When I was a child, my brothers and I had once gone to spend the Diwali holidays with my aunts in Pune. We all piled into the family Daimler and drove to the market to buy crackers and sweets. After buying out almost the entire cracker shop, my aunts went on a spree of ordering sweets that would last an ordinary household over a month. The mithaiwalla was a delightfully fat man with three layers of stomach. He sat cross-legged in a dhoti, amidst the gorgeous array of sweets, weighing and packing the sweets as they were being ordered from the car. When he appeared to have some difficulty cutting the chikat halva (sticky sweet), one of my aunts remarked that he needed a sharper knife The mithaiwalla said that he did not think it necessary, and to demonstrate the sharpness of the knife, lifted his arm and shaved off the hair from his armpit! All the children doubled up with laughter and amidst hysterical shrieks of horror from the aunts, the chauffeur was ordered to depart post-haste, leaving the astounded mithaiwalla gaping, with knife in hand and arm still raised!

The average Parsi loves his food. Some have an excellent palate for different types of food and are true gourmands, which is not to be mistaken for gluttony as is commonly done. 'Gourmand' is a French word meaning a connoisseur of good food and wine, whereas in English, it is mistaken for gluttony.

Just as they have assimilated and adapted the different cuisines they have come into contact with, they have also taken a number of charming and beautiful customs and traditions that have caught their fancy from the land of their adoption, and adapted them in their own inimitable way.

The Parsis have adjusted to the ways of their adopted land and mingled with the people; respecting their way of life, while maintaining their own identity and remaining faithful to their religion. They came to India bringing with them only their fire and their religion and both continue to burn bright.

1

Torans and Chalk

In the mofussil towns of Gujarat, Parsi homes were usually beautiful bungalows with verandas where the family relaxed in the evenings, gardens, stables for horses, garages for carriages and outhouses for the servants. This was also true of the more affluent Parsi homes in the larger cities like Bombay.

The bungalows have now given way, in many instances, to blocks of flats but whether flat or bungalow, the entrance to a Parsi home always has a string of flowers like jasmine or marigold hanging over it. This is the toran, always fresh and scented. The toranwalla brings a new one every morning, or the cook who does the daily shopping buys one in the bazaar, and the toran is changed every day. It is usually a simple, single string unless it is a birthday or some other festive occasion, when a special ornate one is ordered.

For navjotes, weddings and births there are specialists who produce extravagantly beautiful torans to adorn the gate or doorway. Some homes have beautiful glass bead torans copied from those which hang in the fire temples.

Entrance to a Parsi Home

The torans in the fire temples are made of pentagonal flat plates of silver, each one with a symbol of the religion like the aferghaniyu (urn for the fire), asho farovar or swastika carved on it and strung on a silver string. In Gujarat, torans are usually made from mango leaves for daily use and marigold flowers for auspicious occasions.

This beautiful custom of hanging flowers on the entrance door has been taken from the Hindus. Another tradition borrowed from the Hindus and adapted in typical Parsi style is the placing of chalk (lime powder) on the floor of the entrance. In days gone by, the floor of the exterior of the house, just around the entrance door, was covered with lime powder. This served as a disinfectant when the roads were not tarred. A visitor entered the home by first removing his slippers and dipping his feet in the lime, and then wiping his feet on a mat thereby killing the germs and preventing them from entering the home. The Hindus, especially in the south and Bengal, have developed the beautiful art of rangoli where elaborate designs are made with lime paste at the entrance of homes. The Parsis have designed chalk boxes which have their own traditional designs etched out in dot form. The chalk powder is put inside the box and stamped onto a damp floor, producing an artistic pattern.

These two delightful customs are still followed in most Parsi homes and, even in an impersonal block of flats, a Parsi home is easily recognized by the toran and chalk at the entrance. The traditional Parsi home always had a room or a small corner, usually in the kitchen, reserved for the aferghaniyu, divo (lamp), flower vase and other symbols used during the muktad prayers, said in remembrance of the dead. In larger homes there was a separate room reserved for the muktad prayers. There was also a separate kitchen attached to the prayer room where the food for the prayers was cooked.

Some homes had a separate room kept aside for births but

where this was not possible, one of the bedrooms was thoroughly washed, disinfected and reserved for the mother and child, for the duration of the delivery and forty days thereafter.

The aferghaniyu is a vessel in which a fire of charcoal or sandalwood and loban (frankincense) is lit and carried around the entire house twice a day. In the mornings, it is usually the lady of the house who performs this task after she has completed her morning prayers. In the evening, after sundown, the aferghaniyu can be taken around by any member of the household. It is offered to each person in the house to place some incense in the fire. This not only perfume the home, but keeps out the mosquitoes at night and clears the air in the mornings.

Every Parsi home had a divo or diya lit twenty-four hours. Now, though some families still do this and many light one at night, such customs are fast disappearing.

For lifestyles have changed all over the world and so too with the Parsis. In the days of my childhood, fresh bread would be toasted on a wood and charcoal fire and the aroma of this freshly toasted bread still lingers in my mind. As I grew up, I saw these chuhlas of wood and charcoal being replaced by those of gas and electricity. With them came the loss of great flavours that can never be replaced, no matter how sophisticated the modern stove may be.

Thankfully, not all traditions have died out. Some ceremonies like the sagan and achoo meechoo are performed at the drop of a hat in a Parsi home—on birthdays, the first day at school or college, the first day of a new job, on the first visit of a new bride and groom or of a newborn baby, before starting on a journey, when greeting an important guest, on the navjote or on a wedding day.

Traditionally, the Parsi day is divided into five gehs or sections. The first is Havan from dawn to 12.40 p.m.; the second is Rapithwin, upto 3.40 p.m.; the third is Uziran upto sunset; the fourth Aiwisruthren upto midnight; and the last is Ushochin from midnight till dawn. No Zoroastrian sagan or auspicious ceremonies are performed between twelve noon and 3.45 p.m., that is during the Rapithwin geh—as this period is considered inauspicious due to the Hindu influence. However, all religious prayers and ceremonies continue to be performed during this time.

Even numbers are considered inauspicious and odd numbers are considered auspicious according to the ancient science of numerology. Thus Parsis always use odd number in their ceremonies. Whenever chalk marks are stamped there will always be an odd number. Cash gifts are always given in odd numbers. The number seven is most auspicious because it reminds us of the seven amesha-spentas or archangels.

The right side of a person is considered auspicious because it indicates light, and the left is considered inauspicious, as it indicates darkness. As such, whenever a person has to step onto a patlo, or the place reserved for the ceremony, or enter a house, it is always done with the right foot first.

SES

A ses is required for all auspicious occasions. It consists of a silver or silver-plated tray or thali on which is kept a pigani, which contains the kum-kum (red powder) for the teeli, a gulabus which contains rose-water (this is very much a Persian container and is commonly found in many Arab countries even today), and a paro which is a conical-shaped vessel containing sakar (large sugar crystals). There may also be a paan and sopari (betel leaf and areca nut) and a fish which have been adopted as auspicious symbols from the coastal Maharashtrian Hindus. All these items are made of silver or silver plate. A garland of flowers is twisted around the paro and another one is kept on the side for the recipient of the ceremony. A few pieces of sakar, some rice, a few kharak (dried dates which are an auspicious Iranian symbol), two coconuts, one for the recipient and one for the ses and a gift are placed on the tray.

SAGAN

Sagan is usually performed by the seniormost lady of the home. Five or seven chalk marks are stamped on the floor. On top of the chalk is placed a patlo which is a low stool, made of a single piece of wood, without a joint, and the chalk is stamped on it as well. The person for whom the sagan is being performed steps onto the stool with the right foot forward.

The person performing the ceremony, dips her right thumb into the kum-kum from the ses and touches the tip of each shoe with it. She then puts the teeli on the forehead. This is a long vertical mark for a man and a round one for a woman. The vertical mark symbolizes the rays of the sun and the round one symbolizes the moon indicating that as the rays of the sun are absorbed by the moon, so also in life is the relationship between the man and the woman. The use of kum-kum and placing the teeli on the forehead is a custom that has been taken from the Gujarati Hindus.

The recipient is then garlanded with the flowers, and the gift is given. A piece of sakar, sometimes dipped in sweet curd, is put into the mouth to sweeten the tongue and grains of rice are pressed onto the teeli as a sign of plenty. Tradition has it that the number of rice grains that stick to the teeli indicates the number of children one will have, and it is a great sport of the young children to count the rice grains stuck on to each person's forehead.

The remaining rice is then sprinkled over the recipient and an overna is done. For this the person performing the sagan first raises her hands to the face of the recipient, then down in a U-shaped motion and upwards to her temples where she cracks her knuckles. This act is said to remove nazar or the evil eye. The recipient then touches the feet of the elder and steps off the stool, again with the right foot first. Rose-water from the gulabus is then sprinkled lightly over the chalk marks to prevent the chalk from flying all over the room, as it is not cleared away for some time, and to spread a delicate fragrance in the room.

ACHOO MEECHOO

Achoo meechoo is performed to remove the evil eye. This is always done to a person at the entrance of the house, and is performed during navjotes and weddings, when future brides and grooms enter their prospective in-laws' homes for the first time, when newly-married couples or newborn babies enter the homes of close relatives or even over a new house or car.

A silver or silver-plated tray is required for this ceremony. On it is kept a kutli (a mug without a handle) of water, some rice, sakar, rose petals, an egg, a coconut and some kharak. Again the lady of the home performs the ceremony. A family member, usually a girl, holds the tray and stands at one side.

The person performing the ceremony first takes the egg and rotates it over the head of the recipient six times in a clockwise motion and once in an anti-clockwise motion, and then breaks it on the ground at the side of the doorway. The egg is said to remove the evil eye completely, and it is destroyed when the egg is broken. The same is repeated with the coconut and it is believed that it is auspicious to break the coconut at the first blow.

The sakar, kharak and a little rice are kept aside in the hand by the girl holding the tray. Some rice is left in the tray and a little water from the kutli is poured into it. The kutli is held by the girl. The tray is rotated around the recipient in the same way and then the water is sprinkled on both sides. The girl then hands over the rice and sakar to the person performing the ceremony. The sakar is put into the recipient's mouth, rice is thrown over the head and an overna is done. Again the recipient touches the feet of the elder and then enters the house, stepping forward with the right foot first.

THE PARSI CALENDAR

The Parsi calendar consists of twelve months of thirty days each with five days at the end of the year for the muktad, making a total of 365 days.

There are three Parsi calendars belonging to the Fasli, Shahenshai and Kadmi groups. The Fasli group maintains 21 March as their Navroz (New Year's Day) and adjusts the calendar by having one extra day during the muktad during the leap year. The other two calendars ignore the extra day in the leap year and so their muktad days and the New Year Day go back one day every leap year. The Kadmi New Year Day is exactly one month ahead of the Shahenshai New Year Day.

The names of the months and days are the same for all three calendars. The names of the days i.e. roj are the names of the thirty yazastas or guardian angels. The names of the months are also taken from the yazastas. The yazastas are spiritual beings and there are two types—those who preside over the spiritual world and those who preside over the physical world. Seven of these are called the amesha-spentas who are the archangels. The remaining yazastas are the hamkaras or co-workers who help the amesha-spentas in their work. The first seven days of the month are named after the amesha-spentas and the remaining are named after the hamkaras.

The thirty days of the months are:

Hormuzd	Khorshed	Ram
Bahman	Mohor	Govad
Ardibehesht	Tir	Daepadin
Sheherevar	Ghosh	Din
Asphandarmad	Daepameher	Ashisvangh
Khordad	Meher	Ashtad
Amardad	Sarosh	Asman
Daepadar	Rashne	Zamyad
Adar	Farvardin	Marespand
Ava	Behram	Aneran

The last five days of the year are the gatha days, and are the most important days of the muktad. On each of these days one gatha is to be prayed completely. The five gathas are the songs of Zarathushtra and are the only original works of the prophet that have been handed down. These days are, Ahunavaiti (the gatha of free choice); Ushtavaiti (the gatha of supreme bliss); Spenta Mainyu (the gatha of the sacred spirit); Vohu Khshathra (the gatha of divine sovereignty) and Vahishtoishti (the gatha of highest wish-fulfilment) .

The twelve months of the year are:

Farvardin	Amardad	Adar
Ardibehesht	Sheherevar	Dae
Khordad	Meher	Bahman
Tir	Ava	Asphandarmad

The amesha-spentas, their hamkaras and their responsibilities are given below.

Amesha-spenta	Hamkaras	Responsibilities
Hormuzd	Daepadar Daepameher Daepadin	Represents Ahura Mazda and is the protector of man

Bahman	Mohor	Protector of
	Gosh	cattle
	Ram	
Ardibehesht	Adar	Protector of
	Sarosh	fire
	Behram	
Sheherevar	Khorshed	Protector of
	Meher	metals
	Asman	
	Aneran	
Asphandarmad	Ava	Protector of the
	Din	earth
	Ashisvangh	
	Marespand	
Khordad	Tir	Protector of
	Farvardin	water
	Govad	
Amardad	Rashne	Protector of
	Ashtad	plants and
	Zamyad	vegetation

In remembrance and reverence of the amesha-spentas certain rituals and customs are observed on their important days or roj. Not only are they remembered on their own roj, but also on the roj of their hamkaras.

The Farvardin month is the first month of the Zoroastrian calendar, but the muktad starts from roj Ashtad mah Asphandarmad, when dhan (boiled rice), dar (plain dal) and patio are eaten. The muktad ends on Amardad roj and mah Farvardin, the seventh day after Navroz.

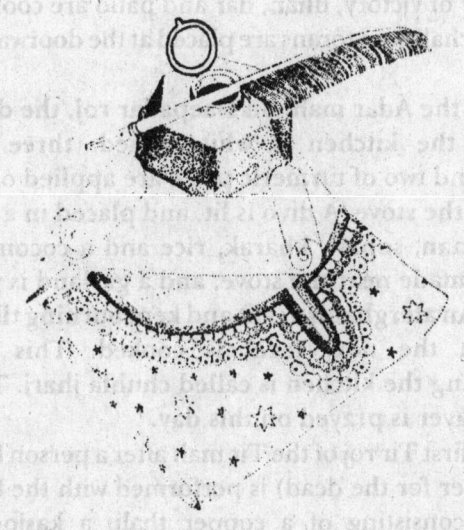

Farvardin mah (month) Khordad roj is celebrated as the
birthday of the prophet Zarathushtra. Dhai (curd), sev (sweet
vermicelli) and dhan dar ne patio is made on this day.

On Hormuzd roj, God is remembered and many people go
to the fire temple to pray and worship him. They also go on the
days of the Hamkaras i.e. on Daepadar roj, Daepameher roj
and Daepadin roj.

Bahman roj is the day to remember the protector of cattle
and so no meat is eaten on that day as also on the days of the
hamkaras i.e. on Mohor roj, Gosh roj and Ram roj. So
important is this amesha-spenta that, meat is not eaten by
most Parsis during the entire Bahman mah. On Bahman mah
Bahman roj, traditionally, khichdi, pumpkin and ghee are
eaten.

Ardibehesht roj is the day of the fire, and again many
people go to the fire temple to pray on that day and also on the
days of the hamkaras i.e. on Adar roj, Sarosh roj and Behram
roj. The dead are remembered on Sarosh roj, and on Behram

roj, the day of victory, dhan, dar and patio are cooked in the house and chalk and torans are placed at the doorways of Parsi homes.

During the Adar mah, on Daepadar roj, the day before Adar roj, the kitchen is whitewashed, three teelis of kumkum and two of turmeric paste are applied on the wall in front of the stove. A divo is lit, and placed in a ses which contains paan, sopari, kharak, rice and a coconut. Chalk marks are made near the stove, and a garland is placed on the stove. An aferghaniyu is lit and kept burning till the next day, when the next meal is cooked. This ritual of whitewashing the kitchen is called chuhla jhari. The Atash Nyaesh prayer is prayed on this day.

On the first Tir roj of the Tir mah after a person has died, a Baj (a prayer for the dead) is performed with the baj vaasan (utensils), consisting of a copper thali, a kasio (a small, straight-sided bowl) and a karasio (a mug without handles) along with a shiav (a set of clothes).

On Tir roj Tir mah the Tirya nu jashan is performed in the fire temple. The Tir yasht is prayed. Tir is supposed to help eyesight.

On Meher mah Meher roj, the Meherengan jashan is performed in the fire temples. Dhan dar is cooked in the home and a special divo is lit. Meher roj is a day of blessings.

On Ava mah Ava roj, the Ava izad nu parab (remembering and revering of water) is performed. People go to the river, sea or well to pray and a coconut is consigned to the water. Traditionally on this day dar ni pori (a flat cake stuffed with sweetened lentils) is eaten. The Ava Yasht is prayed for forty days. Ava is a female angel and helps expectant mothers.

On Adar mah Adar roj, the Adar izad nu parab is performed. Traditionally keri nu gosht or kanda keri nu gosht (meat cooked with mangoes or with mangoes and small onions) is eaten on this day, as it is the start of the mango season. If, however, the Shahenshais and Kadmis carry on with their calendar, in another few years, they will not be able to do so!

On Aneran roj, the devout pray the Siroja Yasht.

Hormuzd, Ardibehesht, Behram, Sarosh, Daepadar, Daepameher and Daepadin roj are supposed to be special days of Ahura Mazda and dhan dar ne patio is eaten on these days.

In addition to these customs, the Parsis have taken some from their Hindu friends and on Manekthali poonum which is the full moon after Diwali and is the largest full moon of the year, doodh pava (pressed rice cooked in milk) is usually eaten. It is also eaten on the other full moon nights.

Chand raat, which is the new moon day is a most auspicious day and so the Parsis eat dhan dar ne patio on all new moon days and try and arrange their important functions on this day. According to tradition, one should look at the face of a dear one on the first sighting of the new moon, then both should look at a silver coin for luck during the coming month. My husband however, refused to look at my face because whenever he did, he was transferred!

The amaas or moonless night is considered most inauspicious and no journey or important work is started on that day and no important functions take place.

2

A Birth in the Family

A birth in the family is an occasion for great rejoicing. The expectant mother is not allowed to be sad, read depressing books or attend funerals. She is to be pampered and allowed to eat whatever she likes and as much as she wants, as 'she is eating for two'! Now, of course, medical science has changed all this and strict diets are followed.

PANCH MACIUM (FIFTH MONTH)

The fifth month of pregnancy is something of a landmark and the panch macium ceremony is performed. Sagan is done to the mother and she is given a set of new clothes by her mother-in-law. An additional divo is lit in the home for that day. This ceremony was probably performed in earlier days as a thanksgiving, because of the number of pre-natal deaths and miscarriages in the early months of pregnancy. It is hardly ever performed these days.

AGHERNEE

When the pregnancy has reached the seventh or ninth month,

the expectant mother is sent from her husband's home to her own mother's home where the confinement and birth of the child takes place. She leaves on an auspicious day, preferably on a Thursday or Sunday. Her mother-in-law sends her off with a new set of clothes and sometimes with jewellery which she wears before leaving the house. The sari is worn in the traditional style. A mathubanu (white muslin scarf worn by Parsi ladies at all times in the old days, even in the home to cover the head, under the sari) is placed in the chhero or end of her sari. In the mathubanu is placed a coconut which has a teeli on it, an aghernee no larvo (a conical shaped sweet made from gram flour), some unshelled almonds, dried dates, sweet batasas (a type of biscuit), paan, sopari, a pomegranate, unhusked rice and wheat, and one rupee and four annas. The mathubanu is folded over, and sagan is done to the girl, while she is holding it in the chhero. She is then escorted by her mother-in-law and other relatives from her husband's family, to her mother's home.

Here they are greeted at the door with the achoo meechoo. After the welcome, they enter the house and the girl empties the contents of her chhero into the chhero of her mother's sari. This is to signify that the mother-in-law has sent her daughter-in-law to her mother's home well provided, for the duration of her stay there, though a rupee and four annas will not last long today! The larvo is taken out and the tip is broken off by the mother and put into her daughter's mouth. It is believed that if the expectant mother gives the tip of the aghernee no larvo to a married woman who has no child, she is bound to conceive!

The ceremony is now over and refreshments are served. Along with more larvo, other dishes like khajoor nee ghari (a type of paratha stuffed with date paste), mava na khaja (clotted cream encased in a type of puff pastry), and mava or narial na larva (sweetened coconut or cream encased in a rice paste and steamed), are served. The more common dishes which are a 'must' are ravo (sweet semolina), sev (sweet vermicelli), sweet curd and tareli machhi (fried fish which is considered auspicious by the coastal people). Additionally, cakes, sandwiches, ice-cream, kulfi, soft drinks, tea and coffee are also served. Fortunately it is not necessary to serve all these dishes! These are served at tea time or in the morning to the ladies, after the ceremony. Like all other Parsi ceremonies the aghernee is also performed before 12 noon or between 4 p.m. and sunset. The men join the ladies later for lunch or dinner as the case may be, and the aghernee no larvo is served again after the meal.

Both sides of the family send some larva to each other and their close friends.

In the old days, the room which was to be used for the delivery was thoroughly cleaned and disinfected, and if desired an Aferghan ceremony was performed.

The first drink given to the mother in labour was a few drops of hoama juice as it was believed to give healthy babies and was associated with immortality. If the hoama juice was not available a few leaves of pomegranate were simmered in water and given instead. Diluted hoama juice was also given to the baby to sip. Now due to the unavailability of hoama, the baby is given gor nu pàni (jaggery water) or more probably, glucose water.

After the child is born a divo is lit and kept in a corner of the room where the mother and child rest. They are isolated from the rest of the world, so that the mother can rest and recover her strength and both can be kept away from infection. No one who has a cold or cough is allowed into the room and those who enter have to be perfectly clean so that no infection is brought in by them.

For four days after the birth of the child, the mother is kept on a semi-liquid diet. She is given sooji kanji (semolina cooked in milk), ghau nu doodh (milk extracted from soaked wheat and dried) which can be bought readymade in the shops or can be made at home, light chicken broth and perhaps a piece of soft, boiled chicken, soft boiled eggs, porridge, fruit and fruit juices. As an Air Force officer's wife, I used to make a delicious liquid chicken for all the young Air Force wives who had no one to look after them after they had their babies, along with pish pash, a great favourite in our family.

PACHORI NU BHONOO

On the fifth day after the birth of the child, close relatives and friends are called for the famous pachori nu bhonu. This is a custom we have adopted from our Hindu friends after coming to India.

Pachori nu bhonu is cooked without spices for the benefit of the suvavri (nursing mother). Seven dishes are cooked in all. These are kharu ghost (savoury lamb), khari murghi (savoury chicken), tareli machhi (friend fish), bhaji bheja (lambs' brains cooked with fenugreek leaves), khara safed booka ne khara booka (savoury sweetbread and kidneys), bheja na cutlets (brain cutlets), and ghau nu doodh. Hot poori or ghau ni rotli (Parsi chapaties) are served throughout the meal.

The new mother is made to taste all these dishes, but just a little of each, as this meal is a kind of breaking of the fast of the last four days.

An enchanting custom is followed on the night of the fifth day after the delivery of the baby. Vermai, the guardian angel of all newborn babies, is believed to visit the child on this night to write his or her fortune. Therefore the mamai (maternal grandmother) prepares a tray in which a glass inkwell filled with wet kum-kum is placed, along with a feather pen and a blank sheet of paper for the angel to write the child's fortune. Seven rupees (guineas in the old days) are left in the tray as a gift for Vermai. A ses is also prepared

with a lit divo, a jhabla (a loose dress with an opening cut in front) which must have a kor (border), and a topi (skull cap) for the child.

At about 10 p.m. or before the household retires for the night, the mamai lights the aferghaniyu with sandalwood and frankincense, prays for the well-being of her grandchild, and asks Vermai to give saru naseeb (good fortune) to the newborn.

She also prays to God while sprinkling loban at each request to give the baby tandarosti bakhusjo (good health), jaasti akalvalu bakhusjo (extra good brains), ghanuj bhayakshai bakhusjo (good fortune), khasta dil no bakhusjo (a big heart), and to make him mayalu bakhusjo (lovable to the less fortunate, dayalu bakhusjo (kindhearted), garibnu posan karnar (look after the poor), sada maan paan no bharelu rakheavo bakhusjo (always looked upto with respect, honour and prestige), ghano khubsurat belu akhvalu ne soonari bal valu bakhusjo (extremely handsome or beautiful with blue eyes and golden hair—presumably an attempt to retain the

Iranian strain), dus lok ma baatkernavalu hojo (hold his or her own in the midst of ten persons), beek vagarno hojo (without fear), sari bhook valu hojo (with a good appetite). This last request has always made me smile when I have prayed for my grandchildren, and believe me, they have all got good appetites!

Horoscopes are made for the child and the raas (starting letter for the child's name) is seen. The child is named according to the raas, or after a near and dear departed member of the family.

Traditionally in the days gone by, the mother and baby stayed in the special room for forty days and forty nights. During this time the mother was supposed to rest and take nourishing food such as strength-giving soups; milk, porridge, suva (a mixture of fennel, pumpkin seeds etc.) to help produce milk; gunder pakh (made out of edible gum) to strengthen her back after the delivery; and badam pakh. She was not allowed to climb stairs or carry heavy loads. It was believed, and it is now a scientifically proven fact, that the uterus takes forty days to return to normal, hence the rest was required.

After the birth of my first daughter, my mother began giving me all these rich pakhs. My father, a gynaecologist watched for a few days and then told me to continue if I wanted to get fat. Naturally I refused to eat them. Well, I remained slim, but had backaches, and I would advise all young mothers to have a little of these delicious and strength-giving foods—but not to overdo it.

On the fortieth day, the mother is given five types of baths. The first is an oil massage; in the second the body is rubbed with fine rice flour paste to help remove all the dead skin; in the third, the body is rubbed with a paste of gram flour and milk to help the skin glow; the fourth is a bath in neem water (water in which neem leaves have been boiled), to remove any prickly heat that may have erupted during the summer months and act as a disinfectant; and the fifth is a head bath after the head is massaged with oil. The mattress is turned over and after fresh sheets have been placed on the bed, a small aferghaniyu lit with smouldering sandalwood and frankincense is placed under the bed for about half an hour, or until it dies out naturally. This was done in the olden days to kill germs. These five baths leave one with a wonderful languor, where one just wants to sink into a deep sleep.

The mother can now have a nahn or sacred bath, where she sips hoama nu pani and chews the leaves of a pomegranate tree while the priest chants some prayers. She dons new clothes and after the baby has also been bathed and dressed in the jhabla and topi kept in the ses when Vermai visited, the mother takes her child to the fire temple for the first time.

On the fortieth day, the mamai gives her grandchild jori-pori—all the clothes necessary for the baby for the next one year, including sheets, towels and blankets. The bapai (paternal grandmother) gives the child the vadhavo, which is the same as the jori-pori.

BESVANU

Around the time when the child is five or six months old there is a ceremony called the besvanu, meaning, to sit. As soon as the baby is able to sit this ceremony is performed. The baby is made to sit on a patlo and sagan is done. The child is given its first morsel of solid food in the form of dhan dar (rice and yellow lentils), and sweet dhai, the auspicious food for all occasions. Of course, things have changed now and the baby is weaned much earlier, but it is a charming ceremony and should still be done.

PUGLARVA

Another delightful custom is the puglarva ceremony which is performed when the child is about nine months old and has started taking its first steps. Two larva (sweets) in the shape of feet are placed in front of the baby who is made to step on them. A soft spank is then given to the baby on its bottom, to help him or her take its next step forward.

Khaman na larva are served to every one attending the ceremony, followed, of course by the traditional lunch or dinner.

3
The Navjote

The next important event in the life of a young Zoroastrian child is the navjote ceremony. This is the ceremony in which the child is invested with the sudreh (the sacred shirt) and kusti (the sacred thread) of the religion, bringing him into the folds of the Zoroastrian religion.

The ceremony is usually performed when the child is between the ages of seven and nine. By the age of seven, even in earlier times, the education of a child had usually commenced. It is the duty of good Zoroastrian parents to impart a sound moral and religious education to their children and this too is started at the age of about seven years.

The child is told the story of Zarathushtra, and through his life story is taught the fundamentals of the religion—a very rare and free religion, where nothing is imposed on one except the advice of good thought, good words and good deeds. The child is taught that there is only one God, and that He is all-knowing, all-wise and everywhere. The fravashi or the immortal spark of God is in all of us and guides the urvan, the soul and the baodha, the discerning intellect.

The Navjote

The lie is considered one of the greatest sins and the importance of telling the truth, no matter what the consequences is emphasized. The concept of freedom of choice—to choose between right and wrong is introduced. The child is taught that God or Ahura Mazda wants us to choose the good path of our own free will, and thus the duality of the good and evil forces is also introduced. The religious motto of humata, hukta, havereshta or manashni, gavashni, kunashni (good thoughts, good words and good deeds) is taught, along with the great traditions of charity towards all, kindness and consideration to the less fortunate, care of, and respect towards the elements and environment as laid down in the scriptures (long, long before today's worry over the degradation of the environment and destruction of the ecological balance), so that these become a way of life as indeed they were in the days of the great forefathers of the Parsi community.

By this stage the basic daily prayers (Ashem Vahu, Yatha Ahu Vairyo, Ahura Mazda Khodai, Kem na Mazda, Jas Meavangheo, Dil no Kalmo, Tandarosti) which will also be said on the navjote day are learnt, along with their meanings. The child is taught how to tie the kusti and instructed that the daily prayers are to be said every morning and night and after the daily bath. In the old days the kusti was to be untied and tied before meals and every time one visited the toilet. It was laid down that the hands and face had to be washed before tying the kusti and this was used as a method of ensuring hygiene. Today, with the pressures of modern living and a better sense of cleanliness, this is no longer required or practised by all.

The sudreh and kusti are the visible symbols of the religion. The sudreh is made of white cotton cloth. White is the symbol of purity and cotton is used so that poor and rich can afford to wear it. Should a poor person not have a large enough piece of cloth, the sudreh may be made up of any number of pieces joined together. That is why every sudreh has an additional cut along the sides which is stitched——to show that in God's eyes rich and poor are equal.

There is a small crescent-shaped patch at the nape of the neck which is supposed to remind one that one has come into this world with the weight of the obligations of the past life. It has a V shaped neck in front. The tip of the V has the most important part of the sudreh, the gireh-ban or kisseh-i-kerfeh. This is the pocket of good thoughts which also holds the khoreh, an individual's personal integrity which he or she tries to keep alive throughout his or her life. It has a slit in the centre for the good thoughts to enter and is a one-inch square piece of the same cloth. It reminds one of one's duties as a good Zoroastrian and, lest one become proud of one's good deeds, it also reminds one that no matter how much good one does, it only measures one square inch in comparison to God's goodness. The sudreh must be worn next to the skin to remind one of purity and righteousness.

The kusti is made of wool from a lamb which has pure white fleece. The wool is combed and spun into fine thread. Two of these threads are twisted into one, on two spindles called chaatris and then woven into a kusti on an adjustable loom called a jantar. The kusti consists of seventy two threads representing the seventy two verses of the Yasna, which is the book of worship, and is woven by the women of the priestly class. It is a hollow cylindrical girdle, and when the weaving is nearly complete it is given to the priest of the household to be cut and consecrated. After that it is turned inside out and the weaving is completed by hand. The ends consist of three tassels of twenty-four threads each.

The navjote ceremony is preferably performed in the morning between 10 a.m. and 11.30 a.m. as the sun's rays are most beneficial during this time. An auspicious day is chosen and invitations are sent out to relatives and friends. In typical

Indian fashion, they are handed over personally to elders and respected members of the family and friends.

A little before the ceremony starts the child is given the nahn or purification bath. The child is then dressed in an ijar (pyjamas), which has a kor or border on either leg, cap, and sapat (slippers) made of velvet. The cap and borders are usually embroidered with silk, silver or gold thread. The upper part of the body is bare and covered with a shawl.

The mother and aunt accompany the child and priest with a ses containing the new clothes to be worn by the child after the ceremony. Traditionally these were an ijar and badian (a long blouse nipped at the waist and flared to the hips) for a girl, and a dagli (a white coat made from fine cotton cloth, very much like the coats we see worn by men in the old Persian and Mughal paintings), with a red satin ijar for a boy. The girl's ses contains a sari which she will wear the first time she puts on a sari. Any jewellery gifted to the child and to be worn after the navjote is also placed in the ses. Now of course, the children wear any clothes they choose, according to the fashions of the times. The sudreh and kusti which is to be worn during the ceremony is kept right on top.

The grandmother or an aunt meets the child at the entrance of the hall and does the achoo meechoo. The child is then led to the place where the ceremony is to be performed.

A carpet is covered with a white sheet and on it is placed a patlo, also covered with a white sheet. Lamps are lit on either side.

On one side of the patlo, where the ses is placed, is a lit divo along with a thali or tray filled with rose petals, rice and pomegranate seeds, which will be sprinkled on the child after the investiture, while the priest prays the Tandorosti.

On the other side of the patlo is a lit aferghaniyu, along with a tray containing the sandalwood and incense used to keep the fire burning throughout the ceremony.

Four priests sit at the four corners of the sheet and the officiating priest stands in front of the child. The child is made to sit on the patlo facing east and the sudreh and kusti are placed in his hands. The Papet prayer is recited by the priests and then the child is made to stand up facing east. The officiating priest holds the child's hands and together they pray the Din no Kalmo or confession of the faith. He then puts the sudreh on to the child while they pray the Yatha Ahu Vairyo prayer. The priest then stands behind the child, holding the kusti while the child holds onto his last finger, and together they recite the kusti prayers and the kusti is tied around the child's waist for the first time. The priest then does sagan to the child, makes him sit down again and prays the Tandorosti, while sprinkling the rose petals, rice and pomegranate seeds on the child.

The ceremony is now over and the child's parents come forward to wish their child. The new clothes are put on and the rest of the family and friends come forward to greet the child with good wishes and blessings, and give their gifts, after which the child goes to the fire temple with his parents.

Music is played before and after the ceremony and drinks are served immediately it is over. During the ceremony, of course there is, or should be, total silence.

I still recall the excellent bands we had to play for us on these occasions in my childhood. There were the Police Band and regimental bands; there was Nelly's band which has received the Rajiv Gandhi award for contribution, achievement and outstanding service to western music. We also had young Parsis aspiring to be Caruso who would get up to sing semi-classical songs like *O Sole mio* with the guests and friends clapping and asking for more! Then we had our own Goody Servai, who would play whatever we asked him to. I still recall how, at my daughter Sherna's navjote which was held at my parents home at Oomer Park, while the guests were having their lunch, my aunts gathered round him and sang all the favourites of their youth. Goody played and played, long after all the other guests had gone and only a handful were left. He has taken his music to heaven and must be keeping the feet of the angels tapping!

Now, unfortunately people play taped music and no matter how good it may be, it cannot give the ambience that the live bands used to and the entire atmosphere of the navjote or lagan (wedding) is lost forever.

Lunch is served in two or three sitting, depending on the number or guests and size of the garden or hall. The superlative food served at the navjote and lagans will be described later.

4
Lagan

According to the ancient Zoroastrian texts, marriage is favoured by Ahura Mazda. The religion encourages marriage and family life with children, as it brings contentment and happiness. In ancient Iran, the State encouraged marriage as it was felt that a married man could tolerate the stresses and strains of life far better than an unmarried one.

It is considered a great boon to give financial aid to poor couples who wish to get married, and if one can arrange seven marriages then one will surely go to heaven!

From ancient times, marriages were usually arranged by parents with the consent of the children, and till very recently professional matchmakers were quite common.

Nowadays of course the children choose their own partners and generally receive the consent of their parents.

As always, marriage is a time of great gaiety, laughter, fun and confusion. Relatives and friends from, all over the country come to the city or town where the wedding is to take place, well in advance of the date, and this period is a round of ceremonies, lunches, dinners and shopping. The actual wedding ceremony is preceded by a series of other ceremonies and there is much going to and fro between the homes of the bride and groom, much food made and consumed, sagans and achoo meechoos performed, and presents given and taken. Today only two or three of the important ceremonies are performed. They may be performed on the same day or on different days, according to the wishes of the families.

Auspicious days, preferably Hormuzd roj (the first day of the month) or Behram roj (the twentieth day of the month when the angel of victory presides over the day) are chosen for the ceremonies. Saturdays or amaas (moonless nights) are avoided, again due to the Hindu influence. As usual the ceremonies are before 12 noon or between 4 p.m. and sunset. The doorways and gateways to the homes are decorated with chalk marks and ornate torans specially ordered for the occasion.

RUPIA PERAVANU

This is the unofficial engagement, when the marriage is acknowledged to be accepted by both sides. On this day the ladies of the bridegroom's family (usually five or seven and never more than nine) go to the home of the bride. They are met at the door by the bride's mother, where achoo meechoo is done and the party enters the home. The bride is presented with a gift of silver coins in a red or brocade bag with the usual sagan. Refreshments with the traditional sev, dhai and ravo are served, sometimes with tareli machhi as well. The bridegroom's family then return home with the bride.

The bride's family now add some more coins to those presented, and go to the groom's home where the same procedure is repeated. The bride's mother does sagan to the groom and gives him the gift. Once again the refreshments are served and the bride and her family return home.

A wedding in progress

Nowadays this ceremony is rarely performed, and if it is, it is combined with the engagement.

ADRAVANU

This was an important ceremony in earlier days, as according to Parsi custom the girl's name was always connected with that of her father before betrothal, and with that of her husband after betrothal, in all the religious ceremonies. This was called the nam padvun. Now the nam padvun is associated with the actual marriage, but the betrothal or adravanu ceremony is still performed.

The participants in the adravanu ceremony consist of the bride, groom, their mothers and five to nine ladies of the immediate families on both sides. On the adravanu day the bridegroom's mother and the other ladies of his family go to the bride's home where they are greeted with songs. In the olden days professional singers were hired to sing the songs. The bride's mother does the achoo meechoo to the party before they enter the home.

As soon as they enter the home, the ceremony of the divo is performed. A divo is kept burning in the room and when the party enters, the bridegroom's mother puts a silver coin in it.

The guests are served cold drinks and amidst much laughter and gaiety the bride is invited by the groom's mother to step onto the patlo—kept ready in the room with the usual chalk marks. Sagan is done to her in the usual way and she is given a set of clothes to wear. She retires to her room with them and returns wearing her new clothes. In the old days the sari would be first cooled by her prospective mother-in-law by sprinkling the corner with rose-water. (This was meant to help the person wearing the sari and to protect her from harm. Even today, a new sari is supposed to be cooled with rose-water or perfume, before it is worn for the first time.) She would help her daughter-in-law to wear the sari. Red glass bangles are put on the bride's arms as a symbol of her engagement.

The actual ceremony now begins. The bride and groom both stand on the patlo together. Sagan is done to both of them by each mother in turn. A piece of sakar is dipped in curd and given to each one and the rings are exchanged. Then the relatives and friends greet the couple and give them their engagement gifts.

After that each member of the bride's family, starting with the mother, is invited on the patlo. Sagan is done to her, and she is given a gift.

The mothers, grandmothers and sisters of the bridal couple are usually given a set of new clothes by the in-laws. All the relatives who are taking part in the ceremony are given gifts of cash. The amount depends on the closeness of the relative to the person getting married and of course, on how much one can afford.

Traditional refreshments are served like tareli machhi, sweet dhai, sev, malai na khaja, (a superlative sweet made with fine layers of puff pastry, stuffed with sweetened rose-flavoured cream), jalebis and sooterfani. Sooterfani is a sweet made from sugar—it looks like fine thread rolled into a large circle the size of a plate. It has a light rose flavour and is sprinkled with rose petals, chopped pistachios, cheronji, crushed cardamom and nutmeg. (This is not made at home and has to be bought). Cold coffee or kulfi is served if the weather is hot. Now as a result of the western influence, cakes, pastries and delicate sandwiches are also served. One of the favourite sandwiches is the chutney sandwich—a beautiful 'marriage' of east and west!

The groom's family then leave for their home, taking the bride with them.

The bride's family now add some more cash to whatever was presented to the ladies of their family and go to the groom's home where the entire process is repeated. The ceremony of the divo is performed by the bride's mother and the members of the groom's family are the recipients of the sagan and gifts. This takes me back to the divo ceremony I had to perform for Sherna. As I was carrying the ses when we went to her mother-in-law's home, I had not taken my purse. As soon as I entered the house and saw the divo I realized my mistake and believe it or not, not a single member of our party could rustle up a silver coin! Amidst much laughter and ribbing from the host party, I had to borrow a coin from my future son-in-law! I promised him that he would get it back, and not in silver but in gold. I kept my word, and he carries the gold coin with him to this day.

The bride is usually asked to stay for dinner, after which her mother-in-law does sagan to her again, and gives her a gift of cash before sending her home.

These ceremonies may be performed any time after both sides have given their consent and have agreed to the marriage, or they may be combined with the aderni ceremony which is performed four days before the actual wedding ceremony.

MANDAV SARO

This is the first of the ceremonies that take place four days before the wedding. It takes place in the morning and each side performs their own ceremony independently.

An auspicious day, preferably a Thursday or Sunday is chosen. Chand raat (new moon's day) or Punam raat (full moon day) are also much favoured. Wednesdays are never chosen for any of the marriage ceremonies, as it is believed that if a girl is given away on a Wednesday, she will never return to her mother's home. Some people also have a very strong superstition about Tuesday and Saturday being very inauspicious for any kind of festivity.

Items needed for the mandav saro ceremony are:

— A mango sapling. If a garden is available, then a hole is dug for planting it. Where there is no garden, a flower pot is kept ready.
— A small bowl of curd.
— A coconut.
— A garland.
— Four supra. These are special cane trays used all over India to separate the rice or wheat from the husk and stones.
— A khal butto—mortar and pestle.
— A thali or basket containing about 200 grams of whole turmeric, twelve leaves of paan, twelve sopari, 200 grams each of unhusked rice and wheat grains, moong (green beans), twelve pieces of dried coconut, twelve unshelled almonds, and a dozen each of dry dates, sakar (large sugar crystals), and batasa.
— Kherputu. This is made with two tablespoons flour, one teaspoon turmeric, and half a teaspoon kum-kum, all mixed together with a little water to make a stiff paste.
— A ball of cotton thread.
— Four stools.
— A small red handkerchief or cloth in which sona rupa na pariku is tied. This is available in all Parsi shops where sandalwood, kustis etc. are sold. It consists of scrapings of silver, gold, emerald, rubies and diamonds. Instead of this a few gold and silver teelis (five gold and seven silver) with which our sari borders are embroidered may be used.
— A small aferghaniyu (urn used for the fire) lit with sandalwood and frankincense.
— One new coconut for the bride or groom, with a tuft of husk left on the top.
— Sweet batasa, kharak, sopari, rice, egg, coconut, and a bowl of water kept in a tray for the achoo meechoo.
— Pigani with kum-kum.

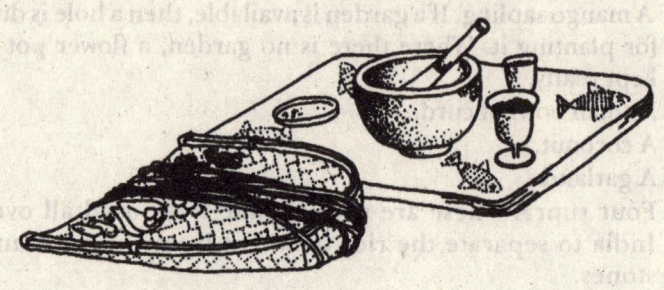

Articles used during the Mandav Saro

The ceremony is performed by four or sometimes five married women who have children, preferably the mother and married sisters or aunts of the bride or groom. One man is also required later on for the tree-planting ceremony. There is a controversy (in typical Parsi fashion), on whether he should be a married man who has children, or a young minor boy. However, it is agreed that he has to wear a red turban.

The four stools are arranged in a square formation and in the centre is the khal or mortar, with chalk marks all around it and a teeli of kum-kum on it. Near it lies the basket or thali with all the items mentioned above. The whole turmeric is placed in the mortar.

The ladies now sit, heads covered, on the four stools and together hold the butto or pestle in their right hands, and crush the turmeric in it. The mortar and pestle are then left in its place.

Next each lady dips her right thumb in the kum-kum and marks five elongated teelis at the base of the supru, leaving place in between to mark three elongated teelis with turmeric or kherputu paste. That done, each lady winds the cotton thread seven times around her supru from the top to the bottom and twists the ends together (no knots are allowed).

She then takes a few of each of the items from the basket and places them in her supru along with a handful or rice, dal and wheat.

When everyone is set all the ladies simultaneously toss their supru seven times. It is then exchanged with that of the lady sitting in front, tossed seven times, returned and tossed again. This procedure is repeated with the lady on the right and then on the left and ends with the last exchange, which is the seventh one, when the supru is swapped with the lady in front once again.

The mother of the bride or groom now takes the coconut in her hand and winds the cotton thread seven times around it, praying the Ashem Vahu with each round. The ends are once again twisted and the coconut is kept safely in the cupboard until the wedding day, when the mother marks a teeli on it and hands it over to her child just before the wedding ceremony.

Next comes the planting of the tree. The bowl of curd is poured into the hole made in the ground or in the flower pot. Some also add a few grains of rice and wheat. Then all the ladies with the help of the married man, or young boy as the case may be, plant the sapling. The handkerchief with the silver and gold in it is tied to a branch or twig of the sapling and a garland is put on it. The mother then does the achoo meechoo over the tree, wishing the couple prosperity and many healthy children. The egg is broken in the flower pot or at the base of the sapling. The coconut is broken and the water is sprinkled over it. Lastly the aferghaniyu is passed around the sapling and all present put loban (frankincense) on the fire and pray for the happiness and prosperity of the couple.

All the supra are collected and kept aside. These are taken by the bride to her new home, or given to the ladies who have taken part in the ceremony. The remaining items used in the ceremony are collected and kept aside. On the varova day (eighth day after the wedding) these, along with the garlands and bouquets of flowers, used during the wedding ceremony are collected and thrown into the sea or river near the city or town.

After the ceremony a 'light' lunch is served, consisting of the traditional sagan nu bhonu.

ADERNI

The next ceremony to be performed is the aderni. This ceremony is usually performed in the evening of the same day as the mandav saro. The two ceremonies may also be combined, and performed either in the morning or evening, but the mandav saro always precedes the aderni.

On this day the other ceremonies that are performed are the gor rupia, sakar tapka and dhai maachli ceremonies.

Items required for these ceremonies are:-

— A silver or plated tray with five or seven medium sized boi (grey mullet) or pomfret, each fish with a kum-kum teeli mark on its head.
— A silver or silver-plated tray with sakar
— A bowl of sweet dhai (curd)

If one does not wish to carry fresh fish, mava nee machhi (mava is a thick semi-solid paste of condensed milk), or a chocolate fish may be used. These are set in fish moulds.

As mentioned earlier, fish is a sign of plenty in the coastal areas and dhai is considered auspicious in all Indian homes; hence these are used in these ceremonies.

For the aderni the ladies of the bridegroom's family (as for the adravanu) go to the bride's home. Apart from the clothes and usual gifts, they also carry the trays of fish, and sakar and the bowl of dhai. They are greeted at the door by the mother of the bride. Achoo meechoo is done and in the old days delightful nuptial songs in Gujarati, now mostly forgotten were sung.

Soft drinks are served and the bride is invited to stand on the patlo by her prospective mother-in-law, sagan is done and she is presented with a new set of clothes. As in the adravanu she goes to the bedroom to wear these clothes, and returns to stand on the patlo when her mother-in-law ties on the sari for her. She is then given the jewellery for the wedding and again red glass bangles are put on her which are kept on till the wedding day. The jewellery is usually put on her after the wedding ceremony by her father or mother-in-law, and is called khoreli dhana which literally means 'taken onto the lap'—that is, the girl has now been taken as the daughter by the in-laws.

The entire procedure of presenting clothes and cash to the accompanying party is repeated as for the adravanu.

Refreshments are served and the groom's party depart, taking with them their trays in which the fish and sakar were brought, all of them filled with sakar.

The bride's family then prepare their own trays with the fish brought by the groom's family plus some more added, along with more sakar, and their own bowl of dhai. More cash is added to the cash gifts given by the groom's family and they go with these and their own gifts to the groom's home.

Once again they are greeted in the usual fashion by the groom's mother and after the achoo meechoo is done, they are invited in. The groom is given the lagan no vago (described under wedding gifts), by the bride's mother and his family members are given the usual sets of clothes and cash.

Once again refreshments are served. All the trays, with the fish and other items brought by the bride's family are left at the groom's home and the bride's party depart, leaving the bride behind. She stays on for dinner. The trays and bowls are a part of the gifts for the bride from her parents.

At this ceremony, the fathers are also given a shawl each, material for a suit and some cash. The youngest brother of the bride is given a ring called sala nee veetee.

The two mothers call each other vehvan and the two fathers call each other vehvai. The groom's eldest brother and sister-in-law are called jeth and jethani by the bride and the other brothers and sisters-in-law are called der and derani. The groom's sisters and brothers-in-law are called naran and narvai by the bride. The brother's wife is called bhojai. The bride's brothers and sisters-in-laws are called salo and sali by the groom. The son-in-law is called jamai and a daughter-in-law is called vahu.

Just before the bride returns to her home, after the dinner at her in-laws' home, sagan is done to her and she is presented with another set of clothes or cash for the ghertarana patli raat na kapra. This was the second marriage ceremony performed in the old days, just after midnight, and these clothes were meant for the second ceremony. Often they were the same set of clothes given to the groom's mother by the bride's mother.

The next day is a day of rest. It is called the khichdi nee reet and nothing special is done except that khichdi and sas is cooked. A game called ookadi lootvan was played, but it is difficult to get an accurate description.

The third and fourth days are known as varadh parta days. Prayers of Satum and Baj are performed in the fire temple in honour of the dead and they are hypothetically invited to the marriage.

Varad vara (a type of cake), saria (rice papads) and papad are sent to the homes of the bride and groom by the respective mothers-in-law.

In the old days when the entire village had to be invited and fed, it was not possible to do so on one day and so this was done over these four days. The Parsis have of course taken this custom into the larger towns where lunches and dinners galore are given by all sides and there is much partying, general exhaustion and fun!

THE MARRIAGE DAY

As stated earlier, a Parsi marriage usually takes place in the evening just after the sun has set. This is because at this time, the day melts into the night, and as they merge into each other, so it is believed will the married couple and they will then live in happiness and contentment.

A marriage is an event to be celebrated with great joy and pomp, and not quietly! It should be performed in the presence of an anjuman (assembly) of at least five people, who are the witnesses to the marriage.

Early in the morning all the relatives of the bridal couple decorate their homes with chalk marks and beautiful sweet-smelling torans. It is a quiet time when very close relatives and the immediate family are together.

The afternoon meal is a light one with sweet dhai, sev, dhan dar ne patio, and any other traditional dish of chicken or meat, with ravo completing the meal.

Just before the wedding ceremony both the bride and groom have to undergo the sacred bath or nahn, and then wear their wedding clothes.

The bridegroom is dressed in traditional white dugli (coat), and white trousers, with a pagri or phento (male Parsi head gear). In the old days some grooms also wore the jama pichori or sahyo which is a long flowing cloak we see worn by the men in old Persian paintings, but this is rarely worn today. The traditional long kum-kum teeli mark is on his forehead and he wears a garland of roses around his neck. He also holds a bouquet of roses in his hand along with the coconut (with the cotton string tied around it seven times), preserved from the mandav saro ceremony. Over his arm, he holds a shawl.

Shawls in India are a token of respect and greatness. At a Parsi wedding the fathers of the groom and bride usually exchange shawls and one is always presented to the officiating priest.

The traditional colour for a Parsi bride is white or, at the very most a pale shade of rose. The sari is of silk, or any other fine material like net or lace.

Until the late sixties, Parsis had beautiful saris embroidered for their weddings and important teerats (auspicious occasions). They were worked on with silver and gold thread, silk thread, beads, and silver and gold teelis (flat disks). Parsi ladies would employ men to work for them and take orders for the saris. One of these was my aunt, Manekbai Mulla. She was an artist whose blending of colours and patterns was incomparable. She would take down designs from old books, wall plates or anything that took her fancy and design a sari or border.

My own wedding sari was embroidered with fine white silk, dull pulled silver and shining silver threads. The pattern was copied from an exceptional piece of exhibition lace bought by my mamaiji in Europe. That piece of lace was placed in my mother's wedding ses as a sudreh piece and eventually became my wedding blouse. The pattern was then embroidered on a georgette sari for me.

Another great artist was Piroja Narielwalla, who also embroidered exquisite saris; then there were shops like Karanjiawalla who took orders for saris. These highly prized saris are a sad casualty of modern times but I am glad that our beautiful garas and borders are now being revived.

All ladies until recently used to cover their heads all the time with a mathubanu (this is a custom brought from Iran, where the ladies still cover their heads) and when they went out of the house the sari was put over it. Even if this was not done as a regular routine, it was certainly done when going to the fire temple and attending navjotes and weddings. Times have changed, and with the fast pace of life, girls going to the fire temple, on their way to work, cover their heads with a scarf.

The bride too covers her head with a mathubanu under her sari. She wears a garland of roses or moghras around her neck and holds a bouquet of flowers, more elaborate than that of the groom, and the coconut with the string tied around it, marked with a teeli, preserved from her mandav saro ceremony in her hands. She wears a round kum-kum teeli on her forehead and the jewellery given to her by her in laws at the aderni ceremony. In some cases the bride's father-in-law puts the jewellery on her after the ceremony is over.

The gates and grounds or hall where the wedding is to take place are beautifully decorated with elaborate torans, floral arrangements and chalk. The senior members of the families stand at the gate to welcome the relatives and guests attending the ceremony.

The dais where the ceremony is to be performed is also elaborately decorated with beautiful floral arrangements. In the centre are two chairs, facing east, with a small table on either side of the chairs, where the wedding lamps or lights, brought by the bride from her home are placed, along with a tray on each table containing rice and rose petals (sakar, almonds and sultanas were also included in the old days). This is showered on the bridal pair during the ashirwad or blessing by the priests, and must be placed within easy reach of them. Near the bride's chair is a small stool where a kutli of ghee (clarified butter) and gur (jaggery) is kept. Gur is considered a symbol of sweetness and good temper and ghee is a sign of gentility and courtesy. It is also a sign of luxury, as it is derived from milk. (Many a doting parsi mother pours a kutli of milk and rose petals over her children before their baths on birthdays and on the wedding day). There is a man standing at the back of the dais, holding a small aferghaniyu with sandalwood and frankincense, as the fire is a sacred and important symbol.

When the bridegroom arrived at the place of marriage, in the old days, he was welcomed with bridal songs. This is no longer done in the big cities as most people have forgotten the songs. He is followed by two married ladies from his family, who hold the ses containing new clothes for him. He takes his seat in front of the assembly of men called sajan (assembly for the royal bride), with his father, brothers and other male members of his family to await the arrival of the bride. The women used to sit opposite the men, but now all mingle together and the atmosphere is more lively and friendly.

Just before the bride arrives, the groom is taken to the dais, and his mother does the achoo meechoo over him. She may slip on a ring which has a precious or semi-precious stone, called arugani veetee, and he sits on the chair on the right. The ses is placed on the table next to his chair.

The bride enters, on the arm of her father or elder brother, and is followed by two married women, close relatives, holding the ses with a sari set on it. Her mother does the achoo meechoo over her and she takes her place beside the groom. Her ses is placed on the table near her chair.

Just before the ceremony starts, a younger unmarried sister or relative of the bride comes with a chamboro made of German silver filled with water or milk, as a gift for the groom, who dips his hand into it and leaves seven silver or gold coins in it. After the marriage ceremony his feet are symbolically washed by the same girl or by another sister or relative, by sprinkling a few drops of milk on his new shoes, and the dropping of the coin is repeated. The gift of the kutli is called var behevoon (a kutli presented to the groom).

Two married men with children, one from each side of the family stand as witnesses on either side of the couple. They are usually an uncle or elder brother of the groom and bride. Three or more married ladies, close relatives of the groom and bride, sit behind the bridal couple. Two officiating priests stand in front of each of the bridal couple.

When all are assembled correctly, the seniormost of the priests asks the young couple if they have consented to the marriage. Either of the couple can say 'no' up to this time. This is important, especially for the bride, who in days gone by may have been forced to marry against her wishes; and if she said 'no' at this stage, the marriage did not take place!

After the bridal couple have both consented to the marriage, the priest then joins their hands together, while praying a benediction; this is known as the Haathevaro. There is another ceremony, the tying of the knot, which symbolizes that the couple are now united, but it is optional and need not be performed.

The actual religious ceremony now starts. The senior priest blesses the couple and then asks the two witnesses for their consent after which he asks the marrying couple thrice if they consent. Once all the consents have been received, both priests recite the Ashirwad and then the Tandorosti (a prayer for good health), while sprinkling the rice and rose petals over the couple. At the end of the ceremony the man holding the aferghaniyu adds more frankincense on the fire and then removes it.

The ceremony over, the custom of washing of the groom's feet with the milk, as described earlier is performed. There is also the custom of making the couple eat dhai koomra, a dish made with sweet curd and vermicelli. The fathers exchange shawls, the groom is given one by his father-in-law and both priests are given a cash gift and a shawl each.

As for the navjote ceremony, so also for the weddings there would always be a live band in attendance, which would start playing when the first guests arrived, stop for the ceremony and start up again after it was over. Relatives and well-wishers come up to the dais, to greet the newly married couple and give them their gifts, after which the couple go to the fire temple. The guests mingle with each other, drinks are served, the younger folk dance to the music of the band, and there is much gaiety and laughter, until the delightful call *'chalo jumva avoji'* (come along to eat).

The married couple and their close relatives—parents, grandparents, brothers and sisters go around the tables, greeting their guests, thanking them for coming and encouraging them to eat well. The traditional saying is *'jamjoji, gher nu bhonu chookia to maaf kerjoji'* (please eat well and forgive us for making you miss your own good food at home).

After all the guests have eaten and departed or are sitting around and talking, the family members, very close friends and members of the band sit down for their meal, after which the bride departs to the groom's home amidst the singing of bridal songs. She is accompanied by the members of her own and her husband's family and once again, as she enters her new home, bridal songs are sung, her mother-in-law does achoo meechoo to the couple and they cross the threshold, right foot forward, into the house.

VAROVA

This is the ceremony that takes place on the eighth day after the marriage.

All the food ingredients used in the mandav saro ceremony along with the wedding bouquets, garlands, and coconuts used in the ceremonies are sent to the sea or river, stream or lake near the town. The mortar and pestle, and the jewellery from the mango tree are kept by the bride to be used for her own daughter's mandav saro.

The bride is sent to visit her parent's home for the first time after the marriage. This could have been due to the fact that in the old days brides were much younger than they are today, and they could well have been homesick. She is usually given a new set of clothes to wear for this occasion. In the evening the jamai (son-in-law), his parents, brothers and sisters are invited for dinner. At the time of departure, the son-in-law is given a large tambri (a pot for storing water), filled with pedas (a delightful sweet made from thick dry condensed milk), with a coconut on top and a garland of flowers around it. If one does not wish to give the tambri, just the sweets may be given.

WEDDING GIFTS

From the bride's parents to their daughter:

Seven sets of clothes consisting of:

— A sari, blouse and petticoat
— Sudreh or material for it, usually a piece of lace
— Jora kusti which, in days gone by was money, usually Rs 7 for the purchase of a kusti and slippers (in the old days Parsi ladies used to wear slippers made of velvet, often beautifully embroidered with silk, silver, or gold thread and beads)
   Underwear and a handkerchief
   These are given for the engagement, aderni, dhai maachli (optional), mandav saro (optional), diva no, wedding and for the wedding ses. Nowadays, a pair of shoes is included for the three important sets for the engagement, aderni and wedding.

The parents also give:

— A pair of chairs and teapoys for the wedding ceremony
— The wedding lamps
— The ses for the bride
— Four cooking vessels containing rice, dal, sugar or gur (jaggery) and wheat
— A tambri (pot) for the varova
— Other pots, pans and items for the kitchen (a detailed list

of utensils used in a Parsi kitchen is given in separate
chapter)
— Crockery, cutlery, glassware, furniture, linen, other
household items, clothes and jewellery according to one's
means.

From the bride's parents to the groom:

The lagan no vago, which is a set of clothes for the groom. This
is usually not given these days. Money is given instead to the
groom to choose the clothes he wishes to buy.
The traditional vago consisted of:
— Warm material for a suit
— Material for seven shirts and seven pairs of trousers
— A tako (a full roll of cloth approximately twelve metres) of
mullmull for sudreh
— A tako of lawn cloth for loose, pyjama-like trousers
called leghas which were worn by Parsi men in the house
while relaxing (hence the expression *sudreh-legha ma
ooto*, meaning he was found relaxing in his informal
clothes)
— Three sets of night suits
— A dressing gown
— A velvet topi which was worn in the house as neither men
nor women kept their head bare
— A pair of sapat or slippers
— A pagri or phento which was the headdress worn when
going out
— A shawl which is put on the groom by his father-in-law after
the marriage ceremony is over
— A wristwatch (optional)
— A set of gold buttons which were worn on shirts in days gone
by
— A pair of shoes

From the brides's parents to the groom's family:

A set of clothes for:
— The groom's mother
— The groom's father
— The narans and naranvais (groom's sisters and brothers)
— The jeth and jethani (groom's eldest brother and his wife)
— The immediate aunts and uncles of the groom.
— The grandparents of the groom
　　Cash may be given in place of the clothes.
　　The father is also given a shawl and nieces and nephews of the groom are given small gifts of cash.

From the bridegroom's parents to the bride:

Five sets of clothes for:
— The engagement aderni, dhai machhli, diva no and ghertarana patliratna
— An engagement ring
— A wedding ring
— Jewellery is given for the wedding at the aderni ceremony.

From the bridegrooms parents to the bride's family:

A set of clothes for:
— The bride's mother
— The bride's father
— The bride's sisters
— The bride's brothers (saala) and their wives (saali)
— The immediate aunts and uncles of the bride
— The grandparents of the bride
　　Cash may be given in place of the clothes. The father is also given a shawl and the nieces and nephews of the bride are given small gifts of cash. The youngest brother of the bride is also given the sala nee veetee.

5

Journey's End

One of the oldest religions in the world, Zoroastrianism teaches respect for the environment and the elements.

In ancient Iran where fertile land was precious and rivers the source of life, nothing was done to desecrate or pollute them, and hence the land was not used to bury the dead nor the rivers polluted by throwing the bodies into them. Cremation was not prescribed as a way of disposal of the dead, as fire was considered sacred and not to be defiled. I do not agree with this as one of the reasons we revere fire is that it destroys all germs and cannot be defiled. It is true, though, that while burning a dead body noxious fumes and gases are generated, polluting the environment, and the amount of wood used is ecologically harmful.

After the funeral ceremony, the dead were disposed of by taking them to a high rocky cliff and fastening them down with heavy stones. There they were left till nature took its course with the help of vultures. The flesh was stripped off the bones in a matter of hours and the bones were then collected and put into a charnel house made of stone or clay, and constructed in such a manner that the rays of the sun could reach the bones and dry them out. The entire procedure was devised to reduce pollution and the time for the body to disintegrate, thus ensuring the safety and wellbeing of the living. From these ancient times and customs were the Towers of Silence derived, and have become what they are today. However now in Iran the Iranian Zoroastrians have discarded the dokhma system and have started burying their dead which may be due to the Islamic influence.

In those early days, kings and princes had their tombs on high cliffheads. The tomb of Darius was on a cliff at Naksh-Rustam. Cyrus the Great was the only king who had his tomb on flat land, though it was erected at a height of seventeen feet. He was entombed in a tub-like coffin made of gold which rested on a couch which had feet of gold. In the tomb were his swords, necklace and clothes, a Babylonion influence. The tomb was at Murgab and on it he had inscribed 'Here I lie Cyrus King of Kings'. Later Alexander's general Aristobulus, who along with his master had great admiration for Cyrus the Great, added to this brief and dignified epitaph 'O man I am Cyrus who acquired the Empire for the Persians and was King of Persia; Grudge me not therefore my monument'. (No Greek would use the word 'Great' for anyone, as in their eyes only Alexander was 'Great').

When a Zoroastrian dies, relatives or close friends stay near the body and recite the Ashem Vahu continuously till the body is removed to the place of the funeral ceremony (either the Towers of Silence or to the ground floor of the home, if the funeral is to be performed at the home of the dead one). The body is given its last bath and laid out in the funeral clothes called the shiav, and the priest takes over.

A divo and a vase of flowers are placed near the bedside of the person who has died and rose petals are sprinkled over the bed. The divo is kept burning for ten days and the flowers are changed every day. The room and possessions of the departed

Articles used during the Jashan Ceremony

one are left untouched for at least one month.

Simplicity is observed in the funeral ritual. Rich and poor are dressed alike and laid out on a stone slab. A divo is lit in one corner near the body and kept alight for four days. A small vase of flowers is placed near the divo and the flowers are changed every day. An aferghaniyu is also kept burning three paces away from the body and is lit to keep away the germs.

The dead body is handled by nassasalars (professional corpse bearers) who place the body on the stone slab after the bath. Two of them then re-enter the room holding a paiwand between them. This is a piece of cloth or tape, held by them to maintain close contact between them and to show that they are in communion and sympathy with each other for the task they have to perform. They cover the body with a white sheet and draw a kasha (a boundary circle drawn with an iron nail) around the slab on which the body is resting, to show that this space has been kept apart and no one should cross it.

A sagdid ceremony is performed at the turn of every geh, for as long as the body is lying on the ground before the funeral. It is the ceremony when a dog, usually a 'four-eyed' dog i.e. one with a spot over each eye, is led to the corpse. 'Sag' means dog and 'did' means sight. It is believed that a four-eyed dog drives away evil spirits.

A priest comes in after the first sagdid ceremony and prays near the body until it is time for the funeral, which is generally performed as soon as possible after death has taken place, to avoid decomposition and to prevent infection from spreading. A funeral is never performed at night. If a person dies in the evening or at night the funeral takes place the next morning. If the person dies during the early part of the day, then it takes place in the evening. Sometimes the funeral could be delayed for a relative who may have to come from afar to pay his or her last respects to the departed one.

Once the body has been washed and laid out only the nassasalars can touch it. There are usually four of them to carry the body, but if it is a child then two are enough. A single person is not permitted to carry the body to the Towers, as a person should not be alone in performing this sad task, and a paiwand must always connect two of them at all times. They come dressed in white, with a white cap on their heads, white socks on their feet and white gloves called dastaneh on their hands. These are to protect them from any infection from the dead body. They bring an iron bier called a gehan. Wood is never used in any Zoroastrian ceremonies as it is porous, can habour germs and is not easily cleaned.

The nassasalars come an hour before the body is to be taken to the Towers. They sit near it and prepare the bier by laying strips of cloth cut from old sudrehs across it in such a manner that the body would be secure on it. The kusti prayers are recited by them and then the Sarosh Baj is recited in muted tones. If the nassasalars have to speak to each other, they do so in suppressed tones with teeth clenched and mouth closed. Once this is over, they sit silently beside the body.

The geh-sarna ceremony is the last of the funeral rites prayed for the dead. The first gatha, Ahunavaiti Gatha is recited. Although it is in a language no one can understand and the translations do not refer to the dead, whoever listens to it is soothed and comforted, and the bereaved get moral courage to bear with fortitude the loss of a dear one.

The prayer is recited by two priests who enter the room or hall holding a paiwand between them. They stand about three paces away from the body, cover their mouths and nose with a paddan (a small square cloth with strings attached to the upper corners to tie it at the back of the head) and start the prayer with the Ahunavaiti Gatha. When half the prayer has been recited there is a pause and the nassasalars lift the body from the slabs and place it on the bier. The prayer is then continued and completed. It is said that one should turn one's face away from the body when it is lifted onto the bier. The probable reason for this is to avoid inhaling the germs when it is moved.

After the prayers are over and the final sagdid is done, the close members of the family approach the body to take a last look at the departed one. The men, who usually sit outside the room file past the body and pay their last respects which is known as sijda.

The face is then covered and the body is handed over by the nassasalars to the khandias who carry the body to the Towers, or Aramgar (burial place) as the case may be. Their number varies depending on the weight of the body, but they are always in pairs. The two priests follow at a distance of three yards followed by the men who attended the ceremony. They are all dressed in white, with the traditional dugli and phento or pagri covering their heads. They too walk in pairs, holding a handkerchief between them. Nowadays close female member of the family also accompany the body upto the Tower gates.

Once there, the bier is placed on a platform and the face is uncovered for the last time, and the last sijda and sagdid is performed. The body is carried into the Towers by the nassasalars who had also accompanied it, and it is left on one of the pavis (sections reserved for the bodies to be placed). The clothes are cut open to attract the eye of the birds of prey. The flesh is removed from the bones in a matter of hours and the bones are dried by the sun.

One of the nassasalars claps his hands to indicate to those outside that the body has been placed in the Tower and when they come out, the gate of the Tower is locked. The men go to a sagri to wash their hands and faces and perform the kusti prayers. The people then return home, where they bathe, wash their hair and change their clothes.

A sagri is slightly different from a fire temple, in that it is specially built in the premises of the Towers of Silence, and quite close to it. A light or divo is kept burning there twenty-four hours and is placed in such a way that from a slit in the wall of the sagri the light falls on the Towers. In many mofussil towns the sagri has an electric bulb burning night and day. This also has another purpose, in that the relatives who spend four days and nights at the bunglis or cottages attached to the Towers have the comfort of praying there, as it has all the facilities of a fire temple.

This was the form of disposal of the dead in ancient Iran, 3000 years ago where arable land was not wasted on the dead, pollution of the environment was avoided and the safety and health of the living was of paramount importance; and we still follow this form.

If the funeral takes place in a home, that area is not used for ten days in winter and thirty days in summer, after which it is to be washed with a disinfectant (cow's urine was used as the disinfectant in early days).

For three days after a death in the family, the close relatives abstain from eating meat. Eggs and fish are allowed with vegetables. This abstinence is called parhezi. Here also it is a matter of health, as during a period of sadness and mourning, meat is more difficult to digest than vegetables. Usually no food is cooked in the home where death has taken place, and some relatives or good friends bring the food from their own homes.

It is believed that the soul of a dead person remains on earth for three days and while it is still on earth it is under the protection of Sarosha, the guardian angel of the soul of man, living or dead. It is for this reason that the Sarosh nu Patru is prayed in honour of Sarosha every evening at sundown after the funeral and before the oothamna. All the prayers start by invoking Sarosha by reciting the Sarosh Baj and praying for his help in protecting the soul of the departed one. The Sarosh Baj is also prayed at the change of each geh during these three days.

Two oothamna ceremonies are performed, one on the afternoon of the third day at the start of the Uziran geh and one at the dawn of the fourth day. The latter is called the charum or patli raat nu oothamnu. The afternoon one is performed for the friends and relatives who would like to attend the ceremony but cannot do so at dawn. The morning one is generally attended by only the very close relatives and friends.

If the funeral is performed in the afternoon, three Sarosh na Patra are performed instead of two as at other times. It is considered fortunate to have three of them performed as three is a sacred number. The soul remains on earth for three days and it also symbolizes the three most important principles of the Zoroastrian religion—humata, hukhta, havareshta—good thoughts, good words, good deeds.

The Sarosh nu Patru prayer asks for the protection of Sarosha for the dead soul still on earth. The afringan ceremony is performed in honour of Sarosha by two priests.

(The priest performing the ceremony is called zaoti and the one tending the fire is called atravakshi). In this prayer a kutli of water is used and flowers arranged in a special way by the priests. The ceremony begins with the Sarosh Yasht in praise of the protection given to the soul and ends with Patet Paseman (prayer of remembrance and for forgiveness for any misdeeds).

The last oothamna is performed by the head priest of the town or fire temple along with four or more priests. It is a very important ceremony, because it is at this time that the soul is supposed to cross the Chinvat Bridge and account for his life to Meher Davar, the judge, Rashne Rast, the angel of justice and Astad, the angel of truth. The soul is now handed over to Meher Davar.

The oothamna ceremony is a beautiful one with flowers arranged all around in silver vases. There is also a tray of seasonal fruits, pomegranate leaves if the fruit is not available, dates, water, sherbet, wine and milk kept in small kutlis. The dates and pomegranate are most essential in these ceremonies. The sacred bread called darun (a thick chapati) is also placed there along with a shiav—a set of clothes consisting a material for five sudrehs, or made up of one sudreh, one jama (a coat), one pyjama, one topi (cap), one pair of petwa (socks) and one pichori (belt), which is usually given to the priest. The aferghaniyu is also there with sandalwood and frankincense. The prayer too is a beautiful one and gives much more comfort to the living than the funeral prayer.

The baj and afringan ceremonies are also performed on this occasion, along with the Arad Farvash prayer for which papri (a crisp, flat poori) and malido (a sweet made with semolina, ghee and sugar) and rotli are placed in the tray.

At the end of the oothamna it is the custom for the eldest son or a relative to announce the charities to be bestowed in the name of the deceased. At this time also, if the person has performed great deeds for the sake of humanity, his country or the community, the head priest or senior citizen may propose to the anjuman (assembly) that the name of the deceased be included in the Dhuj Nirang prayer where all the great men of the Zoroastrian religion are named. This is a custom handed down from Avestan times.

These ceremonies are performed at the site of the Towers of Silence, in the same hall where the funeral took place.

These prayers are also said on the chahram (fourth day), dehum or dusmu (tenth day), masiso or siroj (thirtieth day), chumsi (sixth month) and sal roj or versi (one year), and thereafter on the yearly anniversary of the death, either at home or in the fire temple.

The Yasna, Visparad and the Vendidad are also special prayers said during this time, but can only be recited at the atash behram or agiari where there is a dar-e-meher (a special area kept aside for these prayers). On the third night, at midnight, the chahram nee chasni (chasni means to taste) is also performed at the fire temple. For this a sweet rice called zardo is cooked along with bafelo mitho kand, (boiled sweet potatoes) and wafers.

I was in my teens when I visited the Towers of Silence in Bombay on the death of my paternal grandmother. The Sarosh nu Patru was being recited for three different people in three different bunglis, all within hearing distance of each other. I remember going out to the veranda to see who could be playing what sounded like a kind of strange music in a place like this. Then I realized that it was not music, but the sound of six priests praying together.

I had the same experience when I went to Navsari with some friends and Vada Dasturji Meherji Rana invited us to a jashan in the famous atash behram which has a marble wall containing the image of the first Meherji Rana in the natural grains of the stone. There were eighteen priests praying together and the effect was something I can never forget. It is strange that even though most of us do not understand the language, these prayers still have such an effect on one—it must be the vibrations of the beautiful chant.

There is a belief amongst Zoroastrians that the departed souls of our near ones do not lose touch with the living and their farvashis are with us whenever we need their help—especially of those who have been very close to us and whom we have loved and admired.

I believe I have had many experiences myself of being helped by the farvashis of those whom I have loved, but 1 will not talk about them as they may be wrongly interpreted as figments of my imagination.

However I would like to relate the experience that a doctor had regarding my younger brother Soli, who was an exceptional human being—a musician, sportsman and mountaineer with a wonderful sense of humour. He was lying in the ICU unit at a hospital, recovering from a heart attack when he suffered another one. The patient in the bed next to him was himself a heart specialist. Seeing the nurses in a panic, he disconnected his own leads and rushed to my brother's side to revive him, but unfortunately it was too late. Some years later, when this same doctor was in the USA on a visit, he suffered another very severe heart attack. He realized that his life was slipping away from him, when he felt the presence of my brother in the ambulance and found himself recovering. He believes that it was my brother's farvashi that had saved him.

SATUM

These are prayers said in honour of the dead and are prayed over meals by the gher no panthaki (the family priest) for the four days after the death of a person. These are said three times during the day—in the morning, afternoon and evening at about seven o'clock.

A special room or area in the home is kept aside for these ceremonies. An aferghaniyu is placed on a stone stool and next to it on an aani (a three-legged brass stool) is a tray with sandalwood, frankincense and a divo. On another aani is a tray with the meal.

The morning meal consists of a kutli of tea, fruit, water, a poro (a flat omelette prepared with chopped onions and chillies or just with salt and pepper), rotli, papri, malido, bhakra (small doughnuts made with tari). Tari is the fermented sap of a date or coconut tree. Now, where there is prohibition in various states, this is made with yeast or baking powder and the true taste is lost!

The afternoon and evening meals, especially the ones prepared for the satum on the third day after the death of a person consists of the favourite food of the departed one. There may be upto three or four dishes, and water. Wine, tari or any alcoholic drink was always included in the states where there was no prohibition.

On the fourth day after the death the period of abstinence is broken by preparing a meal of dhan sakh, kababs and gor amli noo kachumber, tari or any other alcohol. This is placed in the afternoon tray for the satum prayers and the family priest is invited to share the lunch with the family. He is given a gift for all the assistance he has provided in making the arrangements for the funeral and subsequent prayers.

At all satums a separate small tray containing milk or food is always kept for the kutra no buk—the morsel for the dog of the house. If there is no family dog, then it is given to any dog in the street. In the old days every Zoroastrian home had a pet dog who faithfully guarded the home and sometimes did the sagdid as well. The kutra no buk, reminds me of Woolie, Mamaiji's dog. Meherbai, our gorani (a lady of the priestly class who cooked the food during the muktad days) would catch the local train from Bandra and arrive at Churchgate station every morning to cook food during the muktad days and give Woolie the kutra no buk. The house was within walking distance from the station, and after the first day, Woolie would accompany her to the station every evening and go to the station every morning to receive her and escort her to the house. This is why the dog is always remembered in our prayers because of his unflinching loyalty, faithfulness and love for the person who feeds him the kutra no buk, his master and his family.

While reciting the satum prayers the priest recites the name of the dead person in whose honour the prayers are being said, and while doing so puts some sandalwood and frankincense on the fire. He repeats this while also reciting the names of other members of the family who have died along with the names of great Zoroastrians of days gone by.

At the end of these prayers family members place some sandalwood and frankincense on the fire, while praying for the peace of the departed soul and others before him.

MUKTAD

The muktad days are the last ten days of the year before Navroz. Some families keep eighteen days for this period—ten days before Navroz and seven after. The first five days are called panje keh or five small days and the next five days are called panje mah or the five big days. These last five are the most important and holy. They are known as the gatha days. One of the five gathas is recited on each of these five days.

The muktad days are especially kept for the remembrance of the dead of the family. They are known as the Farvardin holidays when the souls of the dead are invoked to come to their earthly homes, where prayers are recited in their honour. These are the days when the living members are to reflect on their past deeds and take stock of the good and bad that they did during the year.

It is believed that the souls of our dead want their names

recited in the baj, afringan and satum prayers. Hence they are mentioned by name. The names of the living members of the family are also recited in the Farmaiushni (the people who have authorized the prayers to be said). This complete list of names is called the nam grehan (remembering names).

The muktads of my youth are still very vivid in my mind. How well I recall the special room kept aside for the muktad in my maternal grandmother's home in Bombay. The house had a lovely garden with mango, pomelo, chickoo and pomegranate trees, along with numerous flowering trees. It also had a huge Ashoka tree with an eagle's nest on top. There was a veranda for those alighting from carriages and two gates in the garden for easy manoeuvering of the horses and carriages. Now this has been replaced by a multi-storied building—the price we have to pay for progress! One woke up in the morning to the sound of bird songs and the wafting aroma of charcoal broiled toasts and real coffee being brewed for breakfast.

The room kept aside for the muktad was at the back of the house, with a passage leading to it from the main living area. Behind this was the famous Cross Maidan, from where we could hear the shouts of young boys playing cricket in the evenings.

One entered the room from an adjoining room facing the back garden, where we used to sit and eat the delicious lunches cooked by Meherbai, our gorani, and that is when, at the tender age of five, my love affair with cooking started. One door led to the special kitchen and another door led out to the side of the garden where there was a well and a pomegranate tree. In the old days, the fisherwomen would come with baskets of fresh fish, practically alive from the day's catch across the railway lines (there was no reclaimed Marine Drive at that time) and return with large handas of fresh well-water.

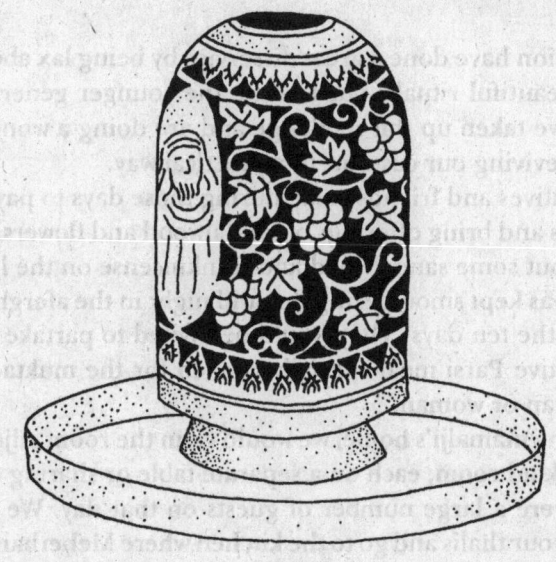

Divo

Inside the room, near the door was a large marble-topped table with brass legs, and on it were the vases of silver and crystal all beautifully arranged with fresh flowers brought from my masi's garden in Pune. There were roses, carnations, dahlias, gladioli and tube roses, which arrived every other day by train and were arranged by the ladies of the house who took turns to do so. They would awaken early in the morning, bathe, wash their hair, put on a mathubanu and come into the room to arrange the flowers. Each departed soul had a separate vase and the flowers were arranged to keep their memories evergreen.

On the right side of the room was the stone stool for the aferghaniyu along with the aanis for the sandalwood, frankincense and divo and the meal for the satum cooked by Meherbai.

The scent of the flowers, sandalwood, and frankincense mingled with the aroma of food and the delightful days of the Farvardin holidays are a cherished memory. I feel very privileged for having experienced this. The people of my generation have done a great disservice by being lax about all these beautiful rituals, but I salute the younger generations who have taken up the challenge and are doing a wonderful job in reviving our customs in a practical way.

Relatives and friends came during those days to pay their respects and bring offerings of sandalwood and flowers. They would put some sandalwood and frankincense on the lit fire, which was kept smouldering day and night in the aferghaniyu during the ten days. They would be invited to partake of the superlative Parsi meal specially cooked for the muktad by a Parsi man or woman.

In my mamaiji's home, we would sit in the room adjoining the muktad room, each on a separate table or sharing one, if there were a large number of guests on that day. We would pick up our thalis and go to the kitchen where Meherbai would be waiting to serve us. We would then return to our chairs and eat the ambrosia she had prepared.

The seventh day after Navroz is called Amardad roj and it is the day the farvashis return to their heavenly abode. On the night before a large thali with the bhat nu bhonu is prepared, tied in a large tablecloth and left on a separate aani. This is supposed to be the hamper containing the food the farvashis may need on their way back. It contains dishes like gharab ne govad no patio (fish roe and cluster bean curry), papeta ma ghost (savoury meat with potatoes), bhakra, tareli boi (fried mullet), papran (large papri); mehsoor (a sweet made with sugar, ghee and gram flour). Some loose coins are also put in the bundle in case it is needed for the journey. At dawn of Amardad roj the flowers and the hamper are removed. The flowers are thrown into a river or the sea. Some of the food is given to the family priest for his family and the rest is distributed to the poor.

Thus ends the muktad for the year.

6

Navroz

The spring or vernal equinox—21 March—is, according to the Parsis, the dawn of a new year. The actual time when the change takes place is recorded in Iran and then the information is sent all over the world wherever there are Zoroastrians.

In my youth Navroz was a day for celebration and meeting friends. We would wake up to the sound of a 'nankhatai' band playing the favourite tunes of the day. The band was perhaps not quite so tuneful but it would cheerfully play a couple of songs for a rupee or two. Our Goan ayahs would make us bathe and don our new clothes, after which we would have the traditional breakfast and visit the fire temple with our mother. There we would meet our relatives and friends and wish them with greetings of Navroz Mubarak or Sal Mubarak (Happy New Year) . We would then visit the elders of the family where gifts would be exchanged, and stay for lunch where we would be joined by our father.

The most traditional drink of this day is falooda which is prepared with milk, flavoured with rose-water and other ingredients. The traditional lunch consisted of sev and sweet dhai followed by pulao and masala ni dar (dal). These are synonymous with the Navroz lunch, but dhan dar ne patio ne ghee kando (rice, plain dal, garnished with onions fried crisp in pure ghee and served with a thick sweet and sour curry made with fish, shell fish, or if vegetarian, brinjal or drumsticks) is also served. Often this dish is served for lunch and the pulao and dal are served at dinner. The meal would end with ravo. There are also other traditional and not so traditional dishes which are served.

The homes are decorated with torans and chalk, and vases are full of flowers. Presents are exchanged and all in all this is a very happy occasion with lots of fun and laughter, when everyone looks forward to a happy and prosperous New Year. In the old days most Parsi homes had a piano and the children were taught the gentle art of piano playing. The parties would usually end with a sing-song, and young and old would join in singing the favourite tunes of the past and present, ending with *Chaye hame Zarthoshti*—we are Zoroastrians.

THE NAVROZ TABLE

This is a lovely Iranian tradition which was practised and observed by the Zoroastrians when in Iran. It is still practised by the Iranian Zoroastrians and also by those who came to India much after the Parsis.

A table is covered with a white tablecloth as white indicates purity. On it is placed a small bowl with a silver coin and on top of it is a pomegranate surrounded with five or seven roses. Next to this is a picture of the prophet Zarathushtra and a book of the Avesta prayers. A mirror is placed in such a way that it reflects the pomegranate and the prophet's photograph. It is believed that at the exact time of the vernal equinox, the pomegranate moves and the mirror catches the movement!

The Navroz Table

Also on the table are placed a lit divo or candle for light, a bowl of water with live fish, if possible and seven food items beginning with 's'—sirka (vinegar), sumac (a spice), samanu (halwa), sib (apple), sir (garlic), senjed (berry of the sorb tree), sabzi (herbs). Along with these are an aferghaniyu with sandalwood and frankincense for perfume, a shallow earthenware plate with sprouted wheat or other beans for prosperity, flowers for colour and a silver coin for wealth. Fresh fruit, dried fruit, seeds of pumpkin and vegetables of every kind available are placed there to welcome the spring. Painted eggs are placed for productivity (perhaps the painted Easter eggs have been derived from this custom), and grains for abundance. Seven food items beginning with 'sh' in Persian—sharab (wine), shakar (sugar), shir (milk), shirini (sweetmeat), shirberenj (sweet), shira (syrup) and shahad (honey) are also placed on this festive table.

The lady of the house greets her guests as they arrive and leads them to the table. She makes them look into the mirror which has already reflected Navroz, so that her friends, for the rest of the year may have good reflections, she makes them look at the silver coin so that they may have wealth during the year, she sprinkles them with rose-water so that they may be as sweet smelling as the rose and then invites them to the table laden with food. This is a beautiful custom which the Parsis should take up as their ancestors used to practise it in Iran.

There is a lot of change for the better in the air. The youth is taking a lead in all matters concerning the Zoroastrians, in India as well as abroad, especially in America. It was the generation who are now in their sixties, seventies and eighties who had allowed the religion to lapse into a type of lethargy and neglect, especially in the days of the Raj. Perhaps with the vitality and zeal of the youth, Parsis may not after all become an extinct and endangered race!

7

Jashan, Ghambars and Faresta

A jashan is a prayer ceremony performed by two or more
priests, on important occasions, happy or sad. Jashans are
also performed on the ghambar days.

When it is performed on a death anniversary it is called the
jashan of that person's baj. If it is to celebrate the anniversary
of a fire temple it is called the jashan of the salgireh. If it is to
celebrate a ghambar, then it is called the jashan of the
ghambar.

Jashans are also performed for joyous occasions such as a
first birthday, wedding anniversary, for thanksgiving after
perhaps recovering from a serious illness, or after an
important work is completed. It is often performed when
one moves into a new home, or in factories, when new
machinery has been installed and before production work
starts. Public jashans are performed at the end of a war or
pestilence in the country. It is performed on Navroz and
other Parsi holidays.

For a jashan ceremony, a white sheet is laid out on a
carpet or durrie. An aferghaniyu is placed in the centre. On
one side is a tray with sandalwood and frankincense for the

fire and on the other side is a tray with all seasonal fruits (dates and pomegranate must be included and if pomegranate cannot be obtained, then the leaves of the tree should be placed in the tray). It also contains kutlis of water, milk, sherbet and any alcoholic drink or wine. A divo and a small tray of cut flowers for the priests to use in the ceremony are placed near this tray.

The officiating or main priest is called the zaota and the assistant priest who tends the fire is called the raspi.

In this ceremony the seven amesha-spentas—the immortal bountiful ones are invoked. They are:-

Hormuzd, guardian of man
Vahu Mana, protector of the animal kingdom
Asha Vahistha whose emblem is fire
Kshathra Vairya, protector of the sky and metals on earth
Spenta Armaiti, protector of the earth
Haurvatat, protector of the water
Ameretat, protector of plant life.

Hence we have in this ceremony, as in all Zoroastrian religious ceremonies, representatives of these seven amesha-spentas. The metals for Kshathra Vairya are represented by the aferghaniyu in which the fire is lit, the chamcho which is the flat spoon and the chipyo, the tongs used to tend the fire. We have the kutlis of water for Haurvatat and milk for Vahu Mana representing the animal kingdom. The earth for Spenta Armaiti is represented by the ground on which the priests sit during the ceremony. The flowers represent the plant life for Ameretat and man is represented by the priests themselves.

The main ceremony performed in the jashan is the afringan ceremony.

After the ceremony is over, everyone eats some of the chasni, the fruits which were prayed upon during the ceremony especially the dates and pomegranate. If it is for a joyous occasion then, in typical Parsi fashion 'light refreshments' of the usual kind are served to the invitees.

GHAMBARS

There are six ghambars which are celebrated. These are seasonal festivals, and they last for five days each. They were originally associated with agricultural activities and are offered as a thanksgiving for a successful season. Thanksgiving for the creation of the heavens, earth, fire, water, vegetation, animals and man were added to the ceremonies later on.

It is considered the duty of Zoroastrians to celebrate the ghambars since we should not remember God only in times of trouble, but also remember to thank Him for his bountiful gifts. Jamshed Pasha was said to be the first person to celebrate the ghambars.

The first ghambar is the Maidhyozarem which is performed in mid spring; the second is the Maidhyoshem performed in mid summer; the third is Paitishhayem performed after the harvest has been collected in autumn; the fourth is the Ayathrem whose meaning is not certain but is performed about a month after the third; the fifth is the Maidhyarem during mid winter and the last is the Hamaspathmaedaem which is performed during the last five days of the year, i.e. just before Navroz.

These occasions are followed by a solemn feast in which all the members of the community in a particular locality take part. Each person may contribute to the function whatever little he has, and rich and poor sit down to eat together. If a person is too poor to contribute anything, he can help manually in the preparation of the food.

The meal is simple—masala ni dar ne chavel (spiced dal and rice) served with kachumber. Sometimes a generous person may contribute an additional dish, which is usually papeta ma gosht (meat cooked with potatoes).

Private individuals and families often celebrate the ghambars for the first year after the death of a member of the family, in his or her remembrance, but the public ones are the important ones wherein the rich learn of the wants of the poor and the poor learn of the manners and good traits of the nobility.

FARESTA

This is a ceremony where all the thirty-three yazatas (angels) are invoked and praised. There are in a fact a very large number of yazatas, but thirty-three are the most important. Thirty of them preside over each day of the month and three are extra. The faresta ceremony consists of reciting the Afringan and Baj for each of these thirty-three yazatas. It is a very lengthy ceremony and is therefore performed by more than one pair of priests.

It is usually performed as a very special thanksgiving, such as on the birth of the first baby in the family, a navjote or marriage, as a housewarming or after a war, or epidemic or the safety of a loved one from great harm.

During the Second World War, during the Battle of Mandalay, my brother Furdoon, an officer in the Indian Artillery was flying his little plane, when he was shot at. It was Navroz day and my mother had gone to the fire temple to pray for the safety of her son. It was as she was praying that not a single hair of this body should be hurt, that the bullet hit him, at exactly 11.30 a.m. The bullet ricocheted off the clip of his ear phones, and went through the top of his cap, tearing it to shreds. The men on the ground thought it was all over for him, but one of the farestas must have heard my mother's fervent prayer and he walked out of the plane alive. That was one occasion when the faresta ceremony was performed, and along with the flowers and other items the torn cap was also placed in a tray near the aferghaniyu, in grateful thanks for a precious life saved.

Recipes

Recipes

Prelude to the Recipes

Much has been said and more is to come, about the traditional and not so traditional dishes of the Parsis. However, there are some that are unusual by any standards.

Amongst the curries, some unusual ones are falsa ni curry, a curry made from a small sweet and sour berry, and cutlets ni curry, made with cutlets instead of meat pieces.

In days gone by, when there were no wayside inns along the seashores of Gujarat, the *Vivid Vani* describes a unique khichdi for travellers. To prepare this khichdi, wash the rice and dal, slightly crush and mix with turmeric and salt (one presumes that one was supposed to carry these ingredients while travelling). Tie the rice and dal in two wet handkerchiefs and bury, not too deeply, on lighted twigs in the sand on the seashore. Light more twigs and dry leaves and place over the rice parcels for three-quarters of an hour. Remove the parcels, turn them around and repeat for another forty-five minutes. Open and eat. For all this trouble, we are informed, that it may not taste as good as an ordinary khichdi would but it will do!

To compensate for the previous recipe there is one which is cooked with chicken or meat, coconut milk, potatoes, almonds, sultanas, turmeric, cumin seeds, ginger, garlic, whole garam masala, nutmeg, star anise, black pepper and bay leaves. I leave it to you to combine the ingredients any way you wish and make up your own khichdi. I feel it should also have onions and a little oil for frying. There is also a khichdi in which fried spiced Bombay duck is added when it is three-quarters done.

I was introduced to another unusual khichdi by my sister-in-law, Sehroo Keki Mody. Medium-sized capsicums are filled with a sharp prawn patio and fried. When the khichdi is half cooked, half of it is removed from the pan, the capsicums are put on top of the khichdi in the pan and then covered with the remaining khichdi which was removed. The dish is then allowed to cook till done.

Uncommon sas to eat with the uncommon khichdi are ones made with cabbage, raw mangoes cocum (dried Indian sour plums), mince and gor-amli (jaggery and tamarind).

Some meat and chicken dishes have the most unusual combinations, which may not suit any but the Parsi palate. Chicken may be cooked with candied sweet potato, gooseberries, raw or ripe papaya, dried apricot and peaches—the latter two would be acceptable to the western palate. Dodhi no dumbo (pumpkin stuffed with meat) is a most unusual and delightful party dish and its recipe is included in the meat and poultry section.

Boomla seera paila is an unbelievable dish—fresh lamprey are deboned, lightly fried, pressed with a light weight for a short while and then dipped in sugar syrup and eaten! I am not sure if even I would like to try it!

As vegetables are not a high priority in Parsi cuisine, not much can be said about them, but drumsticks cooked in toddy or kantolas, a round spiky bitterish vegetable, cooked with jaggery are some specialities.

A typical Parsi soup of the days gone by is called tari ma tarkari no soup, even though it is not a vegetable soup and has pieces of meat in it. The fact is that it has a lot more vegetable than meat and is thus called a vegetable soup! It contains potatoes, onions, sweet potatoes, yam, carrots, green peas, mint, celery and parsley and some meat, and it is cooked with toddy till the meat is done.

An excellent and really unusual vegetarian dish is cutlets made with savoury custard whose recipe is included here. I was introduced to it in Bangalore, when I was asked to be a judge in a cookery competition. I gave this dish the first prize, not knowing that it was prepared by a friend and excellent cook Mrs Parvez Dhunbura, who has also given me the recipes for the khaman na larva and sadhna which are in this book.

Bhajias, or pakoras as they are known in the North, are popular throughout India. These are usually made with different vegetables or paneer, but the Parsis make them with custer, brains, kooto (tiny shrimps), prawns, chicken, mince and even tinned salmon!

There are some interesting variations with poori. Some of them are sweet and some are stuffed—with the famous Parsi estew, crabs, oysters, prawns, savoury mince or even akoori. There are flaky poori, poori made with yeast, or a mixture of gram and rice flour.

Murumbas are made not only with the common mango, pear and pumpkin, but with potatoes as well. Achars are made with chunks of preserved mangoes, peel of orange and sweet lime and chutneys made with sliced mango preserve.

It seems that the imaginative Parsi housewife was not satisfied with making unusual dishes. She has also made a chilli wine (God help the European who drinks it) and a rose-flavoured brandy (let us not tell the French about it), by filing a bottle three-quarters full of red rose petals, pouring over brandy and storing for fifteen days before use!

Food in the Parsi home of yore must have been quite interesting, with never a dull meal and each one to be looked forward to in great anticipation by the household. There was all the time in the world to create the fascinating meals that have made Parsi cuisine so interesting and famous.

INGREDIENTS

Wherever I have mentioned ghee, it is pure ghee. This was the standard fat used in earlier days for cooking, except when frying, for which sesame seed oil was used. This is the oil of choice when frying fish. Peanut oil is also used and some recipes call for mustard oil. Olive oil does not blend in flavour with Parsi cuisine, or for that matter, with any other Indian cuisine.

Ghee gives a special flavour which no other cooking medium gives. However, one has to acquire a taste for it. It is apt to be rather heavy, so one could use a little for flavour along with the regular cooking medium used in the home. Butter may also be substituted for ghee. A few drops of oil added to it, will prevent butter from burning.

Salt

The flavour of rock salt is delicious. One can get it in powdered form or in pieces which can then be crushed.

People living in the coastal areas have the advantage of using sea salt, which I miss so much, living out of Bombay!

I feel these natural salts are so much finer and healthier than the packet salt one buys in the market these days.

Vinegar

The vinegar from Valsad and Navsari has a distinct flavour and this should be used in most Parsi pickles and chutneys, as well as the patias as it gives the right flavour.

Garlic

Garlic available in the West is stronger in favour and has larger cloves. It is suggested that quantities mentioned in these recipes should be halved if used in the West.

Ginger

Whenever ginger is mentioned in this book, use fresh root ginger washed, scraped and either chopped, ground or crushed with a mallet.

COCONUT MILK

> 1 coconut grated with the brown skin removed
> 2 cups hot water

Soak coconut in hot water and leave for about 10-15 minutes. Squeeze with your hand to extract all juice. Strain coconut through a muslin cloth and squeeze out remaining juice, to get coconut milk of a creamy milk consistency.

TAMARIND WATER

> Tamarind the size of a large lime (about 50 g)
> 1 cup hot water

Soak tamarind in hot water for 15 minutes. Squeeze well to extract juice. Strain and rub pulp in strainer with your hand to extract remaining pulp.

GHAU NU DOODH

1-2 kg whole wheat

Soak wheat in water for two days, changing water every day.

Grind wheat and hang in a cloth. Place a flat pan under cloth to catch drippings. When dry, break up into pieces and store in refrigerator. Use as and when required. Cream of wheat may be used as a substitute.

HOW TO MAKE PERFECT WAFERS AND SALI

Wafers and sali are essential to Parsi cuisine.

Peel potatoes and wash well. Slice or shred them. Wash several times in cold water till all the starch has been removed. Steep in iced water and a little salt and keep for half an hour.

Heat oil in a large karai or frying pan. Remove a little of the wafers or sali and dry them in a towel. Sprinkle into hot oil and lower temperature. Add half a teaspoon of concentrated salt water (two teaspoons salt dissolved in half a cup water) to oil, and separate wafers or sali with a fork. The secret is to allow them to fry slowly so that they become crisp without getting brown, and remain yellow. They will rise to the top when they are cooked crisp. Drain well in a large colander and spread out on paper to remove all traces of oil.

Whenever I go to a Parsi lagan or navjote, I can guess the quality of the food to come by tasting the wafers.

SPICES

To get the best flavour from spices, such as coriander, cumin, dry chillies, and garam masala they must be dry roasted on a griddle (tavo) and then powdered and used.

To dry roast correctly, heat griddle. Remove from heat and

put 2-4 spoons of the spice on it. Keep tossing till lightly roasted, but not over browned. Remove from griddle. Reheat griddle and repeat the procedure till all the spice has been roasted. This may be a little troublesome, but is well worth the effort.

In the old days, we used to grind the whole spices every day, according to the day's requirements. Even now, this practice is followed in some homes.

The black curry stone was used for this purpose, and nothing can replace it. I can still recall the rhythmic sound of the grinding in the mornings, which had a somehow soothing effect on me, as if to say, all is well!

In today's hurried lifestyle, new gadgets have come to replace the curry stones, which are helpful to the busy housewife, but the smoothness and texture of a masala ground on the curry stone can never be matched by any machine.

I would strongly recommend that the powdered spices that one uses are bought whole and ground at home for a month at a time. It may be a bit of a bother, but you will taste the difference in the food.

As for ginger and garlic, used in most Parsi dishes—grind about 100 g with a pinch of salt and store in the refrigerator in an airtight glass jar. It will stay very well for a fortnight.

If you are a purist, this is as far as you can go without the curry stone!

I would never use a readymade curry powder. However, I am lenient enough to give you some recipes for curry powders which you can make and store for use in an emergency.

Given below are recipes for a few basic masalas commonly used in Parsi cuisine.

MURCHA NI BHUKHI
(Chilli powder)

This is an excellent chilli powder. It gives colour and taste with
the right amount of pungency.

> 400 g dry red Goa chillies
> 400 g dry red Kashmiri chillies
> 100 g dry red Resumpati chillies
> 100 g dry red local chillies (any good variety)
> 2-3 tbsp oil

Dry roast chillies individually with a little oil. Cool and grind to
a powder.

Store in an airtight glass jar.

Note: Resumpati chillies are a type of red chilli with a smooth
skin grown in Maharashtra and Andhra Pradesh.

BASIC GARAM MASALA

> 15 g cinnamon
> 10 g cloves
> 15 g white cardamoms
> 10 g black peppercorn (optional)
> 10 g cumin seeds (optional)

Grind all ingredients individually, mix and store in an airtight
glass jar.

BHARUCHI GARAM MASALA

> 20 g cinnamon
> 20 g cloves
> 20 g white cardamoms
> 20 g black peppercorn
> 100 g nutmeg
> 20 g mace
> 20 g star anise (badian)

Clean spices and grind to a powder. Do not dry roast or add oil.

Use this masala to sprinkle on top of vegetables or any other cooked dish. If it is fried or dry roasted, it will turn the food it comes into contact with, black

DHAN SAKH MASALA

This is the special masala used for cooking the famous dhan sakh.

There are many recipes for this masala, and this is the one used by my maternal grandmother, an extraordinary lady whom I still recall—especially the delicious morsels of food she would put into my mouth when I would creep up to her while she was eating one of her fabulous brunches!

I thought it produced the best dhan sakh, until I tasted the one prepared by a lady I met in Valsad, Mrs Aloo Shroff, and I had to bow to the better one.

1" piece turmeric (preferably the round variety)
50 g curry leaves
250 g cumin seeds
60 g carraway seeds (shahi jeera)
1 kg coriander seeds
50 g mustard seeds
50 g fenugreek seeds (methi)
50 g cinnamon
50 g cloves
50 g white cardamoms
200 g black peppercorn
50 g poppy seeds (khus khus)
50 g bay leaves (tej patta)
50 g dried orange peel, with pith removed
50 g dried sweet lime peel, with pith removed

Dry roast each ingredient individually with 1-2 tsp of oil on a tava or griddle. Cool, grind and mix. Store in an airtight glass container.

It can be kept for over one year.

SAMBHAR NO MASALO

(Sambhar spices)

100 g dry boria chillies (small round chillies, like cherries)
50 g dry red Resumpati or Goa chillies
100 g broken mustard seeds
250 g broken fenugreek seeds (methi)
20 g asafoetida (hing)
20 g cinnamon
20 g cloves
20 g black pepper
10 g star anise (badian)
1 tsp salt
2 tbsp oil

Grind all spices individually, except asafoetida. Mix and place in a large thali. Make a well in the centre and place asafoetida in it. Pour boiling oil on top and crush it completely with a wooden spoon. Mix well and cool.

Store in an airtight glass jar.

COMPLETE CURRY POWDER

With this curry powder, all you have to do to make a curry is to brown onions, and add curry powder, sauté, add chopped tomatoes if desired.

It is a useful masala to keep and use in an emergency, but please do not use it every time you wish to make a curry, as all your curries will taste the same.

75 g dried red chillies (use a mixture of Kashmiri, Goa and any local chillies)
50 g turmeric
75 g dry ginger powder
75 g dry garlic powder
200 g cumin seeds
10 g bay leaves (tej patta)
10 g dry curry leaves

400 g small coriander seeds
75 g mustard seeds
100 g fenugreek seeds (methi)
100 g poppy seeds (khus khus)
250 g roasted gram (channa)
10 g star anise (badian)
50 g black sesame seeds (til)
5 g cinnamon
5 g cloves
5 g white cardamoms weighed and peeled
10 g black peppercorn
2 nutmegs
5 g salt
2 tbsp oil

Wash and dry coriander, cumin and fenugreek seeds individually, as they are usually full of dust.

Dry roast and grind each ingredient individually and mix all together.

Heat oil till very hot, sprinkle onto spice powder and mix well. This preserves the masala for a longer time, and it does not spoil easily.

Store in an airtight glass container.

BHARUCHI CURRY POWDER

This recipe has been given by Mrs Dhunbai Cama of Bharuch, in whose home we had an excellent breakfast of fried spiced prawns, Bharuchi akoori, hot rotli and gharab nu achar, the taste of which still lingers in my mouth.

100 g dry red Goa chillies
100 g turmeric
250 g cumin seeds
250 g small coriander seeds
250 g poppy seeds (khus khus)
1 kg roasted gram (channa)
10 g cinnamon

10 g cloves
20 g white cardamoms weighed and peeled
10 g black peppercorn
2 nutmegs
10 g mace

Clean all ingredients, dry roast, cool and grind each individually. Mix, sieve and store in an airtight glass jar.

TRADITIONAL VALSAD MASALA (DRY)

This recipe and the following one were given to me by Devji, our cook in my mother's home.

4" piece ginger
1 pod garlic
2 tsp turmeric powder
10-15 dry red chillies
2 tsp cumin seeds
1 tbsp coriander seeds
2" piece cinnamon
6-7 cloves
5-6 white cardamoms, peeled
8-10 black peppercorns
1 tbsp poppy seeds (khus khus)
3 tsp salt

Grind all ingredients and store in an airtight glass jar. It can be kept for 5-6 days, and longer in the refrigerator.

TRADITIONAL VALSAD MASALA (GREEN)

4" piece ginger
1 pod garlic
2 tsp turmeric powder
10-15 green chillies
2 tsp cumin seeds
1 tbsp coriander seeds
2" piece cinnamon
6-7 cloves

5-6 white cardamoms, peeled
8-10 black peppercorns
1 tbsp poppy seeds (khus khus)
3 tsp salt

Grind all ingredients and store in an airtight glass jar.

This will only stay for 2-3 days, and a little longer in the refrigerator.

TABLE OF MEASURES

Teaspoon and tablespoon measures in this book are level unless otherwise stated.

1 cup = 8 oz.

Metric unit	Oz/fl. oz	American pint	cup	Imperial pint	cup	Tbsp
30	1					2
60	2					4
85	3					
115	4	¼	½			8
140	5-1 gill			¼	½	
170	6					
200	7					
225	8-½ lb	½	1			
255	9					
285	10			½	1	
310	11					
340	12		¾			
370	13					
395	14					
425	15				¾	
455	16-1 lb	1				
480	17					
510	18					
540	19					
570	20			1		
1 kg	2.2 lb					
1 litre		2 (1 quart)				1¾

IF YOU DO NOT HAVE SCALES

1 tsp		=	5 ml
1 tbsp	= 3 tsp	=	15 ml
2 tbsp	= 1 oz	=	30 ml

A pinch	=	less than ⅛ tsp (Literally a pinch)
A dash	=	3 drops
Size of a walnut	=	1 tbsp

125 g wheat flour	=	1 cup (8 oz)
125 g flour	=	1 cup
200 g sugar	=	1 cup
150 g semolina	=	1 cup
200 g butter	=	1 cup
125 g curd	=	1 cup
125 g currants	=	1 cup
125 g raisins	=	1 cup
125 g sultanas	=	1 cup
250 g pitted dates	=	1 cup
100 g nuts	=	1 cup
200 g rice	=	1 cup
200 g dal	=	1 cup
100 g green peas	=	1 cup
200 g ghee	=	1 cup
500 g minced meat	=	1 cup
500 g potatoes	=	4 medium-sized or 3 large
500 g onions	=	8 medium-sized or 3 large
500 g tomatoes	=	10 medium-sized or 3 large

SUBSTITUES

½ cup grated coconut + 1 cup water	=	55 g cream of coconut
	=	4 tbsp desiccated coconut
1 cup fresh milk	=	½ cup evaporated or condensed milk + ½ cup water
1 lime	=	2-3 tsp juice
Rind of 1 lime	=	1 tsp grated rind
1 orange	=	6-8 tbsp juice
Rind of 1 orange	=	1 tbsp grated rind
4 chillies	=	1 tsp chilli powder
1" cinnamon	=	½ tsp cinnamon powder
1" piece ginger	=	½ tsp ginger powder
	=	1 tsp ginger paste

1 pod medium garlic	=	1 tsp garlic powder
	=	1½ tbsp garlic paste
1 nutmeg	=	1 tsp nutmeg powder

OLD INDIAN WEIGHTS

1 tola			=	10 g
1 navtank			=	50 g
28 tolas	=	1 seer (Bombay)	=	280 g
40 tolas	=	1 rutal	=	400 g
1 tipri			=	250 g
1 piellee	=	4 seers (Bombay)	=	1 kg 120 g
1 Bombay seer	=	28 tolas	=	280 g
1 Delhi seer			=	1 kg
1 South Indian vis			=	1 kg 350 g
1 South Indian palam			=	40 g
1 gundoo			=	25 kg
1 paa seer			=	180 ml
1 Bombay seer			=	720 ml
1 Delhi seer			=	1 litre 50 ml
1 South Indian ollack			=	500 ml
1 South Indian measure			=	2 litres

OVEN TEMPERATURES

Description	Fahrenheit	Celsius	Gas mark
Cool	225	110	¼
	250	120	½
Very slow	275	135	1
	300	150	2
Slow	325	160	3
Moderate	350	175	4
	375	190	5
Moderately hot	400	200	6
Fairly hot	425	220	7
Hot	450	230	8
Very hot	475	245	9
Extremely hot	500	260	10

8

Pots and Pans

In the old days, at least till I got married, a bride was given a set of kitchen utensils called oria or padra na vasan (copper pots and pans) which were kallied (tinned). Some of them were made of brass as well. Most of these pots and pans are similar to those used in most parts of India.

Nowadays, aluminium, Hindalco, stainless steel, enamelled and non-stick pots and pans are given along with ovenproof glass, pressure cookers, gas or electric ovens and stoves, microwave ovens, refrigerators, and deep freezers.

The traditional utensils used by the Parsis are given below:

Hando or Handi: The hando is the larger of the vessels.

Karasio and kutli: Jugs without handles, usually of German silver. The karasio is the larger of the two.

Boiyu: A colander without legs.

Tapelis: Pans of different sizes and shapes.

Patio: A flat, broad-based pan with a wide mouth usually used for making the dish called patio, hence the name. It can be used for cooking other dishes mostly those with meat or

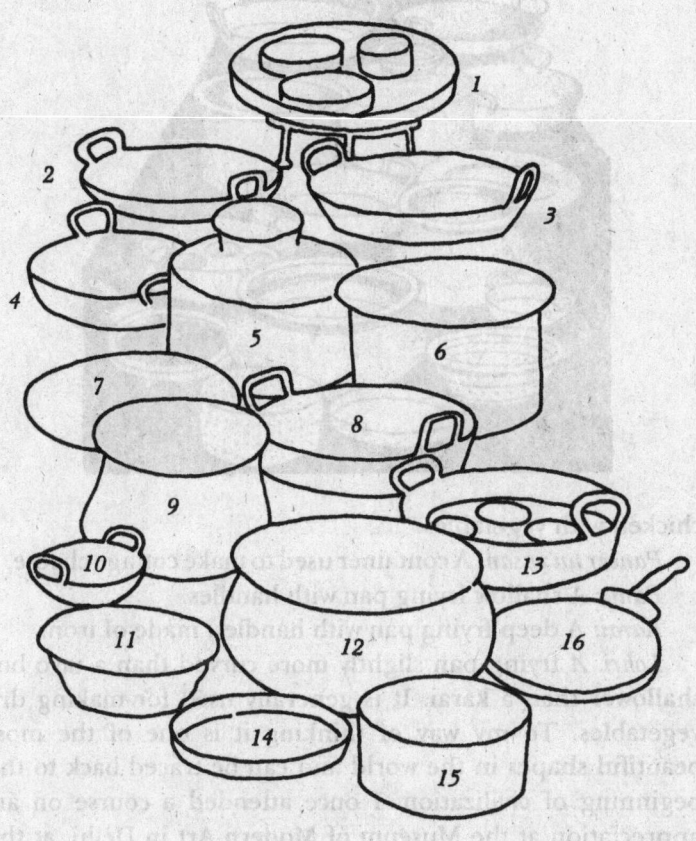

*1. A thali with bowls and kasio placed on an anni 2. Lohri 3. Panu 4.
Lungri 5. Chamboro 6. Tapeli 7. Dhaknu 8. Karai 9. Tapeli 10. Karai
11. Boiyu 12. Patio 13. Popatji nu panu 14. Lungri 15. Paneer nu
vasun 16. Griller*

chicken with vegetables.

Paneer nu vasan: A container used to make cottage cheese.

Panu: A shallow frying pan with handles.

Karai: A deep frying pan with handles, made of iron.

Lohri. A frying pan slightly more curved than a tavo but shallower than a karai. It is generally used for making dry vegetables. To my way of thinking it is one of the most beautiful shapes in the world and can be traced back to the beginning of civilization. I once attended a course on art appreciation at the Museum of Modern Art in Delhi, at the end of which each participant had to write a note on what he or she thought were the ten most beautiful pieces of art. I chose the lohri as one of the pieces of art that I found most beautiful, to the astonishment of many of my friends, 'How can you write about a kitchen utensil!' was the outcry. That's just it! How do you 'educate' the so-called 'educated'!

Tavo: A lightly curved griddle for making rotli.

Dhaknu: Shallow saucer-like curved lids of different sizes to

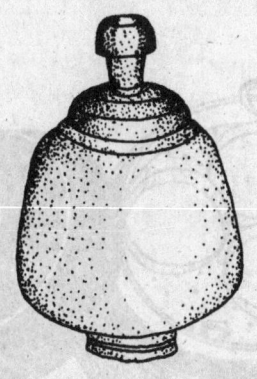

Pani nu matlu ne karasio

fit the tapelis. In the old days, when food had to be left covered to simmer in a pan, some water was always poured onto the lid so that the food did not get burnt.

Popatji nu panu: A type of karai with four round depression to make dishes called popatjis and popatji na pora (omelettes shaped like kababs due to being cooked in this particular utensil).

Sadhna nu vasan: A special steamer used to make the famous dish called sadhna made with rice flour and tari.

Velan ne pato: Rolling pin and board.

Masala no pato: Grinding stone and pestle or the famous curry stone.

Khal butto: Mortar and pestle, usually of brass.

Anni: A three-legged brass stand used to place handas or food on thalis during prayers.

Pani nu matlu: An earthen pot for storing water which keeps it delightfully cool in summer and gives the water a distinct and delicious taste.

Tavato: A flat square slicer.

Karchi: A ladle.

Chamcha: Spoons of different sizes and shapes.

Kata: Forks of different sizes.

Sadhna nu vasan

Chhari: Knives of different sizes.

Chamach: Slightly curved spoons.

Lungri: A flat round tray with a two-inch rim used to bake the famous Parsi custer.

Tambri: A container to hold water which is given to the son-in-law on the Varova day.

Special utensils used for prayers:

Lungri: A flat tray as described above for keeping the daran (sacred bread) or rotli.

Rukabi: A metal plate usually made of silver, silver plate or German silver, to hold the malido and papri in small amounts.

Kathok: A large round tray with a two or three-inch rim to carry sweets, daran and other items from the kitchen to the prayer room and also for making the daran.

Velan ne patlo: Rolling pin made of metal for rolling the rotli. No wooden items are used in Zoroastrian ceremonies as wood, being porous can absorb germs. The rolling pin is usually hollow and some have a bell inside them.

Handi or Kannoo: Used for drawing water from the well. Because of its narrow neck, it is easy to tie a rope around it. (Every fire temple has a well attached to it, from which water is drawn for use in the fire temple and the compound).

Chamboro: Utensil used to store the water drawn up by the Kannoo.

Karasio: A jug without handles to take out the water from the chamboro. This was used to drink water because, due to its shape, you could easily drink from it without touching it to your mouth and contaminating it, so it could be used by others, thus following one of the Zoroastrian practices of purity and hygiene.

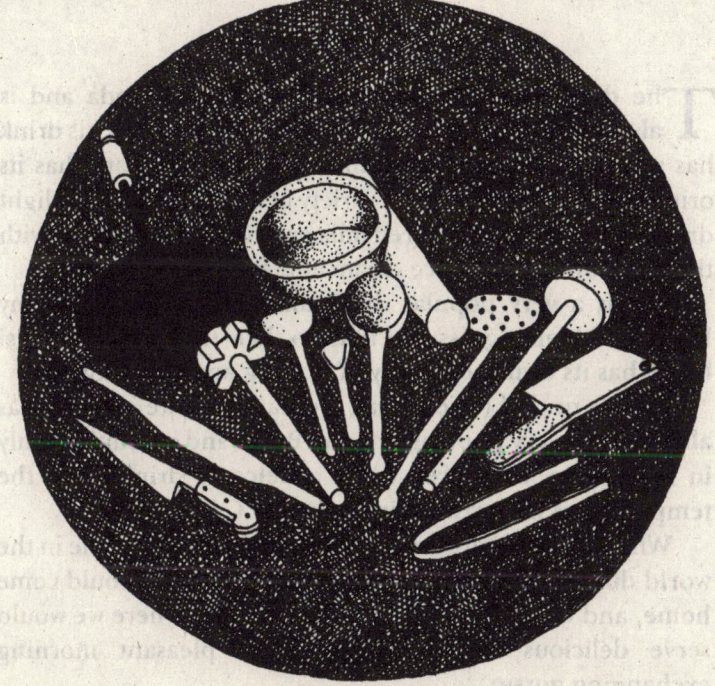

Articles used in the kitchen

9

Beverages

The drink which is traditionally Parsi is falooda and is always drunk on Jamshedi Navroz—21 March. This drink has now become popular in most parts of India and has its origin in Iran. It is made in a variety of ways, and can be a light drink with just rose-flavoured milk or a rich and heavy one with the addition of cream, ice cream and sev.

Tea is a very popular drink amongst the Parsis. Many Parsis add lemon grass and mint to their tea, and each Parsi home has its own special way of making and drinking tea.

Masala ni chai (spiced tea), a great favourite in India has also become very popular with the Parsis and is drunk mainly in the winter, while iced tea is a welcome drink when the temperatures in north India soar to 50°C in summer.

When my generation was young, we had all the time in the world during the mornings, before our menfolk would come home, and we used to have coffee mornings where we would serve delicious snacks and spend a pleasant morning exchanging gossip.

I used to put in a drop of vanilla essence and a pinch of

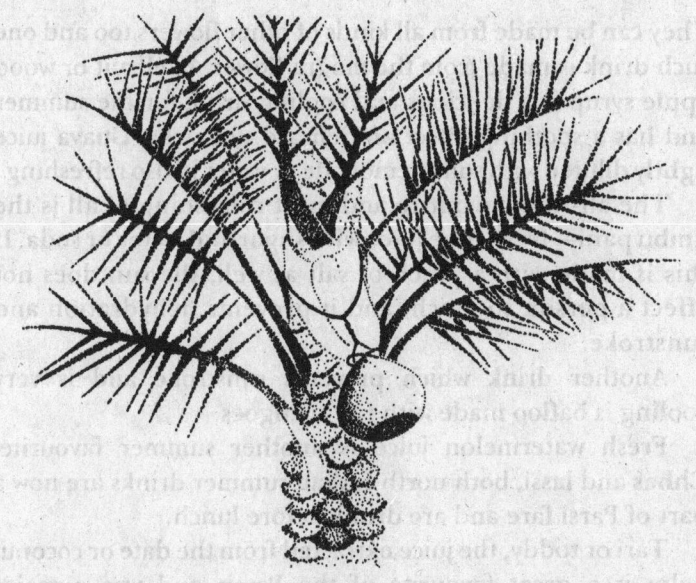

A toddy palm with a matka tied around it for the collection of toddy

cocoa when I percolated my coffee. But one has to be very careful as anything more than a drop and pinch can be disastrous! I recall an occasion when my husband was in the Air Force and the wife of the Chief of Air Staff was invited by the local Commanding Officer's wife for a coffee morning. Luckily she had asked me to come a little early as I had baked a cake and made a few small snacks for her. As soon as I entered the house, I was literally thrown back by a strong smell of vanilla. When I asked her what she was cooking, she told me that she had asked her cook to put some vanilla into the percolator. When confronted, the poor cook admitted to having put in a full tablespoon. Even after the percolator was washed out and fresh coffee prepared without any vanilla, there was enough flavour of the essence in the coffee.

Cold coffee—the richer the better—is another great favourite in summer.

Amongst the sherbets, the rose flavour is the most popular.

They can be made from all kinds of other flowers too and one such drink is made from the mogra flower. Baelfruit or wood apple syrup is a delicious and cooling drink for the summer and has a soothing effect on delicate stomachs. Guava juice lightly diluted with soda, lemonade or water is also refreshing.

The all-time favourite and most refreshing of all is the limbu pani—fresh lime juice with sugar and water or soda. If this is made with a pinch of salt as well, the sun does not affect a person so much, and it prevents dehydration and sunstroke.

Another drink which prevents sunstroke and is very cooling is bafloo made with raw mangoes.

Fresh watermelon juice is another summer favourite. Chhas and lassi, both north Indian summer drinks are now a part of Parsi fare and are drunk before lunch.

Tari or toddy, the juice extracted from the date or coconut palm is a great favourite of the Parsis and was a major money-spinner in Gujarat before the days of prohibition. Tari also has its medicinal values. Ooni ketheli tari—warmed tari with garlic and jaggery is given for upset stomachs.

Matkas or earthen pots are tied to the insertions made in the tree at night by the toddy tappers and the pots are removed early in the morning, before the sun rises. This fresh, light drink newly tapped from the trees before dawn is called neera and is drunk before it ferments. The fresh or slightly fermented juice, taken before ten o'clock in the morning is a delightful drink. In days gone by, we enjoyed many a picnic at Versova where at one time each bungalow had its own vadi or farm. We would watch the toddy tappers descend from the trees in the grove with their matkas and drink the neera or tari they carried down, with a breakfast of tareli machhi made with fresh pomfret, or kooto (tiny shrimps), fried with masala which the owners of the vadis had prepared for us from the fresh catch of the morning.

Many delicious tea time snacks such as bhakra, sadhna,

and popatji, are made with tari. They can of course be made with baking powder or yeast, but the taste is not at all the same. Meat and chicken cooked in tari are also typical Parsi dishes.

A very popular distilled drink was movru. This was made from the grape-like fruit of the movru tree. After it was distilled, it was allowed to mature for a year with dried black grapes and sultanas. This drink was then served as a liqueur, but after prohibition was introduced in Gujarat, one can no longer get movru.

Good wines and spirits are drunk and enjoyed by most Parsis. Wines are served with meals and much appreciated. Spirits, usually whiskey and soda are a regular feature before dinner in most Parsi homes, when the entire family gathers together after the day's work to relax and chat. We even have the famous Parsi peg (three fingers of whiskey), but this was not the norm in most households where at the most one or two drinks were consumed before dinner.

And for special occasions, for those who can afford it, there is always champagne!

Then there are the beverages drunk for strength, which are given to invalids, and women after childbirth. One of these is egg flip. Nursing mothers are given sooji kanji and badam ne makaz ni kanji.

COLD COFFEE
Serves 6-8

6 cups milk
6 tbsp coffee powder (not instant)
Sugar to taste
¾-1 cup cream
½ tsp cocoa
2-3 drops vanilla essence

Bring milk to boil and add coffee powder: Simmer for 2-3

minutes. Strain and add sugar to taste. Chill. Add remaining
ingredients.

   Pour into small glasses. Serve chilled.

Beverages

EGG FLIP
Serves 2

Don't get put off by the name. Believe me, you do not taste the
egg at all and it is really delicious and very strengthening.

   2 eggs, separated
   2 tbsp castor sugar or to taste
   1½ glasses cold milk
   Vanilla essence to taste
   Brandy to taste

Beat yolks and sugar together till thick. Add milk slowly,
mixing well. Add flavourings. Whisk egg whites till stiff and
fold into mixture.

Stir and serve chilled.

Note : If a frothy drink is not liked, beat whole eggs together and add the flavourings.

FALOODA
Serves 6-8

2 tbsp cornflour
1 litre full cream milk
¾ cup cream
½ cup condensed milk
½ cup blanched, peeled and sliced almonds
1-2 tbsp sliced pistachio nuts (optional)
3 tbsp tukhmari seeds soaked in a little water for half an hour
2 tbsp rose-water
Sugar to taste
Vanilla ice cream (optional)

Cook cornflour in one cup water till thick and transparent. Pass mixture through a colander onto a bowl of ice and cold water to form small noodles. Keep aside.

Boil milk and cool. Add all ingredients except ice cream and chill. Mix well before serving.

Pour into glasses and add a dollop of ice cream.

Note: The botanical name for tukhmari seeds is Osymum Pilosum and it belongs to the basil family. These are small black seeds which swell up to double their size when soaked in water.

BADAM NE MAGAZ NI KANJI
(Kanji of almonds)
Serves 1

1 glass milk
1 tbsp almond powder

1 tbsp ground char magaz
¼ tsp crushed nutmeg and seeds of green cardomom
Sugar to taste

Mix milk, almond powder, and char magaz. Put in a pan and bring to boil slowly, stirring constantly. Add nutmeg, cardamom and sugar to taste. Drink hot.

Note: Char magaz is a mixture of melon, pumpkin, cucumber and marrow seeds.

SOOKHA SINGORA NI KANJI
(Kanji of dried water chestnuts)
Serves 1

10 blanched almonds
10 pistachio nuts
1 tbsp char magaz
1 tbsp dried water chestnut powder
6 tbsp water
1 glass milk
Sugar to taste

Powder nuts and char magaz. Mix with water chestnut powder and water to make a paste. Add milk and bring to boil slowly. Add sugar and serve hot.

SOOJI KANJI
(Kanji of semolina)
Serves 1

1 tbsp butter
1 tbsp fine semolina
1 cup milk
Sugar to taste
¼ tsp crushed nutmeg and seeds of green cardamom

Melt butter and sauté semolina for one minute: Add quarter

cup water and bring to boil, stirring continuously. Add milk,
continue stirring and bring to boil again. Remove from heat.
Add sugar, nutmeg and cardamom. Serve hot.

GHAU NU DOODH NI KANJI
Serves 4

2 tbsp ghau nu doodh or dry cream of wheat
300 ml water
200 ml buffalo milk or full cream milk
Sugar to taste
A pinch of salt
12 blanched almonds coarsely crushed
12 peeled pistachio nuts coarsely crushed
2 tbsp char magaz coarsely crushed
1 tsp crushed nutmeg and seeds of green cardamom
Rose-water to taste

Mix cream of wheat with water. Stir well and remove all lumps.
Add milk, mix well and heat slowly. Add sugar and salt. Cool
and add remaining ingredients.

Drink and get strong! Do not think of the calories!

VALSAD NI KANJI
(Valsad-style kanji)

50 g almonds, blanched, chopped and fried
50 g cheronji, chopped and fried
1 cup ghee for frying

Fry in ghee and powder individually:
50 g lotus root
50 g dry water chestnuts
100 g dry ginger (soonth)
50 g ghau nu doodh or cream of wheat
10-15 piprimoor na gath
10 g white peppercorn
2 nutmegs
20 g white cardamoms

50 g edible glue
50 g goghru

Mix all ingredients and store in an airtight jar for upto 2-3 months.

Put one teaspoon in a cup of hot milk, mix well and add sugar to taste.

Excellent after childbirth or long illnesses.

Note: Ingredients for this recipe are available at specialized shops selling spices.

BAFLOO
(Raw mango juice)
Serves 6

6 large raw mangoes
8 cups water
Sugar to taste
Salt to taste

Boil 4 cups water in a pan and add whole mangoes. Boil for 3-5 minutes. Remove from heat and cool. Peel mangoes and remove flesh. Pass through a sieve or liquidize. Dilute with 4 cups water. Add sugar and salt to taste.

MOVRU (1)

500 g movru berries or flowers
100 g sultanas (kishmish)
200 g dried black grapes
100 g raisins (munakka), seeded
50 g almonds
200 g sugar

Put movru in an earthen matka and cover with one litre water. Cover with cloth and tie down. When a film forms on top, distill liquid through a spiral tube and pour into bottles. Half-full each bottle.

Wash and dry fruits. Add fruit, almonds and sugar into bottles. Seal or cork bottles and leave in a dark cool place for 6 months.

Serve as a liqueur.

MOVRU (2)

    2½ litres distilled movru
    1 kg dried black grapes
    ½ kg dried rind of sweet lime
    1 kg sultanas (kishmish)
    1 kg castor sugar
    500 ml rose-water

Mix all ingredients in a covered earthenware pot if possible or in sealed bottles and leave for 2-3 months.

Serve as a liqueur.

MASALA NI CHAI
(Spiced tea)
Serves 6

    6 cups water
    1" piece ginger peeled and crushed
    4-6 green cardamoms
    4-6 cloves
    ½" piece cinnamon
    Sugar to taste
    6 tsp tea

Mix all ingredients except tea in a pan and bring to boil. Boil steadily for 2-4 minutes. Remove from heat and strain. Add tea and allow to stand for 2 minutes.

Pour into cups and serve with or without milk as desired.

OONI KETHELI TARI

(Spiced toddy)

Serves 6

6 large glasses fresh toddy
1-2 tbsp jaggery
3-4 cloves crushed garlic
2 tsp coarsely ground black pepper

Place all ingredients in a pan. Heat, stirring all the time, till jaggery has dissolved.

Serve warm in small glasses.

10
Eggs

BREAKFAST (NASTO)

A love for eggs is a Parsi weakness. In the days of our forefathers having three to four eggs at a time was considered quite normal. I was aghast when my nephew told me about a friend of his who would swim from the beach at Government House in Bombay to Nariman Point and then have a breakfast of twelve eggs! Once, when he was driving to Mahabaleshwar, near Bombay, the people in the car in front started harassing him. He stopped his car in front of theirs, forcing them to stop as well. Then he walked up to the other car, tilted if over with his shoulder and strolled back to his own car! Well, that is what you can do after eating twelve eggs for breakfast!

Breakfast varies with the lifestyles and working hours of individual families. In the old days a breakfast or nasto would consist of eggs, any left-over dishes such as masoor dal, rotli, toast or bread with fresh thick cream of buffalo milk in the winter, jam or murumba, perhaps a cereal, tea or coffee, juice and fruit. If the breakfast was to be a heavy one, fish such as grey mullet or pomfret would also be served, usually in the coastal towns and villages. Some Parsis, depending on their working hours would have a heavy breakfast or brunch at about eleven o'clock in the morning before setting off to work. These brunches would include eggs cooked on mince or any seasonal vegetables, brain cutlets, and other savouries.

In winter doodh na puff (an indescribable confection of light froth spooned off reduced, sweetened, chilled milk) and trotter jelly would be served in glasses. These were some of the favourites of the great breakfasts of yore and one looked forward to the winter when one could have these seasonal dishes.

I well remember the breakfasts served in my mother-in-law's beautiful home on the Mall in Amritsar. We would be served with perfectly made half-boiled eggs, which she would break for each of us, at the table, accompanied with hot toast and butter, after which would come more hot toast, thick cream, her famous kora no murambo (pumpkin preserve), and sometimes kheemo (mince).

The British breakfast of bacon or ham and eggs with all the trimmings like sausages, mashed or fried potatoes and grilled tomatoes has also found its way into Parsi cuisine.

The traditional birthday or Navroz Breakfast consists of hard-boiled eggs, ravo, sev, sweet dhai, fried fish, usually grey mullet or pomfret, and tiny yellow bananas called elchi kera. A tray of this breakfast would be sent to close friends and relatives on birthdays and on Navroz.

Trends have changed and now a breakfast consists of a hurried cup of tea or coffee, with a couple of toasts and perhaps a low calorie cereal, fruit or juice. No wonder the present generation of Parsis do not have the energy or stamina of their forefathers. While I do not recommend twelve eggs for breakfast, a well-balanced breakfast is so necessary for a good day's work.

Before I go on to talk about eggs and give you some recipes

for the various types of eggs cooked by Parsis, I would like to give you the recipes for doodh na puff and kharia ni jelly (trotter jelly), which are synonymous with breakfasts in winter.

DOODH NA PUFF
(Milk froth)
Makes 3-6 Glasses

> 2 litres full cream milk
> 250 g sugar
> Rose-water to taste
> Grated nutmeg to taste

This recipe should be prepared at sundown the day before it is to be served.

Mix milk nd sugar in a pan, put on low heat and cook till sugar has dissolved. Bring milk to boil, 3-4 times. Allow to get cold, stirring all the time while it is cooling.

If you have a garden, pour milk into a ceramic pot , cover mouth with a cloth, tie it down and hang pot from a branch of a tree. Leave overnight.

Next morning, remove pot from tree. Mix the cream formed on top of the milk, stirring in one direction only. Add rose-water and mix well.

Pour half the milk into a cold bowl and churn or beat till foam rises to the top. Spoon foam into chilled glasses till it reaches the top. Fill glasses till the froth is a little over the lip of the glasses. Sprinkle with nutmeg and serve immediately. Scoop this cloud-like mixture into your mouth, and be grateful to have tasted a manna from heaven in the form of doodh na puff!

People without gardens, do not despair. The refrigerator, one of the best of modern inventions, comes to your help. Instead of hanging the pot in the garden, place the mixture in the refrigerator overnight.

Doodh na puff can be kept in the refrigerator in glasses for about one hour only. If kept longer the froth starts sinking. It must be made early, before the sun gets too hot.

KHARIA NI JELLY
(Trotter jelly)
Serves 6

Use trotters of the same size and do not mix lamb's trotters with goat's trotters as the cooking time varies. If using lamb's trotters use twelve.

> 6 trotters of the front legs, with skin, cut into 2" pieces
> Rice flour (as required)
> 3 limes, cut in half
> 2" piece cinnamon
> 5 cloves
> 3 egg whites, lightly beaten
> Egg shells of 3 eggs, washed
> Sugar to taste
> 1-2 tsp tea leaves, for colour
> Brandy to taste
> Lime Juice to taste
> Muslin cloth for straining

Wash trotters well. Rub with rice flour and 2 limes, to remove any smell. Wash again.

Place trotters in a pan with 4 litres water and whole spices. Bring to boil. Lower heat, cover pan and simmer for 1-2 hours till trotters are soft and the bones separate from the flesh.

Strain stock into a pan. Slowly add egg whites, shells, one lime and sugar to taste. Simmer and allow to clear. Strain through two layers of muslin. Add tea leaves for colour, brandy and lime juice to taste. Mix and leave for a few minutes.

Strain out tea leaves and pour into small glasses. Leave overnight to set.

Serve for breakfast the next morning.

EGGS

Parsis cook their eggs on all types of vegetables, and sometimes on small fish as well. Favourites are eggs cooked on savoury potatoes, wafers, tomatoes, or greens. An unusual one is eggs cooked on khari biscot (salted biscuits).

Another speciality is akoori (savoury scrambled eggs), which to my way of thinking, is far superior to the famous Basque piperade! It is a great favourite not only with the Parsis, but also with the rest of their countrymen. Like dhan sakh, each Parsi household has its own recipe which it believes to be the best! There is Bharuchi akoori, which has nuts and sultanas added to it, and other variations containing green garlic and spring onions which are available in Gujarat throughout the year.

The Parsi poro (a flat omelette) is also made in many ways. The eggs may be mixed with chopped onions, chillies, coriander leaves, or with a little ground cumin seed, before frying. My mother used to make a pur no poro, which none of us can make. It was deep fried—a flaky frilly omelette, crisp and lightly layered with egg flakes. Bheja no poro is a delicious way of eating eggs and brains. There is the popatji no poro cooked in a pan with hollows, so that the eggs are formed in the shape of kababs. We even make an 'eggless' omelette (trust the Parsis to do so), especially cooked for our vegetarian friends, called channa atta no poro. Lime juice is usually squeezed on the poro and hot toast, butter and strawberry jam is a favourite accompaniment. Another Parsi eccentricity is gooseberry jam with fried eggs!

Many Continental egg dishes are enjoyed and made in Parsi homes. The soufflé omelette, plain or stuffed with cheese, prawns, chicken, oysters, caviar or smoked salmon is served as a first course as also eggs baked in ramkins with a base of cheese sauce, corn or snail butter. Different types of stuffed hard-boiled eggs are common as hors d'oeuvres or as part of a salad in many a home.

AKOORI
(Savoury scrambled eggs)
Serves 6

Basic recipe:
8 eggs
¼ tsp turmeric powder
Salt to taste
2 tbsp ghee or 50 g butter with 2 tsp oil

Chop:
2 medium-sized onions
3 cloves garlic
2 green chillies, seeded
1 medium-sized tomato
2 tbsp coriander leaves with tender stems

Melt fat in a pan. Add onions and brown lightly. Add garlic and sauté for half a minute. Add remaining ingredients except eggs and cook over high heat for one minute. Remove from heat.

Beat eggs and add to pan. Return to low heat and scramble till just done. Do not overcook eggs as they continue cooking even after they have been removed from heat.

Variations

- Add about 100 g cooked corn just before serving.
- Add 200 g fried prawns.
- Add 2 tbsp finely diced and fried potatoes, one fried shredded Bombay duck, and 1 tsp coarsely ground black pepper.

RICH BHARUCHI AKOORI
(Bharuchi-style scrambled eggs)
Serves 6

8 eggs
400 g potatoes, peeled and julienned
Salt to taste
6 tbsp ghee

Chop:
3 onions
½" piece ginger
4 cloves garlic
1 tbsp coriander leaves with tender stems
3 green chillies, seeded

Heat fat in a pan and fry potatoes till pale gold and crisp.

Remove from pan and drain well. Add onions to pan and fry till light brown. Add ginger and garlic and fry for half a minute. Add coriander leaves, green chillies, salt to taste and well beaten eggs. Cook till just done.

Remove from heat and add fried potatoes. Serve immediately.

Note : The original recipe has 600 g ghee as this particular akoori is supposed to drip with ghee!

LEELA LUSAN NI AKOORI
(Akoori with green garlic)
Serves 6

8 eggs
Salt to taste
4 tbsp ghee

Chop:
25 g green garlic with a little of the greens
4 spring onions with a little of the greens
2-3 green chillies, seeded
4 tbsp coriander leaves with tender stems
½" piece ginger

Heat fat in a pan. Add all ingredients except eggs and sauté for 2-3 minutes. Add beaten eggs and scramble till just set.

Remove from heat and serve immediately with hot rotli or toast.

KHOLI DAR NI AKOORI
(Akoori with pigeon peas)
Serves 8

8-10 eggs, well beaten
250 g pigeon peas (arhar or toover dal)
1 tsp turmeric powder
Salt to taste
6 spring onions with their greens, sliced

3 tsp cumin seeds, dry roasted and powdered
100 g tamarind soaked in 1 cup hot water
4-5 tbsp ghee

Chop:
2 onions
1" piece ginger
6-8 cloves garlic
4 tbsp coriander leaves with tender stems
4-6 green chillies, seeded

Wash and cook pigeon peas in about 400 ml water and turmeric till half done. Add salt and cook till done. Mash coarsely and keep aside. This is the dar.

Heat fat in a pan and sauté onions till light brown. Add ginger and garlic and fry for 1-2 minutes. Add spring onions, coriander leaves, green chillies and cumin powder. Fry for 1-2 minutes more. Add dar and strained tamarind water. Mix well.

Add eggs. Cook till just done. Remove from heat and serve immediately with rotli.

MEVA NI AKOORI
(Akoori with dry fruits and nuts)
Serves 8-10

15 eggs of free-run chicken, well beaten
50 g (⅓ cup) blanched and sliced almonds, cashew nuts and cheronji
Salt to taste
25 g (2 tbsp) sultanas (kishmish)
7 tbsp ghee
2 tbsp extra ghee for frying nuts

Fry nuts in 2 tablespoons fat. Remove from pan and drain well.

Mix remaining fat, eggs and salt and scramble. When half done, add sultanas and when just done add nuts. Serve immediately with hot rotli.

AKOORI OF HARD-BOILED EGGS
(Savoury hard-boiled eggs)
Serves 6

8 hard-boiled eggs cut into fours
2 large potatoes, peeled and diced
Salt to taste
1-2 tbsp Worcestershire sauce or
tomato or mango chutney (optional)
2 tbsp ghee

Chop:
2 large onions
2 tbsp cashew nuts
1 tbsp coriander leaves with tender stems
3-4 green chilies, seeded
2 tomatoes

Heat fat and fry potatoes till pale gold and crisp. Remove from pan and drain well.

Add onions and fry till light brown. Add nuts and fry till light brown. Add coriander leaves, green chillies, tomatoes and salt. Mix well. Remove from heat. Add sauce or chutney, potatoes and eggs. Mix gently and serve immediately.

CHARVELA EEDA
(Scrambled eggs)
Serves 1

Scrambled eggs are eaten all over the world. There is an art in cooking them and it is not easy to get the right consistency always.

There is a difference between butter eggs and scrambled eggs. The later has an addition of a little milk or cream which makes them lighter and there is probably no other egg preparation which is so delicate and digestible, except perhaps half-boiled eggs, which are not easy to get right either.

Scrambled eggs are all too easy to overcook and instead of the dish being soft and creamy, it turns hard and granular. It must be remembered that eggs continue to cook after the pan is removed from the heat. Therefore it should be removed from the heat before they are just done.

A suitable pan for this dish is most important. In my youth, scrambled eggs were cooked in individual kasia (small straight-sided bowls with thick bases) and served in them. One can use a small heavy-based saucepan. The secret of perfect scrambled eggs is to cook on medium heat.

2 eggs, beaten
2 tbsp butter
Salt and pepper to taste
1 tbsp thin cream or milk (the cream gives a delectable flavour)

There are two ways of cooking scrambled eggs. In the first method, melt half the butter in a pan without letting it brown. In the second method spread half the butter over the base of the pan with fingers.

Add eggs, salt and pepper.

Cook slowly and with a metal spoon scoop cooked eggs from base and sides of pan. The mixture should not be mashed. Add remaining butter in bits. Add cream or milk and remove from heat. Continue to scoop eggs till just set and soft. A simpler method is to melt all the butter without browning, add beaten eggs and seasoning and scramble.

Serve immediately.

Variations.

- Most Parsis like their scrambled eggs with finely chopped and seeded green chillies sprinkled on top before serving.
- Add 1 tbsp cooked corn.
- Add 1 tbsp smoked oysters to eggs after they are cooked.
- Add 1 tbsp coarsely chopped smoked salmon to eggs after they are cooked.

- Add 1-2 tbsp caviar to eggs after they are cooked.

The last three variations are not typically Parsi, but are appreciated by those who have acquired a palate for them.

KHARO PORO
(Plain omelette)
Serves 6

12 eggs
Salt to taste
6 tbsp ghee or 150 g butter with 2 tbsp oil

Break eggs in a bowl, add salt and beat well. Heat half the fat in a small frying pan about 8 inches in diameter. Divide eggs into 6 portions.

Add one portion to pan and fry till base of omelette is crisp. Flip over and fry other side until crisp and golden. Remove omelette from pan, drain well and serve.

Repeat with next 2 portions. Add remaining fat and cook last 3 portions.

KAPELA MASALA NO PORO
(Omelette with chopped vegetables)
Serves 6

12 eggs
Salt to taste
6 tbsp ghee or 150 g butter with 2 tbsp oil

Chop:
2 onions
1 large tomato
3 green chillies, seeded
2 tbsp coriander leaves with tender stems
1" piece ginger
3 cloves garlic

Break eggs in bowl and beat well. Add all ingredients except fat and mix well.

Heat half the fat in a small frying pan about 8 inches in diameter. Divide eggs into 6 portions.

Add one portion to pan and fry till base of omelette is crisp. Flip over and fry other side until crisp and golden. Remove omelette from pan, drain well and serve.

Repeat with next 2 portions. Add remaining fat and cook last 3 portions.

Serve with slices of lime, hot toast and butter and if you are cooking for Parsis—serve strawberry jam as well!

PEESELA MASALA NO PORO
(Omelette with ground spices)
Serves 6

This is my mother's recipe and I have never been able to make it the way she did with light frills.

12 eggs
2 tbsp tomato or mango chutney
2 tbsp water
Salt to taste
10 tbsp ghee or 300 g butter with 2 tbsp oil

Grind together:
4 medium-sized onions
4-6 green chillies, seeded
50 g coriander leaves with tender stems
2" piece ginger
6 cloves garlic
½ tsp chilli powder
1 tsp cumin powder

Break eggs in a bowl and beat well. Add remaining ingredients except fat and mix well. Divide mixture into 6 portions.

Heat half the fat in a karai or wok about 8 inches in diameter. Pour one portion of mixture into karai and cook, basting constantly for 'frills' to form. Cook till base of omelette is crisp. Turn over and continue cooking, basting all the time till done. Remove from heat and drain well.

Cook next 2 portions in the same way. Add remaining fat and cook last 3 portions.

Do not put all the fat in the pan in one go as fresh fat creates better frills.

BHOOJELO PORO
(Baked omelette)
Serves 2

5 eggs
Salt to taste
2 tsp rice flour

Break eggs in a bowl, add salt and beat well. Heat a griddle till hot. Sprinkle rice flour and pour in egg mixture. Lower heat, cover pan with lid, and cook till base of omelette is done. Turn over very carefully, cover pan again and cook till done.

LOHRI PER PORO
(Omelette cooked in a griddle)
Serves 2

4-5 eggs
1 tbsp potatoes, boiled and diced
1 fried Bombay duck, with bone removed, crushed
Salt to taste
2 tbsp ghee

Chop:
1 tbsp onion
2 green chillies, seeded
1 tbsp coriander leaves with tender stems
1" piece ginger
4 cloves garlic

Break eggs in a bowl and beat well. Add all ingredients except fat and mix well. Divide into 2 portions.

Heat a lohri and melt fat. When hot pour in one portion of egg mixture. Cover pan with lid and lower heat. Cook till base of omelette is done. Flip over and cook other side.

Remove from pan, drain and serve. Repeat with second portion.

BHEJA NO PORO
(Brain omelette)
Serves 6

12 eggs
1 pair brains, cleaned and chopped
1 tsp turmeric powder
½ tsp chilli powder
Salt to taste
10 tbsp ghee or 300 g butter with 2 tbsp oil

Chop:
2 onions
1 tomato (optional)
2 green chillies, seeded
1 tbsp coriander leaves with tender stems
4 cloves garlic

Break eggs in a bowl and beat well. Add all ingredients except fat and mix well. Divide into 6 portions.

Heat half the fat in a small frying pan about 6 inches in diameter. Add one portion to pan and fry till base of omelette is crisp. Flip over and fry other side until crisp and golden. Remove omelette from pan, drain well and serve.

Repeat with next 2 portions. Add remaining fat and cook last 3 portions.

Serve with slices of lime.

CHANNA NO ATTO NO PORO
(Gram flour omelette or eggless omelette)
Serves 2

100 g gram flour (besan)
1 tbsp garlic, ground
1 tbsp ginger, ground
Juice of 1 lime
½ tsp turmeric powder
½ tsp chilli powder
1 tsp cumin powder
1 tsp coriander powder
1 tsp dhan sakh masala powder
A pinch of sugar
Salt to taste
Oil for shallow frying

Chop:
1 onion
2 green chillies, seeded
1 tbsp coriander leaves with tender stems

Mix all ingredients except oil with enough water to make a paste of dropping consistency. Divide mixture into 2 portions.

Heat a small frying pan. Add enough oil to cover base of pan. Pour one portion of mixture into pan and cook till base is set. Carefully turn over and cook other side.

Repeat with second portion. Serve with slices of lime and hot rotli.

PAU PER EEDA
(Eggs cooked on bread)
Serves 6-8

6-8 eggs
6 slices bread, cubed, with crusts removed
Salt to taste
6-8 tbsp oil
2-3 tbsp ghee

Chop:
3 onions
1" piece ginger
6 cloves garlic
1 tbsp coriander leaves with tender stems
3 green chillies, seeded

Heat oil in a small frying pan. Deep fry bread cubes till crisp and brown. Drain and keep aside.

Remove oil from pan, add ghee and heat. Fry onions till light brown. Add ginger and garlic and fry for one minute. Add salt, coriander leaves and chillies and sauté for a minute. Remove from heat.

Spread cubed bread evenly at the base of another pan large enough to hold eggs, bread and vegetable mixture. Dribble a few drops of oil on top and spread onion mixture evenly over it. Make depressions for eggs.

Lower heat, break eggs into depressions and sprinkle with salt.

Cover pan with an inverted lid. Pour some water on lid and cook on low heat till eggs are set.

KANDA KOTHMIR PER EEDA
(Eggs cooked on onions and coriander)
Serves 6

6-8 eggs
6-8 tbsp oil
2-3 tbsp ghee
Salt to taste

Chop:
3 onions
1" piece ginger
6 cloves garlic
1 tbsp coriander leaves with tender stems
3 green chillies, seeded

Heat oil in a frying pan large enough to hold eggs and vegetable mixture. Fry onions till light brown. Add ginger and garlic and fry for one minute. Add salt, coriander leaves and chillies and sauté for another minute. Spread mixture evenly in pan and make depression in it for eggs.

Lower heat, break eggs into depressions and sprinkle with salt.

Cover pan with an inverted lid. Pour water on lid and cook on low heat till eggs are set.

TAMATAR PER EEDA
(Eggs cooked on tomatoes)
Serves 6

6-8 eggs
4 onions, finely sliced
1½" piece ginger, ground
1 medium pod garlic, ground
½ tsp turmeric powder
1 tsp chilli powder
1-2 tbsp vinegar
A pinch of sugar
Salt to taste
3 tbsp ghee or 100 g butter with 2 tsp oil

Chop:
3-4 green chillies, seeded
1 kg tomatoes
2 tbsp coriander leaves with tender stems

Heat fat in a frying pan large enough to hold eggs and vegetable mixture. Fry onions till light brown. Add green chillies, ginger, garlic, turmeric and chilli powder. Sauté for 2-3 minutes. Add coriander and tomatoes and simmer on low heat till thick. Add vinegar, sugar and salt and mix well.

Spread mixture evenly in pan, make depressions for eggs, break eggs into depressions and sprinkle with salt.

Lower heat and cover pan with an inverted lid. Pour some water on lid and cook till eggs are set.

PAPETA PER EEDA

(Eggs cooked on potatoes)

Serves 6

6-8 eggs
3 onions, finely sliced
1½" piece ginger, ground
½ pod garlic, ground
¾ tsp turmeric powder
1 tsp chilli powder
Salt to taste
6 potatoes, peeled, sliced medium thick, and boiled
3 tbsp ghee or 100 g butter with 2 tsp oil

Chop:
3 green chillies, seeded
2 tomatoes
2 tbsp coriander leaves with tender stems

Heat fat in a frying pan large enough to hold eggs and vegetable mixture. Fry onions till light brown. Add green chillies, ginger, garlic, turmeric and chilli powder. Mix well, add tomatoes, coriander and salt, and simmer on low heat for 3-4 minutes. Add potatoes and toss gently with a slicer till well mixed. Take care that potatoes do not break.

Spread mixture evenly in pan, make depressions for eggs, break eggs into depressions and sprinkle with salt.

Lower heat and cover pan with an inverted lid. Pour some water on lid and cook till eggs are set.

Variations

Use 200g potato wafers or sali instead of boiled potatoes. Cook onion mixture as given above, mix wafers or sali and spread evenly in pan, making depressions for eggs.

Break eggs into depressions and sprinkle with salt.
Cook as above.

BHEEDA PER EEDA
(Eggs cooked on okras)
Serves 6

6-8 eggs
3 onions, finely sliced
1½" piece ginger, ground
½ pod garlic, ground
¾ tsp turmeric powder
1 tsp chilli powder
Salt to taste
½ kg okras (bhindi), finely sliced and deep fried till crisp but green
3 tbsp ghee or 100 g butter with 2 tsp oil

Chop:
3 green chillies, seeded
3 tomatoes
2 tbsp coriander leaves with tender stems

Heat fat in a frying pan large enough to hold eggs and vegetable mixture and fry onions till light brown. Add green chillies, ginger, garlic, turmeric and chilli powder. Mix well. Add tomatoes, coriander and salt. Simmer on low heat for 3-4 minutes. Add okras and mix well.

Spread mixture evenly in pan, make depressions for eggs, break eggs into depressions and sprinkle with salt.

Cover pan with an inverted lid, lower heat, pour some water on lid and cook till eggs are set.

BHAJI PER EEDA
(Eggs cooked on fenugreek leaves)
Serves 6

6-8 eggs
1 bunch large fenugreek leaves (methi) or 20 bunches of the
small variety that grow in the sands of Bombay beaches
3 onions, finely sliced
1½" piece ginger, ground
1 small pod garlic, ground
¾ tsp turmeric powder
1 tsp chilli powder
Salt to taste
3 tbsp ghee or 100 g butter with 2 tsp oil

Chop:
3 green chillies, seeded
2 tomatoes
2 tbsp coriander leaves with tender stems

Wash fenugreek leaves and chop. Mix with salt and leave for
half an hour. Squeeze out the bitter juice.

Heat fat in a frying pan large enough to hold eggs and
vegetable mixture and fry onions till light brown. Add green
chillies, ginger, garlic, turmeric and chilli powder. Mix well.
Add tomatoes, coriander and salt. Simmer on low heat for 3-4
minutes. Add fenugreek leaves, mix well and sauté for 1-2
minutes.

Spread mixture evenly in pan, make depressions for eggs,
break eggs into depressions and sprinkle with salt.

Cover pan with an inverted lid, lower heat, pour some
water on lid and cook till eggs are set.

Variations: This dish can be cooked with spinach in place of
fenugreek leaves.

SEKTA NI SINGH NA PHOOL PER EEDA

(Eggs cooked on drumstick flowers)

Serves 6

6-8 eggs
150 g drumstick flowers, cleaned and washed
600 g onions, finely sliced
1 tsp turmeric powder
Salt to taste
100 ml coconut milk
Pinch of chilli powder
3 tbsp ghee or oil

Chop:
2-3 green chillies, seeded
2 tbsp coriander leaves with tender stems
1" piece ginger
½ pod garlic
2 tomatoes

Blanch drumstick flowers in boiling water for half a minute. Drain and refresh in cold water. Leave in a strainer to drain out water.

Heat fat in a frying pan large enough to hold eggs and vegetable mixture and fry onions till light brown. Add remaining ingredients except tomatoes, coconut milk, chilli powder and eggs. Sauté for 2-3 minutes.

Add tomatoes and coconut milk. Simmer till thick.

Lower heat, spread mixture evenly in pan, make depressions for eggs, break eggs into depressions and sprinkle with salt and chilli powder.

Cover pan with an inverted lid, lower heat, pour water on lid and cook till eggs are set.

KERA PER EEDA

(Eggs cooked on bananas)

Serves 6

In Bombay we have the local cooking bananas which grow in Vasai. We would buy large bunches and put a paste of lime and water at the tips to hasten the ripening process and wait for the skin to turn black. They were then fried or made into this dish. However, the ordinary bananas will also do, provided they are not too ripe.

6-8 eggs
3 onions, finely sliced
1½" piece ginger, ground
1 pod garlic, ground
¾ tsp turmeric powder
1 tsp chilli powder
Salt to taste
8 bananas, sliced
3 tbsp ghee or 100 g butter with 2 tsp oil

Chop:
3 green chillies, seeded
2 tomatoes
2 tbsp coriander leaves with tender stems

Heat fat in a frying pan large enough to hold eggs and vegetable mixture and fry onions till light brown. Add green chillies, ginger, garlic, turmeric and chilli powder. Mix well and add tomatoes, coriander and salt. Simmer on low heat for 3-4 minutes. Add bananas and mix gently.

Spread mixture evenly in pan, make depressions for eggs, break eggs into depression and sprinkle with salt.

Cover pan with an inverted lid, lower heat, pour some water on lid and cook till eggs are set.

This was one of the dishes I demonstrated at the Cordon Bleu School of Cookery in London in 1961, after which I got an admission to the prestigious Advance Course. There were never more than ten students but they made an exception for me and I was the eleventh. There was rampant hysteria from the family when I informed them that I was going to demonstrate this dish—followed by shocked silence—when I told them that I had got my admission—the first Indian to do the Advance Course.

KHEEMA PER EEDA
(Eggs cooked on mince meat)
Serves 6

6-8 eggs
250 g mince
½ tsp turmeric powder
1 tsp chilli powder
2 tsp cumin powder
2 tbsp vinegar
1 tsp sugar
Salt to taste
3 tbsp ghee or 100 g butter with 2 tsp oil

Chop:
2 onion
2 tomatoes
3-4 green chillies, seeded
2 tbsp coriander leaves with tender stems
1" piece ginger
1 tbsp garlic

Heat fat in a frying pan large enough to hold eggs and mince mixture and fry onions till light brown. Add mince and sauté till brown. Add remaining ingredients except eggs and cook till mince is done, adding some water if necessary.

Spread mixture evenly in pan, make depressions for eggs, break eggs into depressions and sprinkle with salt.

Cover pan with an inverted lid, lower heat, pour water on lid and cook till eggs are set.

BHEJA PER EEDA
(Eggs cooked on brains)
Serves 6

6-8 eggs
3 brains, cleaned and cut into pieces
1 tsp turmeric powder
1 tsp chilli powder
2 tsp cumin powder
Salt to taste
3 tbsp ghee

Chop:
3 large onions
3 green chillies, seeded
2 tbsp coriander leaves with tender stems
1" piece ginger
1 tbsp garlic
2 tomatoes

Heat fat in a frying pan large enough to hold eggs and mixture and fry onions till light brown. Add remaining ingredients except tomatoes and eggs. Sauté for 2 minutes. Add tomatoes and mix well.

Lower heat, spread mixture evenly in pan, make depressions for eggs, break eggs into depressions , and sprinkle with salt.

Cover pan with an inverted lid, lower heat, pour water on lid cook till eggs are set.

KOOTA PER EEDA
(Eggs cooked on shrimps)
Serves 6

6-8 eggs
500 g small shrimps the size of rice grains (kooto)
Juice of 1 lime
Salt to rub on shrimps
1 tbsp rice flour
500 g onions, sliced
1 tsp turmeric powder
1 tsp chilli powder
2 tsp cumin powder
2 tsp dhan sakh masala powder
Salt to taste
50 g tamarind infused in ½ cup water
7 tbsp ghee

Chop:
1 pod garlic
2 tbsp coriander leaves with tender stems
4 green chillies, seeded

Clean shrimps well and rub with salt and lime juice. Leave for half an hour and then rub with rice flour. Place in a large sieve and rinse well.

Heat fat in a frying pan large enough to hold eggs and mixture and fry onions till light brown. Add garlic, coriander leaves, green chillies, turmeric, chilli powder, cumin powder, dhan sakh masala powder and salt. Sauté for 2 minutes. Add shrimps and cook for 1-2 minutes. Add strained tamarind juice and cook till juice is absorbed.

Lower heat, spread mixture evenly in pan, make depressions for eggs, break eggs into depressions and sprinkle with salt. Cover pan with an inverted lid, lower heat, pour water on lid and cook till eggs are set.

Note: One can use ambar which is larger than kooto or very small mud fish (levti) which are found in the estuaries of the rivers and streams of Gujarat.

TOORIA NE AMBAR PER EEDA
(Eggs cooked on courgettes and small shrimps)
Serves 6

6-8 eggs
100 g small dried or fresh shrimps (ambar)
½ tsp turmeric powder
1 tsp chilli powder
Juice of 1 lime
2 large onions, sliced
1 kg courgettes (toori), peeled and chopped
Salt to taste
3 tbsp ghee or oil
3 tbsp oil for frying shrimps

Chop:
2" piece ginger
1 pod garlic
2 tbsp coriander leaves with tender stems
3-4 green chillies, seeded
3 tomatoes

Clean shrimps well and mix with turmeric, chilli powder and lime juice. Fry lightly and drain.

Heat fat in a frying pan large enough to hold eggs and mixture and fry onions till light brown. Add ginger and garlic and sauté for one minute. Add coriander leaves, green chillies, and tomatoes and cook for 1-2 minutes

Add courgettes and salt, lower heat and cook till done. Add shrimps and mix well.

Spread mixture evenly in pan, make depressions for eggs, break eggs into depressions and sprinkle with salt.

Cover pan with an inverted lid and lower heat. Pour water on lid and cook till eggs are set. Serve with hot rotli.

SOOKHA BOOMLA PER EEDA
(Eggs cooked on Bombay duck)
Serves 6

6-8 eggs
12 Bombay duck
4 onions, sliced
2" piece ginger, ground
½ tsp turmeric powder
½ tsp chilli powder
1 heaped tsp cumin powder
1 tbsp vinegar
Salt to taste
A pinch of sugar
3 tbsp ghee or oil

Chop:
½ pod garlic
1 tomato
1 tbsp coriander leaves with tender stems

Soak Bombay duck in water for 10 minutes. Drain and dry well. Remove centre bone and shred.

Heat fat in a frying pan large enough to hold eggs and mixture and fry onions till light brown. Add Bombay duck, ginger, garlic, turmeric powder, chilli powder and cumin powder. Sauté for 2 minutes. Add vinegar, tomato, coriander leaves, salt and sugar. Mix well and cook for 2-3 minutes.

Lower heat, spread mixture evenly in pan, make depressions for eggs, break eggs into depressions and sprinkle with salt.

Cover pan with an inverted lid and lower heat. Pour water on lid and cook till eggs are set.

Serve hot with rice or whole wheat flour rotli.

KHARI BISCOT PER EEDA
(Eggs cooked on flaky biscuits)
Serves 6

Khari biscot are biscuits of a puff pastry variety, but their layers are much lighter and finer. This is a delicious dish.

    6-8 eggs
    3 onions, finely sliced
    1" piece ginger, ground
    ½ pod garlic, ground
    ¾ tsp turmeric powder
    1 tsp chilli powder
    Salt to taste
    150 g khari biscot, lightly broken up
    3 tbsp ghee or 100 g butter with 2 tsp oil

    Chop:
    3 green chillies, seeded
    2 tbsp coriander leaves with tender stems
    2 tomatoes

Heat fat in a frying pan large enough to hold eggs and biscuit mixture and fry onions till light brown. Add green chillies, ginger, garlic, turmeric, chilli powder and coriander leaves. Mix well and add tomatoes and salt. Simmer on low heat for 3-4 minutes.

Spread mixture evenly in pan, and sprinkle biscuits on top. Make depressions for eggs, and break eggs into depressions. Sprinkle with salt and a pinch of chilli powder.

Cover pan with an inverted lid, and lower heat. Pour water on lid and cook till eggs are set.

Note: On all eggs cooked with vegetables:

The eggs may be separated, the whites beaten till semi stiff, then yolks beaten in and spread on top of vegetables and cooked in the same way.

The whites may be beaten till stiff and spread on top of vegetables and the yolk placed on top of the egg whites and cooked in the same way. The preparation can be placed in an oven proof dish and baked in an oven at 175°C (350°F) for 20 minutes.

11

Vegetables

One seldom heard of a Parsi vegetarian in my youth. Vegetables were usually cooked with a meat or an egg dish and if served individually, they were served as accompaniments to meat or fish dishes.

Nowadays, however, more and more Parsis are turning vegetarian in keeping with the times and vegetarian dishes are much to the fore.

BHAJI DANA
(Savoury green peas and fenugreek leaves)
Serves 6

4 onions, sliced
1 tsp cumin powder
1 tbsp coriander powder
Salt to taste
2 onions cut in thin rings (optional)
1 cup green peas, boiled
2 tsp crushed nutmeg and seeds of green cardamom
2-3 tbsp ghee

Chop:

18 bunches of the small variety or
2 bunches of the large variety of fenugreek leaves (methi)
4-5 green chillies, seeded
1 cup coriander leaves, with tender stems
2" piece ginger
1 pod garlic

Mix fenugreek leaves with one teaspoon salt and leave for 15 minutes. Squeeze out bitter juice and keep aside.

Heat fat in a pan and fry sliced onions. Do not let them brown. Add all ingredients except green peas, onion rings and cardamom and nutmeg powder. Mix well, put onion rings on top of dish and simmer till all liquid has dried. Add green peas and cardamom and nutmeg powder.

Variations:

• Use 200 g coriander leaves instead of fenugreek leaves.
• Add this dish to kharu gosht (savoury meat) and serve it as bhaji dana ma gosht.
• Use common spinach or cholai bhaji—green or red.
• Eggs may be baked on this vegetable mixture.

Note: The small leafed variety of fenugreek leaves is available almost throughout the year in Maharashtra and Gujarat. They are grown in the sands of the beaches and are preferred to the large leafed variety in Parsi cuisine.

PAPETA NI TARKARI
(Savoury potatoes)
Serves 8

1 kg potatoes, boiled in their jackets, peeled and quartered
1 tsp mustard seeds
1 tsp whole cumin seeds
1 tsp turmeric powder
Salt to taste
2 tbsp ghee

Chop:
4 green chillies, seeded
4 tbsp coriander leaves

Heat fat in a pan and add mustard seeds. When they start spluttering, add cumin seeds and turmeric powder. Fry for one minute and add remaining ingredients.

Mix well and serve with poori.

KHARA PAPETA
(Savoury potatoes)
Serves 8

1 kg potatoes, peeled and quartered or cut into eights if large
3 large onions, finely sliced
1 tbsp ginger paste
1 tbsp garlic paste
½ tsp turmeric powder
1 tsp chilli powder
2 tsp cumin powder
Salt to taste
2 tbsp oil

Chop:
2 tomatoes
1-2 green chillies
1 tbsp coriander leaves with tender stems

Heat fat in a pan and fry onions till light brown. Add ginger, garlic, turmeric, chilli and cumin powders. Add a little water and sauté for 2-3 minutes. Add remaining ingredients and cook till light brown.

Add some water to pan and cover with an inverted lid. Pour a little water onto lid and allow to simmer, adding more water if required, till potatoes are done. This prevents the food from burning.

Note: The water from the lid should be put into the pan and replaced with fresh water when potatoes are half done.

Variations:

Add any combination of the following vegetables:

- 250 g green peas, shelled and added with potatoes
- 250 g carrots, peeled, cubed and added with potatoes
- 500 g capsicum, cut into cubes, with pith and seeds removed, added 10 minutes before potatoes are cooked
- 100 g spring onions, sliced obliquely with a little of the green, added just before removing pan from heat.
- 6-8 drumsticks, peeled and cut into 3" pieces, added 10-15 minutes before potatoes are cooked. In this dish, increase the gravy by adding one cup water with drumsticks.

PAPETA NU SALNU
(Savoury potatoes)
Serves 8

Potatoes cooked in this way go well served with poori.

> 1 kg potatoes, peeled and cubed
> 1 tsp turmeric powder
> Salt to taste
> 1 tbsp mustard seeds
> 2-3 strips curry leaves
> 3 onions, sliced
> 3-4 green chillies, chopped or 1 tsp chilli powder
> 2 tbsp ghee or oil

Boil potatoes with turmeric powder and salt till done. Strain.

Heat fat in a large frying pan and add mustard seeds. When they start spluttering, add curry leaves and onions. Saute till onions are soft. Add chillies, potatoes and one cup water. Adjust seasoning and simmer for 2-3 minutes.

Serve hot with poori.

PAPETA NE VATENA NI SOOKHI TARKARI
(Savoury dry potato and green peas)
Serves 8

> 8 medium-sized potatoes, boiled in their jackets till half done
> 2½ cups shelled green peas
> 1 tbsp mustard seeds
> 1 tbsp cumin seeds
> 1 tsp turmeric powder
> 2 tomatoes chopped (optional)
> Salt to taste
> 2-3 green chillies, chopped
> 1 tbsp chopped coriander leaves
> 2-3 tbsp ghee or oil

Peel potatoes and cut into cubes. Boil green peas and refresh immediately in cold water so that they do not lose their colour.

Heat fat in a pan and add mustard and cumin seeds. Add turmeric powder when mustard seeds start spluttering. Add potatoes, salt and tomatoes, if used and saute till done.

Add green peas, chillies and coriander leaves, mix well and serve hot.

NARIEL NA DOODH MA PAPETA NE SEKTA NI SING

(Potatoes and drumsticks cooked in coconut milk)

Serves 8

8 medium-sized potatoes, peeled and quartered
8-10 drumsticks, peeled and cut into 3" pieces
2 medium-sized onions, finely sliced
1 tbsp mixed whole cinnamon, cloves and black cardamom
2½" piece ginger, ground
1 large pod garlic, ground
1 tsp turmeric powder
2-3 tsp cumin powder
Salt to taste
2 tomatoes, chopped (optional)
4-5 green chillies, slit or
4-5 dried red chillies broken into 2-3 pieces
2 cups coconut milk, extracted from 1 coconut
4 tbsp ghee or oil

Heat fat in a pan and fry onions with whole spices till onions are light brown. Add half a cup water and simmer till onions are mushy and water has evaporated. Add ginger, garlic, turmeric, cumin powder and salt. Sauté for 1-2 minutes. Add tomatoes if used and continue to sauté. Add chillies and potatoes and cook on low heat till potatoes are three-quarters done.

Add drumsticks and coconut milk and simmer till vegetables are done and gravy is thick.

TARELA PAPETA NE VENGNA
(Fried potatoes with aubergines)
Serves 4-6

2 large potatoes, peeled and cut into 8 pieces each
1 kg long aubergines (baigan), cut lengthwise into 4 pieces
each
2 tsp cumin seeds
3 whole red chillies, broken into 2-3 pieces each
Salt to taste
3 tbsp oil

Heat oil in a pan and add cumin seeds and chillies. Fry for 1-2 minutes and add vegetables and salt. Sauté for a few minutes, cover and cook on low heat till vegetables are done. If it appears to be sticking, add 1-2 tbsp water.

PAPETA NE MOTA MURCHA
(Savoury potatoes and capsicum)
Serves 8

8 potatoes, peeled and quartered
2 capsicum, cut into quarters, with pith and seeds removed
Salt to taste
3 tbsp ghee or 100 g butter with 2 tsp oil

Heat fat in a pan and add potatoes and salt. Cook on low heat till potatoes are done, taking care not to let them colour. Add a little water if required. Add capsicum and simmer for 2-3 minutes.

PAPETA NA PATTIS
(Potato patties)
Serves 6

1½ kg potatoes
3 tbsp gram or plain flour
Salt to taste
Oil for shallow frying

Filling:
250 g green peas, weighed in their pods and shelled
1 tbsp chopped coriander leaves with tender stems
¼" piece ginger, chopped
½ tsp garam masala powder
1 tbsp grated coconut
1 tbsp lime juice
Salt to taste

Grind Coarsely:
2 tbsp almonds
2 tbsp pistachio nuts
2 tbsp cashew nuts

Boil potatoes in jackets. Peel, mash well and mix with flour and salt.

Boil green peas. Drain and mix with remaining ingredients except oil and potatoes. Crush mixture roughly with a fork.

Wet your hands and take up a spoonful of potato mixture. Flatten and put 1½ teaspoon green pea mixture in the centre. Cover peas with edges of potato disc and shape into a ball. Flatten into the shape of a small flat cake. Repeat with remaining potatoes and green peas.

Heat oil in a frying pan and shallow fry patties till golden brown, turning them over only once.

Serve hot.

VEGETABLE JALEBI
Serves 6-8

At all Parsi lagans and navjotes there is a vegetarian thal for our vegetarian friends. This is one of the dishes that is often served.

Dough:
¾ kg whole wheat flour (atta)
½ kg fine semolina
2 tsp chilli powder
Salt to taste
Pepper to taste

Mix to a paste with a little water:
1 tsp chilli powder
1 tsp garam masala powder
2 tbsp dhan sakh masala powder

Clean, chop and fry individually:
3 onions
100 g French beans
2 carrots
¼ kg cauliflower
1 large sweet potato
2 long aubergines (baigan)
¼ kg red pumpkin (kaddu)
2" piece ginger
1 large pod garlic

Filling:
1 cup shelled green peas, boiled
4 potatoes, boiled, peeled and mashed
2 tbsp coriander leaves with tender stems, chopped
4 green chillies, chopped
2 tbsp cornflour
Salt to taste

Juice of 2 limes
Salt to taste
¼ kg ghee for shallow frying

Make a stiff paste with ingredients for dough, with a little water. Knead well and beat on the table till pliable. Keep aside.

Fry paste of spices in a little ghee. Add fried vegetables and ingredients for filling. Mix well and mash coarsely. Season with salt and lime juice. It should have a sharp taste.

Roll out dough thinly in a rectangular shape, like a Swiss roll. Spread mixture on it and roll up, Wet ends so that they stick together firmly. Cut with a sharp knife into quarter-inch thick slices.

Shallow fry and scrve with wedges of lime.

KHARU DODHI
(Savoury marrow)
Serves 8

1 kg marrow (ghia), peeled and cut into 1" cubes
3 large onions, finely sliced
1 tbsp ginger paste
1 tbsp garlic paste
½ tsp turmeric powder
1 tsp chilli powder
2 tsp cumin powder
6 cloves
2" piece cinnamon
4 black cardamoms
Salt to taste
2 tbsp oil

Chop:
2 tomatoes
1-2 green chillies
1 tbsp coriander leaves with tender stems

Heat fat in a pan and fry onions till light brown. Add ginger, garlic, turmeric, chilli and cumin powders. Add a little water and saute for 2-3 minutes. Add remaining ingredients and cook till slightly brown.

Add one cup water to pan and cover with an inverted lid. Add water to lid and allow to simmer, adding more water if required, till marrow is done.

KHARU KORU
(Savoury pumpkin)
Serves 8

Use the yellow variety of pumpkin (kaddu) and cook in the same way as kharu dodhi.

KORU NE MOTA MURCHA
(Yellow pumpkin with capsicum)
Serves 8

¾ kg ripe yellow pumpkin (kaddu), peeled and cubed
½ kg capsicum, cubed, with pith and seeds removed
3 onions, sliced
1 pod garlic, peeled
¼ kg spring onions, sliced
4 ripe tomatoes, chopped
6 green chillies, chopped
1 tsp turmeric powder
Salt to taste
3 tbsp oil

Heat fat and fry onions till light brown. Add peeled cloves of garlic. Sauté for 2 minutes. Add pumpkin and cook for 3-4 minutes, stirring all the time. Add remaining ingredients and simmer for 2-3 minutes. Add half cup water and simmer till pumpkin is cooked.

TARELA BHEEDA (1)
(Fried okras)
Serves 8

1 kg young, small tender okras (bhindi)
Salt to taste
Oil for shallow frying

Wash and dry okras completely. Remove heads, cut into quarter-inch slices and sprinkle with salt.

Heat oil in a frying pan and fry okras a few at a time, till crisp, but still green.

TARELA BHEEDA (2)
(Fried okras)
Serves 8

1 kg young, small, tender okras (bhindi)
4-6 eggs, well beaten
Salt to taste
4-6 tbsp flour
Breadcrumbs as required
Oil for deep frying

Wash and dry okras completely. Add salt to eggs.

Heat oil in a deep frying pan. Roll okras in flour, dip in beaten eggs, roll in breadcrumbs and fry till crisp and light golden.

Note. This is not a Parsi dish, but this is the way our Goan cooks served okras with fried chops and mashed potatoes. It is a delicious way of eating okras, especially for those who do not much care for this vegetable.

KHARA BHEEDA
(Savoury okras)
Serves 8

1 kg young, small, tender okras (bhindi)
2 large onions, sliced
1 tsp turmeric powder
Salt to taste
2 tbsp oil

Chop:
2 medium-sized tomatoes
4 green chillies, seeded
2 tbsp coriander leaves with tender stems

Wash and dry okras completely. Remove heads, cut into quarter-inch slices and sprinkle with salt.

Heat oil in a pan and fry onions lightly. Add remaining

ingredients and cook till okras are tender.

Note : You may cut okras even finer, and deep fry them till crisp, but still green, and then add them to onions and remaining ingredients, just before serving.

You may also add ½ kg fried or boiled, cubed potatoes.

DHAI MA BHEEDA
(Okras cooked with curd)
Serves 8

1 kg young, small, tender okras (bhindi)
Salt to taste
2 tbsp ginger paste
2 tbsp garlic paste
1 tsp turmeric powder
2 tsp chilli powder
3 tsp cumin powder
350 g thick curd, beaten till smooth
4-6 tbsp oil

Wash and dry okras completely. Remove heads, cut into half-inch slices and sprinkle with salt. Heat oil in a pan and fry till crisp but green. Drain.

In the same pan add ginger, garlic and spices. Fry for 1-2 minutes, adding a little water if needed. Add curd and mix well. Lower heat and simmer for 1-2 minutes. Add salt and fried okras. Simmer for a further 2-3 minutes

Serve hot with rotli or khichdi.

TARELA VENGNA
(Fried aubergines)
Serves 8

¾ kg thick, long aubergines (baigan), washed, dried and cut into ½" rounds
2 tsp turmeric powder

3 tsp chilli powder
3 tsp cumin powder
Salt to taste
Oil for shallow frying

Mix spices and salt with 3-4 tablespoons water to make a paste. Apply on both sides of aubergines and allow to marinate for 15 minutes.

Heat oil in a shallow frying pan and fry a few slices of aubergines at a time, turning once only.

Serve hot with any meat dish.

VENGNA NU BHURTU
(Dry roasted aubergines)
Serves 6-8

500 g large round aubergines (baigan)
Salt to taste
1 tbsp cumin seeds
1 cup curd (optional)
2 tbsp groundnut oil

Chop:
1 onion
2 tomatoes, peeled
3 green chillies, seeded
1 tbsp coriander leaves

Rub aubergines with a little oil and put them under a grill or in hot ash till skin is brown and slightly burnt. Cool, peel and wash off all black skin.

Mash aubergines, add all ingredients except oil, curd and cumin seeds. Mix well.

Heat remaining oil, add cumin seeds and saute for one minute. And aubergine mixture. Stir well and add curd if used.

Serve warm with khichdi or cold as a salad.

RAVEYA VENGNA
(Stuffed aubergines)
Serves 8

8 thick aubergines (baigan), 2-3 inches long
Salt to taste
1 cup coconut milk extracted from ½ coconut
50 g tamarind infused in the coconut milk
Ghee or oil for shallow frying

Grind together:
1 grated coconut
3 onions
2" piece ginger
6 cloves garlic
6 dried red chillies
1 tsp turmeric
1 tbsp dhan sakh masala powder

Wash and dry aubergines. Make four slits, keeping stem point intact. Fill aubergines with ground spices and salt.

Heat ghee or oil in a patio or broad-based pan. Add aubergines, and any leftover ground spices. Lower heat, strain in coconut milk and tamarind mixture and simmer till aubergines are cooked, taking care that they do not break.
Note. To keep the stuffing in place, wind a thin string around the aubergines.

VENGANA NE DHAI NI BURIANI
(Savoury aubergine stew with curd)
Serves 4-6

800 g long aubergines (baigan), slit in ½ and cut into ½" pieces
Salt to taste
3-4 green chillies, chopped
3 tbsp chopped coriander leaves with tender stems
1 kg curd, beaten till smooth
4 tbsp ghee

Grind together:
2" piece ginger
6 cloves garlic
3 tsp cumin seeds

Grind to a powder:
1" piece cinnamon
8 black cardamoms, peeled
¼ nutmeg

Mix both ground spices with salt, chillies and coriander. Divide into two portions.

Rub one half of spices into aubergines, and mix remaining with curd.

Heat ghee in a pan and fry aubergines on very low heat till done. Add curd and mix well. Simmer for 1-2 minutes.

Serve with pulao or vagharela chawal.

Note. This dish can also be made with marrow or mixed vegetables.

TARI MA SEKTA NI SING
(Drumsticks cooked in toddy)
Serves 8

8-10 drumsticks, peeled and cut into 3" pieces
300-500 ml fresh toddy
Salt to taste
1 tbsp ghee

Grind finely:
3 green chillies, seeded
3 tbsp chopped coriander leaves with tender stems
1" piece ginger
6 cloves garlic
3 tbsp grated coconut
1 tsp turmeric powder

Tie drumsticks in bundles of three or four, or leave loose. Heat fat in a pan and fry ground spices for 1-2 minutes.

Add toddy, salt and drumsticks and simmer till done.

KHARA TOORIA
(Savoury courgettes)
Serves 8

1 kg courgettes (toori), peeled and sliced
4 onions, sliced
2 tbsp ginger paste
2 tbsp garlic paste
1 tsp turmeric powder
2 tsp chilli powder
2 tomatoes, chopped
3-4 green chillies, slit and seeded
Salt to taste
2 tbsp chopped coriander leaves with tender stems
2 tbsp ghee or oil

Heat fat in a frying pan and fry onions till light brown. Add ginger, garlic, turmeric powder and chilli powder. Saute for 2-3 minutes, adding a little water if required. Add tomatoes and simmer for 3-4 minutes.

Add courgettes, green chillies and salt. Mix well, lower heat and simmer till tender. Add coriander leaves and serve.

Note : Fried kooto or ambar (tiny shrimps) may be added to this dish. Eggs can be baked on the vegetable, cooked in this manner.

KHATU MEETHU ESTEW
(Sweet and sour stew)
Serves 8

This is one of the favourite vegetable dishes of the Parsis and is often served at weddings and navjotes.

250 g green peas, weighed in their pods and shelled
150 g French beans, trimmed and cut into pieces
300 g pickling onions, peeled
4 carrots, peeled and cubed
300 g cauliflower, cut into flowerets (optional)
300 g baby potatoes, peeled or
3 large potatoes, peeled and cubed
300 g elephant's foot or yam, peeled and cubed
2 medium-sized sweet potatoes, peeled and cubed
3 onions, sliced
3 tbsp vinegar
2 tbsp sugar
Salt to taste
Oil as needed for shallow frying prepared vegetables

Chop fine:
3 tomatoes
3-4 green chillies, seeded
3 tbsp coriander leaves with tender stems
½ bunch mint leaves
2" piece ginger
1 pod garlic

Heat oil in a frying pan and lightly shallow fry individually all prepared vegetables except sliced onions, and finely chopped ingredients.

Heat 2 tbsp oil in a pan and fry sliced onions till light brown. Add all finely chopped ingredients and simmer for 3-4 minutes. Add fried vegetables and mix well. Add vinegar, sugar and salt and simmer for another 5 minutes.

The dish should have a predominantly sweet and sour taste.

Note : All vegetables should be cut to approximately the same size.

VENGNA NE TOORIA NO PATIO

(Aubergine and courgette patio)

350 g long aubergines (baigan), sliced in ½" rounds
500 g courgettes (toori), peeled and sliced in ½" rounds
2 large onions, sliced
Salt to taste
2 tomatoes, chopped
Tamarind the size of a walnut infused in ½ cup hot water
1 tsp jaggery
2 tbsp ghee

Grind together:
2 onions, dry roasted till the skin is black, cooled and peeled
3 green chillies, seeded
6-8 cloves garlic
4 dried red chillies
1 tsp turmeric powder
2 tsp cumin seeds, dry roasted
1 tbsp coriander seeds, dry roasted
1 tbsp dhan sakh masala powder
1 tbsp poppy seeds (khus khus)
1" piece cinnamon
4 cloves

Keep sliced vegetables immersed in salted water till required.

Heat ghee in a pan and fry onions till light brown. Add half cup water and salt, lower heat and cook till onions are mushy and water has evaporated. Add ground spices and sauté for 2-3 minutes. Add tomatoes and simmer for 2-3 minutes until liquid from tomatoes is reduced.

Add courgettes and aubergines. Lower heat and simmer till vegetables are cooked. Add strained tamarind and jaggery. Adjust seasoning and serve with yellow dal and white rice.

The taste of the patio should be sweet and sour.

DHAI TAMATAR NO SAS

(Hot sweet and sour sauce with curd and tomatoes)

Serves 6

300 g thick curd, beaten till smooth
500 g ripe tomatoes, blanched and chopped
2 large onions, finely chopped
1-2 tsp Navsari vinegar
Sugar to taste
Salt to taste
2 tbsp ghee

Grind together:
2-3 green chillies, seeded
1 tbsp chopped coriander leaves with tender stems
1" piece ginger
6-8 cloves garlic

Heat ghee in a pan and fry onions till light brown. Add ground spices. Sauté for 1-2 minutes. Add tomatoes and simmer till soft and well amalgamated with spices. Add curd and simmer on low heat, stirring continuously for 4-5 minutes.

Add vinegar, sugar and salt.

Serve with khichdi or pulao or rotli.

This is a very tasty dish and you may add 500 g filleted or sliced fish or prawns to it.

TARELA KERA

(Fried bananas)

Serves 8

Many types of bananas are grown in India. The ones used for cooking are usually the long large yellow variety which grow in Vasai. They are made to turn completely black before cooking, by making a paste of edible lime powder or choonam used in paan and water and applying it to the tip of the bananas. However, ripe, green and yellow bananas can also be used.

There is also a variety of bananas which grow in South India, which are used for making chips.

8 long yellow bananas, turned black
Ghee or oil for shallow frying

Peel and slice bananas into round slices or cut them in half and then lengthwise.

Heat ghee or oil and fry bananas slowly till crisp.

Serve hot or at room temperature as an accompaniment to any dish like meat curry and rice, savoury meat, etc.

CUSTER NA CUTLETS
(Savoury custard cutlets)
Serves 8

This is a prize-winning recipe given to me by Parviz P. Dhunbura.

600 ml full cream milk
10 eggs
Salt to taste
Breadcrumbs
Ghee or oil for deep frying

Grind together:
6 green chillies, seeded
3 tbsp coriander leaves with tender stems
1" piece ginger
6 cloves garlic
2 tsp cumin seeds

Cook milk on low heat until quantity is reduced by a quarter. Cool. Beat 5 eggs and add to milk with salt and half the ground spices. Mix well and spoon into a well greased, square or rectangular baking dish, so that it comes to a height of one inch.

Steam for 15-20 minutes by putting the dish in a steamer,

or place in a dish with water reaching about 2 inches above base of custard dish and bake in a medium oven at 175°C (350°F) for 20-25 minutes.

Allow to cool completely and cut into one-and-a-half-inch squares. Carefully coat each piece with remaining ground spices, dip in breadcrumbs and then in remaining beaten eggs. Deep fry till pale gold. Drain and serve.

AMBAKALIO (1)
(Fresh mango cooked in syrup)
Serves 6

1 large ambakalia mango or
500 g ordinary half ripe, half raw mangoes or
1 tin (250 g) sliced mangoes
1 large onion, sliced
1" piece cinnamon
4-6 cloves
4-6 green cardamoms
125 g jaggery
2 green chillies, seeded and chopped
1 tbsp chopped coriander leaves with tender stems
½ tsp salt
3 tbsp ghee or butter

Peel and slice mangoes.

Heat fat in a pan and fry onion with whole spices till light brown. Add jaggery, mangoes, green chillies, coriander leaves, salt and half cup water. If you are using tinned mangoes, use half cup juice from tin.

Simmer for 1-2 minutes and mix well without breaking mango slices.

Serve with dhan sakh or khichdi.

Note : You may add this dish to kharu gosht and serve ambakalia ma gosht.

If you are using tinned mangoes, use half the quantity of jaggery.

AMBAKALIO (2)
(Fresh mango cooked in syrup)
Serves 6

1 kg raw mangoes, peeled and diced
1 kg pickling onions
350 g jaggery
A pinch of salt

Mix all ingredients and cook very gently till jaggery has dissolved and mangoes are just cooked.

BHARUCHI AMBAKALIO
(Fresh mango cooked in syrup—Bharuchi style)
Serves 6

½ kg raw mangoes, peeled and diced
½ kg pickling onions
250 g jaggery
Salt to taste

Mix all ingredients and cook very slowly till mangoes are soft. Serve as a vegetable dish or with khichdi.

CHAS PAIALO KAN
(Sweet potato or yam in syrup)
Serves 8

1 kg sweet potato or yam, peeled and cubed
2" stick cinnamon
4-6 cloves
4-6 black cardamoms
400 g sugar
2 cups water
Salt to taste
Oil for deep frying

Deep fry sweet potatoes or yam and keep aside.

Make a sugar syrup with remaining ingredients and add yam or sweet potato. Simmer for 5 minutes on low heat or till vegetable is tender and serve at room temperature.

Note : You may cook kharu gosht and add this dish to it and serve as chas paialo kan ma gosht.

GOR AMLI NU DORU

(Sweet and sour sauce to serve with khichdi)
Serves 6-8

8 drumsticks, peeled and cut into 3" pieces
Salt to taste
1 tsp turmeric powder
1 tsp chilli powder
2 tsp dhan sakh masala powder
1 tbsp gram flour
300 g tamarind infused in 1 cup hot water with 100 g jaggery
2 tbsp ghee or oil
2 tbsp chopped coriander leaves for garnish

Chop:
3 onions
6-8 green chillies, seeded
¾ cup coriander leaves with tender stems
2" piece ginger
1 large pod garlic

Boil drumsticks till just done. Heat ghee or oil in a pan and fry onions till light brown. Add remaining chopped ingredients, salt and powdered spices and saute for one minute. Add gram flour and continue to saute for 1-2 minutes more, adding a little water if required.

Add strained tamarind and jaggery juice and bring to boil. Add drumsticks and simmer till thick and the drumsticks are cooked.

Garnish with chopped coriander leaves and serve with khichdi and papads.

KORA NU DORU

(Sweet and sour pumpkin sauce)

Serves 8

1 kg ripe pumpkin (kuddu), peeled, boiled and mashed
3 onions, chopped
2 tbsp chilli powder
2 tsp cumin powder
1 tbsp coriander powder
100 g tamarind, infused in 1 cup water with 50 g jaggery
Salt to taste
Juice of 1 lime
3 tbsp ghee

Grind together:
4 green chillies, seeded
2 tbsp coriander leaves with tender stems
2" piece ginger
6-8 cloves garlic

Heat ghee and fry onions till brown. Add ground and powdered spices. Fry for 1-2 minutes, adding a little water if required.

Add pumpkin and mix well. Simmer for 2-3 minutes. Strain juice from tamarind and jaggery mixture into pan. Mix well and add salt and lime juice.

The taste should be sweet and sour.

Serve with khichdi, papad and bafena pickle.

GOBI NI SALAD

(Cabbage salad)

1 kg cabbage, finely sliced
Juice of 2 limes
2 green chillies, seeded and chopped
½ cup coriander leaves, chopped
2 tsp cumin seeds, dry roasted and coarsely ground
A pinch of sugar
Pepper to taste
1 tsp salt

Combine all ingredients, mix well, chill and serve.

RAITU
(Curd based salad)

This is a recipe of my maternal grandmother, Bhickaiji F. Karaka.

½ kg cucumbers, peeled, seeded and cubed or
4 ripe bananas, peeled and sliced
2 cups thick curd, beaten till smooth
3 tbsp strong mustard paste, freshly made
1 tbsp chopped coriander leaves
Salt to taste

If using cucumbers, sprinkle with salt and leave for half an hour. Drain out water. If using bananas, do not peel till ready to use.

Mix curd with mustard, coriander leaves and salt. Add cucumber or bananas and mix well.

Chill and serve as a salad with any rice dish.

KERA NU RAITU
(Banana and curd salad)

6-8 ripe bananas, peeled and cut into ¼" slices
½ kg thick curd, beaten till smooth
1 green chilli, seeded and chopped
3 tsp skinned mustard seeds, coarsely pounded
Salt to taste

Mix all ingredients gently. Chill and serve.

KACHUMBER

4 onions, finely sliced
1-2 green chillies, seeded and chopped
1 tbsp chopped coriander leaves
1 tomato finely sliced (optional)
Salt to taste

Mix all ingredients and serve.

GOR AMLI NU KACHUMBER
(Jaggery and tamarind kachumber)

4 onions, finely sliced
1 tomato, seeded and finely sliced
1-2 green chillies, seeded and chopped
1 tbsp chopped coriander leaves
Salt to taste
2 tbsp tamarind without seeds or strings, infused in ¾ cup
water with 2 tsp jaggery

Mix all ingredients except tamarind and jaggery juice. Strain juice into vegetables, mix well and serve.

DHAI KACHUMBER
(Curd Kachumber)

4 onions, finely sliced
1 tomato, seeded and finely sliced
1-2 green chillies, seeded and chopped
1 tbsp chopped coriander leaves
250 g curd, beaten till smooth
Sugar to taste
Salt to taste

Mix all vegetables together. Add curd, sugar and salt, stir well and serve.

CURRIES

COCUM CURRY
Serves 4-6

Cocum is a dry sour plum. Its botanical name is *Garcinia Indica*. The best variety comes from Goa and it is used extensively in Goan food.

10-12 cocum
2 tbsp coriander leaves, chopped
5 cups coconut milk extracted from 1½ grated coconut
1 tbsp gram flour (besan), slaked in 2 tbsp coconut milk
Sugar to taste
Salt to taste

Grind together:
3-4 green chillies, seeded
2" piece ginger
2 tsp cumin seeds
A pinch of asafoetida (hing)

Vaghar (seasoning):
1-2 dried red chillies broken into 2-3 pieces
1 tsp cumin seeds
2-3 strips curry leaves
1 tbsp ghee

Wash cocum well in running water to remove all grit. Soak in warm water for half an hour, then purée on a curry stone or in an electric blender. Place purée in an enamel or china bowl if it is to be kept for some time.

Mix all ingredients, except vaghar in a pan and bring to boil just once.

Heat ghee for vaghar in a small frying pan and fry vaghar ingredients for one minute. Add to curry. Stir well and remove from heat. Serve with khichdi and papad.

Note : Do not use an aluminium pan to cook this dish. Use a stainless steel, kallied or enamel pan.

GUAVA NI CURRY
(Guava curry)
Serves 6-8

1 kg half-ripe, half-raw guavas, peeled, seeded and quartered
2 onions, sliced
2 cups coconut milk extracted from ½ grated coconut
Juice of 2-3 limes

Salt to taste
2 tbsp oil

Grind together:
2" piece ginger
8 cloves garlic
2-3 tsp chilli powder
2 tsp cumin seeds
1 tbsp coriander seeds
½" piece cinnamon
3 cloves

Heat ghee in a pan and fry onions till light brown. Add half cup water and salt, lower heat and cook till onions are mushy and water has evaporated. Add ground spices and saute for 3-4 minutes. Add guava and simmer for 2-3 minutes. Add coconut milk, salt and lime juice and simmer for 5 minutes more on low heat.

Serve with white rice.

Note : This is an unusual curry and quite delicious. You can use this recipe for a mixed vegetable curry, or okra and potato curry or a drumstick and potato curry.

You may use tamarind the size of a large lime, infused in half a cup hot water, instead of lime juice.

The guavas should not be too raw. They should be firm and just ripe.

KUDHIS

Kudhis are light curries, if you can call them curries. They are mainly curd or buttermilk based and are basically vegetarian dishes. The Parsis have borrowed their kudhis from the Gujaratis, though this dish is made all over India with slight variations. It is a cooling, light dish for a hot summer afternoon.

DHAI NI KUDHI
(Curd kudhi)
Serves 6-8

1 litre sour curd
4-6 tsp gram flour (besan) or rice flour
6 green chillies, seeded and chopped
4 strips curry leaves
3" piece ginger, ground
1 tbsp dhan sakh masala powder
Salt to taste

Vaghar (seasoning):
4-5 dried red chillies, broken into pieces
3 tsp cumin seeds
A pinch of asafoetida (hing)
1 tbsp ghee

Add 3-4 cups water to curd and beat well with a rotary beater for about 10 minutes, or in an electric beater for about 5 minutes. Make a paste of gram or rice flour, with a little water. Add to curd with remaining ingredients except vaghar and pour into a pan.

Place pan on fire and bring curd to boil, stirring continuously. Reduce heat and simmer for 2-3 minutes, stirring continuously.

Heat ghee for vaghar in a small frying pan and fry vaghar ingredients for one minute. Add to curd. Stir well and remove from heat.

Serve with white rice and papad.

VALSADI DHAI NI KUDHI
(Curd kudhi—Valsad style)

1 litre sour curd, beaten till smooth
2-3 strips curry leaves
1 tbsp crushed cocum (dried sour plum)
1 tbsp cumin seeds, dry roasted and crushed

Salt to taste
1 tbsp rice flour, slaked in 2 tbsp water
2 tbsp ghee

Chop:
1 onion
10 green chillies, seeded
2 tbsp coriander leaves
2 pods garlic

Heat ghee in a pan and fry onions lightly. Add remaining ingredients except curd and rice flour and fry for 1-2 minutes

Add rice flour and 2 cups water and bring to boil, stirring continuously.

Lower heat, add curd and warm through. Do not heat for too long. Serve hot with rice and papad.

Note : You may add fenugreek seeds before adding onions, or 6-8 chopped green garlic and one pod garlic instead of two.

CHHAS NI KUDHI
(Buttermilk kudhi)
Serves 6-8

1 litre buttermilk
5 onions, roasted on a fire, peeled and sliced
3-4 strips curry leaves
2 tbsp cumin powder
Sugar to taste
Salt to taste
6 tbsp rice flour
3 tbsp ghee

Chop:
6-8 green chillies, seeded
2 tbsp coriander leaves
1 medium sized pod garlic

Heat ghee in a pan and lightly fry onions. Add remaining

ingredients except rice flour and buttermilk, Sauté for 1-2 minutes. Add rice flour, mix well and gradually add buttermilk, stirring continuously to avoid lumps. Bring to boil, adjust seasoning and sugar and serve hot with boiled rice and papad.

TARI NI KUDHI
(Toddy kudhi)
Serves 6

750 ml fresh toddy
1 tsp cumin powder
1 tsp dhan sakh masala powder
1 tbsp gram flour (besan)
1 tbsp ghee
Salt and sugar to taste

Chop:
2 onions
2-3 green chillies, seeded
1 tbsp coriander leaves
1" piece ginger
6-8 cloves garlic

Heat ghee in a pan and fry onions till light brown. Add remaining ingredients except toddy. Sauté for 1-2 minutes. Add toddy and simmer for 5 minutes.

Serve with boiled rice or khichdi and papad.

KERI NI RUS NI KUDHI (1)
(Mango juice kudhi)
Serves 6-8

6-8 ripe mangoes
1 cup curd, beaten
2 cups water
2 tbsp gram flour (besan), slaked with 4 tbsp water

4 green chillies, seeded and chopped
½ tsp turmeric powder
1 tsp chilli powder
1 tsp dry ginger powder (soonth)
Salt and sugar to taste

Vaghar (seasoning):
1 tbsp mustard seeds
A pinch of asafoetida (hing)
1 tbsp ghee

Press mangoes between your hands to soften them and then cut off tops. Squeeze out pulp and remove remaining pulp by scraping with a spoon. Sieve or liquidize pulp and pour into a pan.

Beat curd with water and add to mango pulp with slaked gram flour. Stir well and add remaining ingredients except vaghar. Place pan on heat and bring to boil, stirring continuously. Remove from heat.

Heat ghee for vaghar in a small frying pan and fry vaghar ingredients for one minute. Add to kudhi. Stir well, warm through and remove from heat.

Serve with white rice and papad.

KERI NI RUS NI KUDHI (2)
(Mango juice kudhi)
Serves 6-8

6 cups strained mango juice
1-2 cups water
6 strips curry leaves
Sugar to taste
Salt to taste
2 tbsp ghee

Dry roast individually and grind coarsely:
6 seeded and broken dry red chillies

2 tsp cumin seeds
1 tbsp coriander seeds
2 tsp mustard seeds

Heat ghee in a pan and add ground spices and curry leaves. Fry for 1-2 minutes.

Add mango juice and just enough water to make a thinnish liquid. Add sugar and salt to taste. Bring to boil and remove from heat.

Serve with boiled rice or khichdi and papad.

12

Fish

Fish is an intrinsic part of a Parsi meal. Having settled on the western coast of India, the Parsis not only enjoy eating it, but also consider it auspicious, as do the fishing folk. There are many varieties of fish which are popular.

The white and black pomfret are highly prized. The black pomfret is more popular in Bombay for its great flavour and is more expensive. The boi or grey mullet is another favourite. It should be about 6-7 inches long for individual servings, and 12-16 inches if it is to be sliced.

Imagine a breakfast of fresh crisply fried boi, meva ni akoori, hot rotli and fresh toddy! There are fish belonging to the surmai or tuna family, others like the bhangra or mackerel, and the boomla which belongs to the lamprey family which are also popular. Levta and levti, large and small mud fish found in the river estuaries of Gujarat are more popular in the smaller towns and cities than in the larger ones. The usual shell fish—lobsters, prawns, shrimps, crabs are of course highly prized as are clams and oysters.

In my youth there was a machhi bazaar or fish market near

the Chowpatty beach in Bombay where fresh fish, many still flapping, brought in from the evening catch would be sold. We would get our boomla for the night from there. No one ever ate the fish caught in the morning for dinner or that caught in the evening for lunch the next day. It was always the morning's catch for lunch and the evening's catch for dinner. This was because we did not have proper refrigerating facilities in those days. Now with these facilities, we have forgotten what it is to eat taji terferti machhi (fresh fish).

All fish taste best when fresh. When the flesh is pressed it should spring back and leave no depression. The prawns should be firm to the touch and the heads firmly fixed on the rest of the body. Boomla should be firm and straight and not curved and floppy. The eyes should not be sunken and the gills should not be sticky and slimy when touched.

TARELI MACHHI
(Fried fish)
Serves 6

This is the most common and popular way of preparing any type of fish in India.

6 large or 12 small slices of fish ½" thick cut through the bone, or filleted
1 tsp turmeric powder
1 tsp chilli powder
1 tsp cumin powder (optional)
Juice of 1 lime
Salt to taste
Sesame seed oil for shallow frying

Wash fish. Mix remaining ingredients together except oil and rub into fish. Leave to marinate for half an hour.

Heat oil in a frying pan till hot. Add fish and lower heat. Cook till underside is crisp, turn pieces over and cook other side. The secret of crisp fried fish is to fry it in this manner.

Serve immediately with slices of lime.

PATRA NI MACHHI
(Fish in banana leaves)
Serves 6

This is a universal favourite and perhaps the most popular of all the fish preparations of the Parsis.

12 pieces pomfret sliced ½" thick through the bone and marinated with salt and lime juice for ½ an hour
3 tbsp oil
4-5 medium-sized banana leaves
Cotton string

Coconut chutney made by grinding together:
1 coconut, grated

6 green chillies, seeded
6 tbsp chopped coriander leaves with tender stems
1 tbsp chopped mint leaves
1½" piece ginger
1½ pods garlic, medium-sized
½ tsp turmeric powder
1 tsp cumin powder
Juice of 2 limes
Pinch of sugar
Salt to taste

Add oil to chutney. (I know this is not done in the traditional recipe, but the oil keeps the fish moist). Soften banana leaves by holding them over a low fire.

Cut banana leaves into 12 large pieces, removing central stem. Spread chutney on both sides of fish pieces. Wrap each piece in a banana leaf like a parcel. Tie parcels with cotton thread.

Place fish in a large steamer and steam for 20 minutes.

It can also be cooked in an oven at 175°C (350°F). Put half an inch of water mixed with two tablespoons oil in a tray and place fish in it. Put tray into oven and bake for 15 minutes. Turn fish pieces over and bake further for 5 minutes.

Remove fish from tray, remove string, and if serving at a buffet, open leaves and place fish on top, so that it is easy for the guests to handle.

Variation:
• This preparation can also be shallow fried.
• Fill chutney into a deboned mullet, fresh pomfret or salmon. Rub fish with a paste of salt, chilli, turmeric and cumin powders, a little lime juice and oil. Bake in a moderate oven, at 175°C (350°F) for 20-25 minutes.
• Mix chutney with lightly fried prawns, stuff salmon, mullet or pomfret and bake.

BHOOJELO BHARUCHI BHING

(Barbecued shad—Bharuch style)

Serves 6

This fish is sometimes called the king of fish. It is the tastiest though boniest of all fish. This recipe was created in the Parsiwad, with its clean narrow winding lanes, of Bharuch. Unfortunately, today only the older generations of the community appreciate this dish enough to prepare it. Bharuch is a lovely historic city, which has Towers of Silence built over 100 years ago (now out of use) and a fire temple over 800 years old. It overlooks the Narmada river and the town of Ankleshwar across it.

1 medium sized shad (about 2½ kg)
100 g prawns, shelled, cleaned and deveined, if fish is without roe
Juice of 2 limes
Salt to taste
Tamarind the size of a large lime soaked in ¼ cup hot water
3-4 tbsp sesame seed oil, heated and cooled
2-3 large banana leaves
A piece of muslin cloth to cover fish
River mud or damp sand to cover fish

Chutney made by grinding together:
7-8 green chillies, seeded
3 tbsp coriander leaves with stems
1 pod garlic
2 tsp cumin seeds, dry roasted
1 tbsp coriander seeds, dry roasted
1 tsp sesame seeds (til), dry roasted
1 tsp poppy seeds (khus khus), dry roasted
¾ grated coconut (optional)
Salt to taste

Scale and clean fish. Remove roe if present and clean. Rub fish and roe or prawns with salt and lime juice and leave for half an hour.

Strain tamarind juice into chutney and mix well. Rub chutney all over fish, inside and out. Put roe or prawns inside fish and close flaps.

Press centre of banana leaves and flatten by holding over fire till soft. Place leaves on a kitchen board, put fish on top, and wrap completely with leaves. Place fish parcel in cotton or muslin cloth and sew it. Cover this with damp sand or river mud.

Place in hot charcoal ash, cover completely with ash and cook for one hour. It can also be cooked in an over at 120°C (250°F), for 30-40 minutes. Break open mud, cut open cloth, remove banana leaves and lo and behold, one of the classics of Parsi cuisine!

Serve with slices of lime.

Another way to cook it is to heat sand on a lohri, put fish on top and place an inverted pan over it. Half way through turn fish to cook other side.

Note : Those of you with gardens, do try and cook this dish in the classic way. It is not so difficult—just keep ashes hot with small pieces of live coal and twigs.

TARELA BOOMLA
(Fried lamprey)
Serves 4

12 boomla
12 green chillies
1 tsp turmeric powder
2 tsp chilli powder
2 tsp cumin powder
Salt to taste
Lime juice as required
Rice or wheat flour as required
Sesame seed oil for shallow frying

Remove head, fins and bone jutting out above tail of fish.

Remove insides without tearing the soft skin. Wash well. Insert a green chilli into empty sack where fish was cleaned. Rub fish with mixed spices, salt and lime juice and leave for half an hour.

Roll each fish in flour. Heat oil on a hot griddle. Add boomla, lower heat and fry till crisp on one side. Turn gently to fry the other side.

Serve hot and crisp with slices of lime and hot rotli.

TARELA MASALA BOOMLA
(Fried spiced lamprey)
Serves 4

12 fresh boomla
1 tsp cumin powder
½ tsp fenugreek powder (methi)
Juice of 2 limes
Salt to taste
Rice flour as required
Sesame seed oil for shallow frying

Grind together:
4 green chillies, seeded
2" piece ginger
6 cloves garlic
1 tsp turmeric powder
5 dried red chillies, seeded
1 tsp cumin powder
2 tsp coriander powder
1 tsp fenugreek seeds (methi)
1 tbsp poppy seeds (khus khus)
2" piece cinnamon
2-3 cloves
3 white cardamoms
4 black peppercorns

Clean fish by removing head, fins and bone jutting out above tail. Remove insides without tearing the soft skin. Wash well.

Mix fenugreek and cumin powder and rub into empty sack where fish was cleaned. Add lime juice and salt to ground spices, rub all over fish and leave for half an hour.

Roll each fish in flour. Heat oil on a hot griddle, add boomla and lower heat. Fry till crisp on one side. Turn over and fry the other side.

Serve hot with slices of lime and hot rotli.

DEVJI'S KHARA BOOMLA
(Savoury lamprey)
Serves 4

Devji was the cook in my home when I was a child. This was one of his masterpieces.

> 12 boomla, cleaned and cut into three pieces each
> 1 tbsp ground ginger
> 2 tbsp ground garlic
> 1 tsp turmeric powder
> 2 tsp chilli powder
> 2 tsp cumin powder
> Salt to taste
> 2-3 tbsp sesame seed oil
>
> *Chop*:
> 3 onions
> 2 tomatoes
> 2 tbsp coriander leaves with tender stems
> 4 green chillies, seeded

Heat oil in a pan and fry onions till light brown. Add ginger, garlic, and spices and sauté well, adding a little water if necessary.

Add tomatoes, coriander leaves, chillies, salt and a cup of water and simmer for 2-3 minutes. Add fish and simmer for a further 3-4 minutes till just cooked.

Serve with boiled rice or rotli.

Note : Any other fish, cut in pieces, or filleted, or prawns can be cooked in this manner.

DEVJI'S MASALA NA BOOMLA
(Devji's spiced lamprey)
Serves 4

12 boomla
2 onions, chopped
Tamarind the size of 2 large limes infused in ½ cup hot water
Salt to taste
2 tbsp chopped coriander leaves
4 tbsp sesame seed oil

Grind together:
4 green chillies, seeded
2" piece ginger
6 cloves garlic
1 tsp turmeric powder
5 dried red chillies, seeded
1 tsp cumin powder
2 tsp coriander powder
1 tsp fenugreek seeds (methi)
1 tbsp poppy seeds (khus khus)
2" piece cinnamon
2-3 cloves
3 white cardamoms
4 black peppercorns

Clean fish by removing head, fins and bone jutting out above tail of fish. Remove inside without tearing the soft skin. Wash well.

Heat oil in a pan and fry onions till light brown. Add ground spices and sauté for 1-2 minutes, adding a little water if necessary.

Add strained tamarind juice and salt, and simmer till gravy is thick. Add fish and simmer for a further 2-3 minutes on medium heat. Add coriander leaves and rotate pan to mix. Do not stir with a spoon, in case fish breaks. Cover and cook for 2-3 minutes longer.

Serve hot with rotli.

TARELA SOOKHA BOOMLA
(Fried Bombay duck)
Serves 6

18 large Bombay duck, freshly dried
½ tsp turmeric powder
1 tsp chilli powder
3 tsp cumin powder
Sesame seed oil for shallow frying

Soak Bombay duck in water for 10 minutes. Drain and dry. Slit open and remove backbone. Mix spices and rub onto fish.

Shallow fry fish in hot oil on a lohri till crisp.

Serve as an accompaniment to any dish, especially curries and sas.

Note : Bombay duck is the name given to dried boomla. It is a misnomer to call the fresh fish by this name. It is believed that the name was given by an Englishman travelling past an area where the fish was being dried. He wanted to know what the smell was and due to a misunderstanding in the languages, the name Bombay duck, somehow got attached to the dried fish. To clean Bombay duck, snip off heads, slit soft belly and clean out the inside.

MAPPY'S TARELA SOOKHA BOOMLA
(Fried Bombay duck)
Serves 6

18-20 Bombay duck, freshly dried
2 eggs, beaten
Breadcrumbs as required
Sesame seed oil for deep frying

Green chutney made by grinding together:
2 green chillies, seeded
50 g coriander leaves with tender stems

1 small bunch mint leaves
6 cloves garlic
½ grated coconut
Juice of 1 lime
Salt to taste

Soak Bombay duck in water for 20 minutes. Drain and pat dry. Slit open and remove backbone. Fill with chutney, fold back and press.

Dip into beaten eggs and roll in breadcrumbs.

Deep fry in hot oil.

Serve with khichdi and sas.

BHARUCHI TARI MA SOOKHA BOOMLA

(Bombay duck cooked in toddy—Bharuch style)

Serves 6-8

24 Bombay duck
Gram flour (besan) as required
Salt to taste
4 tbsp oil
½ litre toddy

Grind together:

2 pods garlic, medium-sized
2 tbsp cumin seeds
8 dried red chillies
1 tbsp jaggery
½ cup vinegar

Wash Bombay duck well. Slit open and remove backbone. Rub with gram flour and wash again. Cut each into 2 pieces. Rub with salt, oil and ground spices and leave to marinate for 2 hours.

Place fish in a clay pot, add toddy and simmer on low heat for about 15-20 minutes, till cooked.

TARAPORI PATIO
(Bombay duck patio—Tarapore style)
Serves 8-12

This is perhaps one of the most prized patia amongst the Parsis. It can stay in a refrigerator for over a month, or 4-5 days without one. It used to be a very popular picnic dish and was created in the town of Tarapore, hence its name.

30 large Bombay duck, freshly dried
Tamarind the size of a walnut
2 tbsp jaggery
2 cups strong Navsari vinegar
1 tbsp cumin seeds, dry roasted and ground
1 tbsp black pepper, dry roasted and ground
Salt to taste
3 tbsp ghee
4 tbsp sesame seed oil

Grind coarsely in half cup Navsari vinegar:
3 pods garlic, medium sized
6-8 green chillies
3 tbsp coriander leaves with tender stems
1 tsp turmeric powder
6-8 dried red chillies
2 tbsp dhan sakh masala powder

Wash and dry fish. Lightly pound and remove backbone. Cut into 2-3 pieces with scissors. Soak tamarind and jaggery in vinegar for half an hour.

Mix dry and ground spices with salt and rub into fish. Strain vinegar mixture.

Heat ghee and oil together in a kallied patio or broad-based pan. Add fish, and fry for 1-2 minutes. Add strained vinegar mixture and simmer till fish is cooked.

Serve with rotli or rice and mori dar.

LOHRI PER SOOKHA BOOMLA NO PATIO

(Bombay duck patio cooked on a lohri)

Serves 4

10 medium-sized Bombay duck, freshly dried
2 onions, finely sliced
2 potatoes, peeled and cubed
1 tsp turmeric powder
1 tsp black peppercorn, ground
1 tbsp dhan sakh masala powder
Tamarind the size of a walnut, infused in ½ cup hot water
2 tbsp ghee
2 tbsp sesame seed oil
Salt to taste

Slit open fish, remove backbone and wash well. Cut into 6-7 pieces.

Mix all ingredients including oil and ghee with fish.

Heat a lohri and put fish in it. Lower heat and cover with a lid. Stir occasionally, and cook till potatoes and fish are done.

Serve with boiled rice and plain dal or rotli.

TAJA BOOMLA NO PATIO

(Lamprey patio)

Serves 6

18 fresh boomla
Lime juice as required
Rice flour as required
Salt to taste
6 green chillies, seeded
3 tbsp coriander leaves with tender stems
2 pods garlic, medium-sized
1 tbsp cumin seeds
2 tbsp dhan sakh masala powder
Clean tamarind without seeds or strings, the size of a large lime
3 tbsp ghee
3 tbsp sesame seed oil

Clean fish by removing head, fins and bone jutting out above tail of fish. Remove insides without tearing the soft skin. Wash well, rub with lime juice and rice flour and wash again. Rub with salt and keep aside for half an hour.

Grind remaining ingredients except ghee and oil with a little water to make a semi stiff paste. Rub onto fish.

Heat ghee and oil in a lohri and fry fish a few at a time. Fry till one side is done, then carefully turn over and fry other side.

Serve with rotli or boiled rice and plain dal.

DEVJI'S MACHHI NO PATIO
(Devji's fish patio)
Serves 4-6

500 g white pomfret, sliced ½" thick through the bone or
500 g prawns, shelled, cleaned and deveined
Tamarind the size of a walnut
Juice of 1 lime
Salt to taste
8 drumsticks or 6 small aubergines
2 onions, sliced
3 tbsp ghee or sesame seed oil

Grind together:
1 large onion, dry roasted with its skin (remove skin before grinding)
3 green chillies
2 tbsp coriander leaves with stems
1 large pod garlic
3 dry red Goa or Kashmiri chillies, dry roasted
2 tsp cumin seeds, dry roasted
3 tbsp coriander seeds, dry roasted
3 tsp poppy seeds (khus khus), dry roasted
½" piece cinnamon, dry roasted
6 cloves, dry roasted
3 tbsp dhan sakh masala powder

Clean tamarind, remove any seeds or strings and infuse in one cup hot water.

Rub fish with salt and lime juice and leave for half an hour.

Peel and cut drumsticks into 3" pieces or slice aubergines.

Heat fat in a patio or broad-based pan and fry onions till light brown. Add a little water and simmer till onions are mushy. Add ground spices and salt to taste. Sauté for 2-3 minutes, adding a little water if required.

Add fish, drumsticks or aubergines and strained tamarind juice. Lower heat and simmer covered till fish and vegetables are cooked.

Serve with boiled rice and plain dal.

MAJA'S PRAWN OR FISH PATIO
Serves 4-6

This recipe was given to me by my niece Maja Daruvala, an excellent cook.

¾ kg prawns, shelled, cleaned and deveined or any other fish
Juice of one lime
8 medium-sized onions, grated
1 tbsp vinegar
Salt and sugar to taste
2-3 tbsp tomato ketchup
4 tbsp sesame seed oil or ghee

Grind together in a little Valsad vinegar:
6-8 cloves garlic
6-8 dry red Goa chillies
2 tsp cumin seeds

Marinate prawns with salt and lime juice for half an hour.

Heat oil in a pan and fry onions till brown. Add ground spices and fry well. Add prawns and simmer till done. Add vinegar, salt, sugar and tomato ketchup.

Serve hot with boiled rice and plain dal.

Note : I know it is unusual to use tomato ketchup in a patio, but this is one of the best patios I have tasted.

AMLI NE MACHHI NO PATIO
(Tamarind and fish patio)
Serves 4

**500 g pomfret or any other fish, sliced ½" thick through the
bone or 500 g prawns, shelled, cleaned and deveined
2 tsp cumin seeds
1 large pod garlic
1-2 tsp chilli powder or 6 dried red chillies
Vinegar for grinding
1 tsp turmeric powder
Tamarind the size of a lime without seeds or strings, infused
in 2 cups hot water
2 tsp sugar
Salt to taste**

Wash fish, rub with a little salt and keep aside for half an hour.

Grind cumin seeds, garlic and red chillies in a little vinegar.
Add turmeric powder, Rub half the ground spices on fish.

Heat oil in a pan and fry remaining spices. Add fish and
sauté for a minute. Strain tamarind water into pan, add sugar
and salt and simmer on medium heat till fish is cooked and
gravy is thick. Serve with boiled rice and plain dal or rotli or
khichdi.

COLMI NE BHEEDA NO PATIO
(Prawn and okra patio)
Serves 6-8

**500 g prawns, shelled, cleaned and deveined
500 g okras (bhindi), sliced ¼" thick and deep fried till crisp
but green
Juice of 2 limes
1 pod garlic**

2 tsp cumin seeds
4 dried red Goa or Kashmiri chillies, soaked in a little
vinegar
1 tsp turmeric powder
2 onions, sliced
2 tbsp chopped coriander leaves with tender stems
4 green chillies, seeded and chopped
Salt and sugar to taste
1 tbsp ghee
2 tbsp sesame seed oil

Rub prawns with salt and lime juice and leave for half an hour.
Grind garlic, cumin seeds and chillies in vinegar in which
chillies were soaked. Add turmeric and mix well.

Heat oil and ghee in a lohri or frying pan and lightly brown
onions. Add ground spices and sauté for 1-2 minutes. Add
prawns and cook for 2-3 minutes.

Add okras, coriander leaves, green chillies, salt and sugar
to taste. Mix well, sauté for 1-2 minute and serve with hot rotli.

Serve with rotli or boiled rice and mori dar or khichdi.

Note : This dish should taste sweet and sour.

Variation:

• Take one bunch of the large variety or fourteen bunches of
the small variety of fenugreek leaves (methi). Wash and
remove stems. Chop leaves and sprinkle with one tsp salt.
Mix well and leave for 10-15 minutes. Squeeze out juice to
remove bitterness, sprinkle on patio and sauté for 2-3
minutes, before adding okras.

SANDHNA NO BHARUCHI PATIO
(Jumbo prawn patio—Bharuchi style)
Serves 6-8

1½ kg jumbo prawns, shelled, cleaned, deveined and salted
Salt to taste
½ cup ghee
3 tbsp sesame seed oil

Chop:
10 medium onions
800 g spring onions
50 g green garlic (if available)
2 pods garlic, medium-sized
1" piece fresh turmeric (if available)
24 bunches small leafed fenugreek leaves (methi)
2 tbsp coriander leaves

Grind together:
6-8 green chillies, seeded
Coriander stems reserved from leaves used above
1 tsp turmeric powder
12 dried red chillies, seeded
5 heaped tsp cumin seeds
2 tsp black peppercorn

Mix half ground spices with prawns and keep aside for half an hour.

Heat half the ghee and oil in a patio, or broad-based pan. Add remaining ground spices, salt, and chopped ingredients. Fry for about 3-4 minutes.

Heat remaining ghee and oil in a frying pan and lightly fry prawns. Add to patio. Mix well and simmer for 3-4 minutes, or till prawns are cooked. Serve with rotli or boiled rice and dal or khichdi.

Note : Do not overcook prawns or they will get tough.

TAAJA KOOTO ATHWA AMBAR NO PATIO

(Small shrimp patio)

Serves 4-6

This patio can stay in the refrigerator for 15-20 days.

500 g fresh small shrimps
1 tsp turmeric powder
1 tsp chilli powder
2 tbsp cumin seeds, dry roasted and coarsely pounded
1 cup Navsari vinegar
Salt to taste
2-3 tbsp sugar
3 tbsp sesame seed oil

Chop:
4 large onions
1" piece ginger
6-8 cloves garlic
2 tbsp coriander leaves with tender stems
8-10 green chillies, seeded

Wash shrimps well and remove all other small fish that may be mixed with it. Drain.

Heat oil in a pan and fry onions till brown. Add ginger, garlic, turmeric, chilli powder, cumin seeds, coriander and green chillies. Sauté for 1-2 minutes. Add shrimps and fry over high heat for 3-4 minutes. Add vinegar, salt and sugar. Simmer for 4-6 minutes till liquid has almost dried.

Serve hot with rotli or hot toast.

This dish can be served at room temperature.

SOOKHI GHARAB NE GOVAD NO PATIO

(Dried fish roe and cluster bean patio)

Serves 6

750 g dried salted fish roe
750 g cluster beans (gwar ki phali)

3 onions, finely sliced
1 tsp turmeric powder
2 tbsp cumin seeds, dry roasted and coarsely pounded
1 tsp black pepper powder
2 tbsp dhan sakh masala powder
2 tbsp coriander leaves with tender stems, coarsely ground
6 green chillies, coarsely ground
Tamarind the size of a lime infused in 1 cup hot water
Salt and sugar to taste
2 tbsp ghee
2 tbsp sesame seed oil

Clean and wash fish roe and cut into two-inch pieces. Wash and trim cluster beans, and keep whole.

Heat ghee and oil in a pan and fry onions till brown. Add a little water and simmer till onions turn mushy. Add spices, coriander leaves and green chillies and sauté for one minute.

Add fish roe and cluster beans and simmer on low heat till beans are cooked. Strain tamarind juice into pan and mix by turning pan with both hands from side to side. Simmer till all moisture has evaporated. Add salt and sugar to taste.

Serve with rotli or boiled rice and mori dar.

Note : If a less salty dish is required, soak fish roe in water for half an hour, dry and use.

GHARUB NE KORA NO PATIO
(Fish roe and pumpkin patio)
Serves 8

1 kg salted roe
1 kg ripe red pumpkin (kuddu), peeled and cut into thin slices
4 onions, finely sliced
2 tomatoes, blanched and chopped
Lime juice to taste
Salt to taste

Tamarind the size of a large lime soaked in ½ cup hot water
with 1 tbsp jaggery
4-6 tbsp sesame seed oil

Grind together:
4 green chillies, seeded
½ cup coriander leaves with tender stems
1 pod garlic
1 tsp turmeric powder
2 tsp chilli powder
2 tsp cumin seeds

Wash roe in water to remove excess salt. Dry and cut into
one-inch pieces.

Heat oil in a frying pan and fry roe till half cooked. Remove
roe from pan. Add onions and fry till light brown. Add ground
spices and tomatoes and sauté for 1-2 minutes, adding water if
required.

Add pumpkin and simmer till cooked. Add roe, lime juice,
salt and strained tamarind paste. Simmer for 3-4 minutes
more. Serve hot with rotli or khichdi.

NARIEL NA DOODH MA BHEEDA NE COLMI
(Prawn and okras cooked in coconut milk)
Serves 4

300 g prawns, shelled, cleaned and deveined
400 g okras, cut into 2-3 pieces
Juice of 1 lime
Rice flour as needed
4 onions, chopped
1 tsp turmeric powder
2 cups coconut milk extracted from 1 large coconut
Tamarind the size of a walnut infused in 6 tbsp Navsari
vinegar
Salt and sugar to taste
3 tbsp ghee

Grind together:
5-7 green chillies, seeded
2 pods garlic
4 tsp cumin powder

Rub prawns with rice flour, salt and lime juice. Wash well.

Heat fat in a pan and fry onions till light brown. Add prawns and cook for 2-3 minutes. Add ground spices and turmeric and fry for one minute. Add okras, and cook for another 2-3 minutes. Add coconut milk and simmer for a further 3-4 minutes. Strain tamarind juice into pan, add sugar and salt and remove from fire.

Serve hot with rotli, rice or khichdi.

MACHHI NO SAS (1)
(Sweet and sour fish)
Serves 6-8

1 kg pomfret, sliced ½" thick through the bone, or filleted or
1 kg prawns, shelled, cleaned and deveined
1 large onion, finely chopped
1 tbsp fine rice flour
1 tbsp cumin seeds, coarsely pounded
2 pods garlic, finely chopped
8-10 green chillies, seeded and chopped
Salt to taste
50 g cherry tomatoes (optional)
3 eggs
Sugar to taste
½ cup vinegar
2 tbsp oil or ghee
Chopped coriander leaves for garnish

Heat oil in a patio or broad-based pan. Fry onion till light brown. Add rice flour and sauté for 1-2 minutes. Add cumin powder, garlic and chillies and sauté for one minute. Add 3 cups water and salt. Mix well and bring to boil.

Add fish and tomatoes, and simmer till fish is three-quarters done. Remove pan from heat.

Beat eggs, add sugar and vinegar and mix well. Pour into pan and swirl pan with both hands, taking care not to break fish. Return pan to heat and simmer on low heat till gravy is thick, swirling pan around so that eggs do not set.

Taste sas as it should be sweet and sour, and adjust vinegar and sugar accordingly.

Garnish with coriander leaves and serve hot with khichdi.

Variations:

- Substitute boiled chicken in place of fish. Add chicken stock instead of water.
- Substitute boiled breast meat in place of fish. Add meat stock instead of water.
- Substitute 500 g okras in place of fish.
- Add 300 g fried Bombay duck, cut into 3-4 pieces.
- Add about 500 g fried fish roe cut into 1" pieces instead of fish.
- Substitute 1 kg boomla, cut into 3 pieces in place of fish.
- Add 500 g fried, fresh or dried small shrimps (kooto) to gravy just before serving.
- Use 6-8 dried red chillies instead of green chillies. Grind chillies and add 2 chopped tomatoes to make a reddish gravy.
- Add half cup coconut milk and reduce quantity of water accordingly.

MACCHI NO SAS (2)

(Sweet and sour fish)

Serves 4

This is my mother's recipe and it is very good—naturally!

8 pieces pomfret, sliced ½" thick through the bone, or filleted
or 500 g prawns, shelled, cleaned and deveined
1 large onion, finely chopped
½ cup coconut milk extracted from ¼ coconut
3 eggs, separated
Salt and sugar to taste
½-¾ cup vinegar
2 tbsp oil or ghee
Chopped coriander leaves for garnish

Grind to a stiff paste:
2 green chillies, seeded
4 dried red chillies, seeded
8 cloves garlic
2 tsp cumin seeds

Heat fat in a pan and fry onion till light brown. Remove onion
and keep aside. Add ground spices and cook for one minute.
Drain fat from pan and keep aside. Add coconut milk, and
fried onion to pan. Mix well and add fish. Simmer till fish is just
done.

Beat egg yolks with sugar, salt and vinegar. Beat egg whites
till stiff and fold into vinegar mixture. Pour into pan and swirl
pan with both hands to mix. Cook on low heat for one minute,
swirling pan all the time, or spoon into a baking dish and bake
for 10-15 minutes in medium oven at 175°C (350°F).

Spoon in reserved fat, sprinkle with coriander leaves and
serve with khichdi.

LAGAN NO MACHHI NO SAS
(Sweet and sour fish cooked for weddings)
Serves 6

**2 pomfret, weighing about 1½ kg, cut into ½" thick slices
through the bone, or filleted
3 tsp cumin seeds, dry roasted and powdered
3 cups water
2-3 tbsp flour
1 cup cherry tomatoes (optional)
5 eggs
1 cup vinegar
Salt to taste
3-6 tsp sugar or to taste
2-3 tbsp oil or ghee
2 tbsp chopped coriander leaves for garnish**

Chop:
**2 onion
1 large pod garlic
6-8 green chillies, seeded
2 tomatoes, blanched and seeded**

Heat fat and fry onions without browning. Add garlic, chillies, chopped tomatoes, cumin powder and 3 cups water. Bring to boil. Slake flour with half cup water and add to pan. Allow to thicken, stirring all the while.

Add fish and cherry tomatoes and simmer till fish is done. Beat eggs with vinegar, salt and sugar and add to pan, swirling pan with both hands to mix well. Continue cooking on low heat, swirling pan all the while, and allow to thicken.

Add coriander leaves and serve hot.

This gravy should be thick and not runny.

Serve with rotli.

BHOOJELO SAS
(Baked sweet and sour prawns)
Serves 6

18 large prawns, shelled, cleaned and deveined
2 tbsp cumin seeds, dry roasted and coarsely pounded
½ cup vinegar
Salt and sugar to taste
2 tbsp gram flour (besan), slaked with 1 cup coconut milk
extracted from ¼ coconut
5 eggs, separated
4 hard-boiled eggs, peeled and sliced in half
3 tbsp ghee

Chop:
6 onions
2" piece ginger
1 pod garlic
8-10 green chillies, seeded

Rub a little salt on prawns. Place in pan, cover and cook on low heat, till half done. Remove from heat and keep aside.

Heat fat in a frying pan and lightly fry onions. Add ginger, garlic, green chillies and cumin powder. Sauté for 2-3 minutes. Remove from heat and add prawns.

Mix vinegar, sugar, gram flour and coconut mixture. Beat egg yolks and add to vinegar mixture.

Spoon prawns into a shallow baking dish and pour vinegar mixture over it. Stir and adjust seasoning. Arrange sliced hard-boiled eggs on top, cover with stiffly beaten egg whites and bake in a medium oven at 175°C (350°F) for 25-30 minutes.

Variation:
• Make sas as given in the above recipe but without the hard-boiled eggs.

COLMI NA KABAB
(Prawn kababs)
Serves 4

500 g prawns, shelled, cleaned and deveined
2 onions, chopped, fried and well drained
3 green chillies, seeded and chopped
6 cloves garlic, chopped
1 tsp turmeric powder
1 tsp chilli powder
1 tsp cumin powder
1 tbsp dhan sakh masala powder
1 egg, beaten
Lime juice to taste
Salt to taste
Sesame seed oil for shallow frying

Blanch and coarsely chop prawns. Mix with remaining ingredients, taking care to add just enough egg to bind kababs. Shape into kababs and shallow fry.

Serve with slices of lime.

SOOKHA BOOMLA NA CUTLETS
(Bombay duck cutlets)
Serves 8

36 Bombay duck, washed, soaked for 1 hour, drained and dried
2 slices bread, soaked in water and squeezed dry
Salt to taste
4-5 eggs, beaten
Flour as required
Breadcrumbs as required
Sesame seed oil for frying

Chop:
6 onions
4 green chillies, seeded
2 tbsp coriander leaves with tender stems

Grind together in vinegar:
1" piece ginger
1 pod garlic
1 tsp turmeric powder
1-2 tsp chilli powder
2 tsp cumin seeds
1 tbsp dhan sakh masala powder
1 tsp jaggery

Fry onions in hot oil till crisp. Drain and crush. Remove centre bone of Bombay duck and crush fish into a paste with mortar and pestle.

Mix all chopped ingredients, crushed onion, fish, salt, ground spices, and soaked bread. Add a little beaten egg and form into cutlets.

Lightly press in flour and then dip into eggs, press into breadcrumbs, redip into eggs and fry in hot oil.

Serve with hot rotli and mashed potatoes made with eight potatoes, into which is added 1 tbsp chopped coriander leaves, 1 tbsp finely chopped spring onions, salt, pepper, 1 cup hot milk, and 60 g butter.

CURRIES

DEVJI NI MACHHI ATHWA COLMI NI CURRY
(Devji's fish or prawn curry)
Serves 4-6

I know there are many excellent recipes for fish curries all over India but the curry made by Devji, the cook when I was a child was such that friends would come to our home just to taste it.

500 g white pomfret, filleted or
500 g prawns, shelled, deveined and cleaned
Lime juice as required

Salt to taste
1 large onion, finely chopped
2 tomatoes, blanched and finely chopped
Tamarind the size of a walnut, infused in ½ cup hot water
1½ cups coconut milk extracted from ½ coconut
1 tbsp sesame seed or any other oil

Grind very fine:
1" piece ginger
1 large pod garlic
1 tsp turmeric powder
6 dry red Goa or Kashmiri chillies
4 tsp cumin seeds
6 tsp coriander seeds
Seeds of 2 white cardamoms
¼ grated coconut

Rub fish with salt and lime juice and keep aside for half an hour.

Heat oil in a pan and fry onion on low heat till light brown. Add ground spices, salt, tomatoes, strained tamarind juice and 3 cups water. Simmer slowly for 5-8 minutes. Add coconut milk and slowly bring to boil. Simmer for 5 minutes.

Strain curry through a muslin cloth. Return to pan, add fish and simmer till done.

Cool completely. Leave for 1-2 hours before serving. Reheat, add lime juice to taste and serve hot with boiled rice.
Note: The longer any curry is kept before serving, the better the taste. In fact it tastes even better the next day and it is a good idea to make it the day before, and keep it in the refrigerator, if it is to be served for lunch, or cook it in the morning for dinner.

MOTHER'S FISH MOOLI
Serves 6-8

1½ kg pomfret cut into ½" thick slices through the bone
Juice of 2-3 limes
Salt to taste

2 cups coconut milk extracted from ½ coconut
2" piece ginger, sliced
4-6 green chillies, seeded and chopped
3 strips curry leaves
3 tbsp sesame seed oil

Dry roast individually and grind together to a fine paste:
1 tsp cumin seeds
1 tbsp coriander seeds
1 tbsp poppy seeds (khus khus)
½ coconut, grated
2 tbsp peanuts
3 tbsp cashew nuts
4 tbsp roasted gram (channa), shelled
1 tbsp rice

Grind together:
2 onions
2 tbsp coriander leaves with tender stems
6-7 dry red Goa chillies or green chillies, seeded
6-9 cloves garlic

Rub lime juice and salt on fish and leave to marinate for half an hour.

Mix both ground pastes. Heat oil in a pan and fry ground spices. Add coconut milk, ginger, green chillies, curry leaves and salt. Mix well. The texture should be that of milk. Add water if necessary. Simmer for 3-4 minutes. Add fish and simmer till done. Add lime juice to taste.

Serve with white rice and papad.

GOA CURRY (1)
Serves 6

The secret of a good Goa curry is the smoothness of its texture. The ground spices must feel absolutely smooth when rubbed between thumb and fingers.

Try to use Goa chillies (soaked in hot water for 15 minutes)

as these are not too hot and have the distinct flavour needed
for this curry.

> 12 pieces pomfret, cut into ½" thick slices through the bone,
> or filleted or 500 g prawns, shelled, cleaned and deveined
> 1 onion, sliced
> Salt to taste
> 6 cocum (dried sour plum)
> Tamarind the size of a walnut, soaked in ¾ cup hot water
> Lime juice to taste
> 1½ cup coconut milk extracted from ¾ coconut
> 100 g small okras (bhindi), optional
> 2-3 green chillies, slit

> *Grind together to a smooth paste:*
> 8 cloves garlic
> 2" piece ginger
> ½ tsp turmeric powder
> 6-8 dry red Goa chillies
> 2 tsp cumin seeds

Mix sliced onion and salt thoroughly with your hand in a
pan and leave for 10 minutes. Add ground spices and mix
well. Add cocum, strained tamarind juice, lime juice and 3
cups water.

Place pan on heat and simmer gently for 15-20 minutes.
Add coconut milk, okras, if used, green chillies and fish and
simmer till fish is cooked.

Cool completely and reheat just before serving. Serve with
hot boiled rice.

This curry is eaten with a variety of rice called ookra chaval
(parboiled rice) in Goa.

Other accompaniments with Goa curry are plain or masala
fried Bombay duck or fried fish such as mackerel.

GOA CURRY (2)
Serves 6

¾ kg fish, sliced ½" thick through the bone, or filleted or
¾ kg prawns, shelled, cleaned and deveined
1 onion, finely sliced
4-6 green chillies, slit and seeded
6 cocum (dried sour plum)
Salt to taste
1 tbsp oil

Grind together to a smooth paste:
6-8 cloves garlic
½ tsp turmeric powder
6-8 dry red Goa chillies
1 tsp cumin seeds
1 tbsp coriander seeds
¼ grated coconut
1 tbsp tamarind without seeds or strings

Heat oil in a pan and fry onion very lightly. Add green chillies, cocum and ground spices. Fry for one minute only.

Add 4 cups water and simmer gently for 15-20 minutes. Add fish and salt and simmer till cooked.

Cool completely and reheat just before serving. Serve with hot boiled rice.

GOA CURRY (3)
Serves 6

500 g fish, sliced ½" thick through the bone, or filleted or
500 g prawns, shelled, cleaned and deveined
1 onion, finely sliced
4-6 green chillies, slit and seeded
10 cocum (dried sour plums)
1 tsp turmeric powder
Salt to taste
1 tbsp oil

Grind together to a smooth paste:
1 tsp turmeric powder

6-8 dry red Goa chillies
2 tsp cumin seeds
¼ grated coconut
Tamarind without seeds or strings, the size of a walnut

Heat oil in a pan and fry onion very lightly. Add green chillies, cocum, turmeric powder and ground spices. Fry for one minute only. Add 4 cups water and simmer gently for 15-20 minutes. Add fish and salt and simmer till cooked.

Cool completely and reheat just before serving. Serve with hot boiled rice.

Variations:
* Goa curry can be made with any fish including mackerel, boomla, crabs, clams, lobsters.
* The onions in all the recipes can be ground with the other spices instead of being sliced.

PHILIP'S GOA CURRY
Serves 8

1 kg filleted pomfret or prawns, marinated in salt and lime juice
2 large onions, ground
5 cups coconut milk, extracted from 1½ coconuts
1½ tbsp tamarind soaked in 2 cups hot water
Salt to taste

Grind together:
20 dry red Goa or Kashmiri chillies
8 cloves garlic
2 tsp cumin seeds
3 tbsp coriander seeds
½ tsp turmeric powder

Put onions, ground spices, coconut milk and strained tamarind juice in a pan. Mix well and bring to boil. Simmer for 10-15 minutes. The consistency should be that of thick milk.

Strain and add fish and salt. Simmer till fish is cooked.

Cool completely and reheat gently before serving. Serve with boiled rice.

ANNA'S GOA CURRY
Serves 6

6-8 mackerels, cleaned, washed and marinated in salt and lime juice
1 onion, sliced
4-6 green chillies, slit and seeded
6 cocum (dried sour plums)
Salt to taste
2 tsp sesame seed oil

Grind together to a fine paste:
8 cloves garlic
½ tsp turmeric powder
8-9 dry red Goa chillies or 2 tbsp chilli powder
1½ tsp cumin seeds
1 tbsp coriander seeds
¼ grated coconut
1 tbsp tamarind without seeds or strings

Heat oil and fry onions lightly with green chillies. Add ground spices and fry for one minute.

Add 4 cups water and cocum and simmer for 10-15 minutes. Add fish and salt and cook till done.

Cool completely and reheat gently before serving. Serve with boiled rice.

ANNA'S GOA CURRY WITHOUT COCONUT
Serves 6

12 slices of any fish cut ½" thick through the bone or filleted
1 onion, sliced
3-4 green chillies, slit and seeded
6 cocum (dried sour plum)
Salt to taste
1 tbsp sesame seed oil

Grind together:
6-8 cloves garlic
1 tsp turmeric powder
6-8 dry red Goa chillies
1 tsp cumin seeds
1 tbsp tamarind, without seeds and strings

Heat oil in a pan and fry onion lightly with green chillies. Add ground spices and fry for 1-2 minutes. Add 4 cups water and cook till thick. Add cocum, salt and fish. Simmer till fish is done.

Cool completely and reheat gently before serving. Serve with boiled rice.

MR FERNANDES' GOA CURRY
Serves 6-8

Mr Fernandes was the chef at Raj Bhavan, Bangalore while I was the catering consultant to His Excellency Mr Dharma Vira, the Governor of Karnataka. What is fascinating is the number of variations there are for this curry!

1 kg pomfret, sliced ½" thick through the bone or filleted
1 onion, sliced
Tamarind the size of a lime, soaked in 1 cup hot water
2" piece ginger, smashed with the heel of your hand
Salt to taste
4-5 cups coconut milk extracted from 1½ coconuts

Grind together to a fine paste:
1 pod garlic, peeled
½ tsp turmeric powder
20 dry red Goa chillies
2 tsp cumin seeds
1 tbsp coriander seeds

Mix ground spices with onion, strained tamarind juice, ginger, salt and coconut milk. Bring to boil and simmer till it reaches the consistency of thick milk. Add fish and cook till done.

Cool completely, remove ginger and reheat gently before serving, but do not boil. Serve with boiled rice.

13

Meat and Poultry

No Parsi meal is complete without a meat or chicken dish. Most of these dishes are cooked with vegetables and the names of the dishes are self-explanatory, e.g. meat cooked with potatoes is called papeta ma gosht where the 'ma' stands for 'in'. The custom of cooking meat and chicken with vegetables is an Iranian one, which has not left us even after nearly fifteen hundred years.

The essence of all these dishes is the savoury spices (kharo masalo), used to prepare the savoury meat or chicken (kharo gosht or khari murghi). The spices used are ginger, garlic, turmeric powder, and green or red chillies or chilli powder. There are variations using cumin, coriander, garam masala (cinnamon, cloves, cardamom and black pepper). Onions are always used and are fried first, before the spices are added. Tomatoes may also be used as a variation.

The frying of onions is crucial. They should be thinly sliced and fried on low heat till brown. If they are fried too quickly they turn leathery and the taste of the dish is ruined. Once the onions have been browned, a little water is added to soften them and the cooking is continued on low heat till they become mushy. Once this art has been mastered, half the battle of preparing a perfect dish has been won.

After the water has evaporated, the spices are added. A little water is added at this stage, just enough for the spices to cook without burning. Here again, the art lies in gentle cooking, so that the flavour of the spices is not burnt out. Parsis do not fry the masala till the oil floats on top, as too much frying destroys the flavours of the spices. The meat is added at this stage and the frying is continued. The dish is then allowed to cook with the addition of a little water at a time, again just enough not to let it burn and to provide a nice thick gravy at the end. The vegetables are added at any time after the meat, depending on the time required for them to cook.

The Iranian influence is again felt in curries with nuts like the hundred-almond curry and the almond and pistachio curry.

The word curry is actually an anglicized version of the South Indian word kari. The curries of today are quite different from the original ones (the most famous of which is the muligatawny) which was created for the British.

The Parsi curry is thick, discreetly spiced and has just the right amount of sourness.

The secret of making a good curry again lies in the slicing and frying of the onions and masala. The masala should be finely ground—the texture obtained on the black curry stone of South India cannot be achieved by any machine. The curry should not be allowed to boil. It should be simmered with the lid half covering the pan and should be cooked at least 2-3 hours before serving, so that all the different flavours are amalgamated and brought out just right. Finally a good curry needs a good rice which should be steamed or boiled.

Potatoes and okra are often added to meat, chicken and fish especially in the Goa curry.

Accompaniments to the curry are fried Bombay duck, kachumber, papad, pickles, chutneys and murumbas.

Other favourites are baby lamb cooked with coconut milk and cashew nut (kid gosht), a classic of the wedding and navjote feasts, Mughlai meat and chicken, and meat cooked in curd (khatu gosht, or dhai gosht), a speciality of Surat. There are the bafats cooked with spiced vinegar and the vindaloos borrowed from the Goans (though not as popular as the Goa curry). We have the famous Parsi kababs eaten with dhan sakh or sheet beans (papri ma kabab), the cutlets with crisp frills of eggs, eaten plain or with tomato gravy, and the patties—mashed potato stuffed with mince. All these dishes are prepared using the basic recipe for Parsi mince, which has a sweet and sour flavour.

Bhoojan is a spiced barbecued meat and in the past we used to have wonderful bhoojan parties. These were often in the garden, in the evening. There was a magical silence in the air, even amongst us children, as the aroma of the barbecued meat would waft towards us, with the oomberiu (a dish cooked with sheet beans and meat in an earthenware pot, placed in a hole in the ground and surrounded with smouldering dry mango leaves and twigs), nearly ready to be unearthed. We would watch the sun set and listen to the bird song and bells of the cows as they were being led to their sheds in the sweet lime fields behind the house, as we sipped our toddy.

Some dishes are very typical of the Parsis, like chicken or meat cooked with mango (ambakalia ma murghi athwa gosht) and chicken or meat cooked with toddy (tari ma murghi athwa gosht).

KHARU GOSHT ATHWA KHARI MURGHI
(Savoury meat or chicken)
Serves 4-6

1 kg leg or shoulder of lamb, cut into pieces with bone, or
1½ kg chicken, jointed
4 medium-sized onions, finely sliced
1 tbsp mixed whole cinnamon, cloves and black cardamom
2½" piece ginger, ground
1 large pod garlic, ground
1 tsp turmeric powder
2-3 tsp cumin powder
4-5 dried red chillies or 1 tsp chilli powder
Salt to taste
2 tomatoes, chopped (optional)
4-5 green chillies, slit and seeded
4 tbsp ghee or oil

Heat fat in a pan and fry onions with whole spices till onions are light brown. Add half cup water and simmer till onions are mushy and water has evaporated. Add ginger, garlic, turmeric, cumin powder, red chillies or chilli powder and salt and sauté for 1-2 minutes. Add tomatoes if used and meat or chicken and continue to sauté till meat is light brown. Add green chillies and one cup water.

Lower heat, cover pan with an inverted lid, put some water on lid and simmer till meat or chicken is tender and gravy is thick. Stir occasionally, adding water to pan or on the lid as required to prevent meat from sticking to base of pan.

This is the basic dish and can be served by itself with hot rotli.

Variations

- **Papeta ma gosht athwa murghi (1)**
  (Savoury meat or chicken with potatoes)

  Add 8 potatoes peeled and cut into fours when meat or chicken is three-quarters cooked.

- **Bheeda ma gosht athwa murghi**
  (Savoury meat or chicken with okras)

  Slice ¾ kg okras (bhindi) into 1" pieces and deep fry till crisp, but still green. Sprinkle on dish before serving.

- **Tamatar ma gosht athwa murghi**
  (Savoury meat or chicken with tomatoes)

  Blanch and chop 1 kg tomatoes. Add to meat or chicken when it is half cooked along with 1 tsp chilli powder, 1 tsp salt and 1 tsp sugar. Simmer till gravy is thick.

- **Vatena ma gosht athwa murghi**
  (Savoury meat or chicken with green peas)

  Add ½ kg boiled green peas to meat or chicken, mix well and serve.

- **Papri ma gosht athwa murghi**
  (Savoury meat or chicken with sheet beans)

  Include 2-3 tsp ajwain with other spices, and add ¾ kg cleaned and trimmed sheet beans when meat is three-quarters done. Cook till meat and beans are done.

- **Jerdaloo ma gosht athwa murghi**
  (Savoury meat or chicken with dried apricot)

  Soak 1 kg dried apricots and stone them. Add to meat, 15

minutes before it is cooked with 3-4 tbsp Worcestershire sauce and 2 tsp chilli powder. This dish should have a sweet and sharp taste and should not be bland.

- **Kera ma gosht athwa murghi**
  (Savoury meat or chicken with bananas)
  Peel and cut 6-8 ripe Vasai bananas (ordinary bananas will do) into 1½" slices and fry in a little oil till brown. Add to meat or chicken just before serving.

- **Kanda papeta ma butack, gosht athwa murghi**
  (Savoury duck, meat or chicken with baby onions and potatoes)
  Duck is used in the classical recipe. Substitute two small ducks for chicken.

  Add 1 tbsp mixed whole cinnamon, cloves and cardamoms just before adding duck. Peel and fry 1 kg baby potatoes and 1½ kg baby onions and add with 2 tbsp Worcestershire sauce a few minutes before duck is ready. Simmer till potatoes and duck are tender.

- **Meva ma gosht athwa murghi**
  (Savoury meat or chicken with dry fruits)
  This is a very typical Parsi dish, but seldom served.

  Fry individually:
  ¾ cup sultanas (kishmish)
  ½ cup almonds, blanched and sliced
  ½ cup pistachio nuts
  ½ cup cheronji
  ½ cup pinenuts (chilgoza), peeled
  ½ cup cashew nuts
  200 g dried apricots or 200 g dried dates, soaked in water and seeded

  Add to meat or chicken just before serving.

- **Sekta ni sing ma gosht athwa murghi**
  (Savoury meat or chicken with drumsticks)
  Peel and cut 8-10 drumsticks into 3" pieces. Tie into bundles of 3 or 4 or leaves separate. Add to meat 15 minutes before it is cooked.

Another variation of the same dish is to add coconut milk extracted from one coconut and 8 medium-sized potatoes, peeled and quartered, half way through the cooking process. Add drumsticks 15 minutes before meat is cooked.

- **Vengna ma gosht athwa murghi**
  (Savoury meat or chicken with aubergines)

Cut 1 kg small aubergines (baigan) in half, lengthwise. Rub with salt and leave for half an hour. Remove all liquid and dip into a mixture of turmeric powder and cumin powder. Shallow fry and add to meat just before serving.

- **Sali ma gosht athwa murghi**
  (Savoury meat or chicken with julienned potatoes)

This famous and very favourite dish is often ruined by not serving it properly or adding tomatoes while cooking the meat. The meat must be placed in a dish and completely covered by very fine julienne of potatoes. It can truly be called a universal dish and finds favour with both children and adults. It can also be prepared with wafers.

Make very fine sali (julienne) from 1½ kg potatoes, place meat or chicken in a dish and cover thickly with sali.

- **Doodh ma gosht athwa murghi**
  (Savoury meat or chicken with milk)

Blanch and slice 50 g almonds. Add to half litre buffalo or full cream milk and cook milk till reduced to quarter. Add to meat just before serving.

- **Mosumbi na chhal ma gosht athwa murghi**
  (Savoury meat or chicken with sweet lime peel)

Remove white pith from peel of ½ kg sweet lime and cut into thick strips. Plunge into boiling water and cook for 10 minutes. Refresh in cold water.

Add to meat 15 minutes before it is ready. Add juice of 2 limes and serve.

- **Dodhi ma gosht athwa murghi**
  (Savoury meat or chicken with marrow)

Use double the quantity of whole spices and include 5-6 dried red chillies. Add 1½ kg peeled and cubed marrow (ghia) with meat. The marrow should be mushy when the dish is ready.

- **Bhaji dana ma gosht athwa murghi**
  (Savoury meat or chicken with greens and green peas)
  Cook bhaji dana as given in Chapter 11 and add to savoury meat dish. Simmer for 3-4 minutes and serve hot.

ANNANUS MA MURGHI
(Chicken with pineapple)

To savoury chicken (khari murghi), add pineapple prepared as given below:

Dissolve half cup sugar in 2 cups water and add one small ripe pineapple, peeled and cut into slices, which should then be cut in half. Strain and add to chicken with 1 tsp chilli powder to equalize the sweetness.

AMBAKALIA MA GOSHT
(Savoury meat with mangoes)
Serves 4-6

Cook ambakalia as given in Chapter 11 and add to Kharu Gosht. Simmer for 3-4 minutes, taking care not to break mango slices. Serve hot.

VALSADI DODHI MA GOSHT
(Savoury meat with marrow—Valsad style)
Serves 4-6

This dish has been adapted from the one given to me by Kekhashru Bhikaji Kamana who caters for all the weddings and navjotes in Valsad.

1 kg leg or shoulder of lamb, cut into pieces, with bone
1 kg marrow (ghia), peeled and cubed

3-4 onions, cubed
4-5 green chillies
4-5 dry red chillies, seeded
3" piece ginger, ground
2 pods garlic, ground
3 small pieces cinnamon
5-6 cloves
Salt to taste
5-6 extra cloves garlic, crushed
3-4 tbsp ghee

Heat 3½ tbsp fat and fry meat till well browned. Add remaining ingredients except crushed garlic cloves. Do not add water. Simmer on low heat till meat is tender.

Heat remaining fat in a small pan and fry crushed garlic and add to meat. Simmer for a few minutes more.

Serve with hot rotli.

DODHI NO DUMBO
(Lamb stuffed in pumpkin)
Serves 6

This recipe has been very graciously given to me by Mrs Bapsy Nariman from her excellent cookery book *Gourmet's Guide to Parsi Cooking*.

750 g tiny cubed pieces of lamb, boneless
¾-1 kg round white pumpkin (kaddu)
½ tsp turmeric powder
½ tsp cumin seeds, powdered
½ cup cashew nuts, chopped
¼ cup sultanas (kishmish)
Salt to taste
2 tbsp oil

Chop:
2 large onions
½" piece ginger

8 cloves garlic
2 green chillies
2 sticks celery

Peel pumpkin, cut a thick slice from the top and keep aside to use later as a lid. Remove pulp from inside pumpkin, being careful not to tear the skin.

Heat oil in a pan and fry onions till golden brown. Add ginger, garlic, powdered spices and sauté for a few minutes. Add meat and all remaining ingredients, including pumpkin pulp, except cashew nuts and sultanas. Sauté on low heat till meat is cooked and dry. Add cashew nuts and sultanas and mix well. This is the stuffing. Fill into pumpkin and cover with pumpkin lid.

Apply a little oil to base of a thick, flat bottomed pan and place pumpkin in it. Cover pan with a tight-fitting lid, and put water on the lid. Cook on low heat for 10 minutes. Pour water from lid into pan and add some more water to lid. Cook for a further 45 minutes to one hour, until pumpkin is fairly well cooked, adding water from lid to pan as and when required, and replacing water on the lid. Take care that the pumpkin does not flop. Serve hot.

This is an attractive party dish and also tastes very good.

Variations

- Use mince instead of cubed lamb
- Instead of meat, use a mixture of the following nuts and sultanas:

  1½ cup cashew nuts
  1½ cup almonds, blanched
  1½ cup cheronji
  1½ cup shelled walnuts
  1½ cup sultanas (kishmish)
  1 cup sugar
  1 tsp crushed nutmeg and seeds of green cardamom
  A pinch of salt

Fry all nuts and chop them. Fry sultanas. Make a sugar syrup with one cup water and boil till quite thick. Add nuts, sultanas, crushed spices and salt.

Fill pumpkin and continue to cook in the same way as dumbo with meat.

TARI MA GOSHT ATHWA MURGHI
(Savoury meat or chicken with toddy)
Serves 4-6

This dish has been adapted from the one given to me by Kekhashru Bhikaji Kama of Navsari.

1 kg leg or shoulder of lamb, cut into pieces with bone or
1½ kg chicken, jointed
4 onions, finely sliced
1-2 small pieces cinnamon
3-4 cloves
1 litre toddy or beer
Salt to taste
2-3 onions, cubed
4 potatoes, peeled and quartered
3 tbsp ghee, not oil

Grind together:
4 green chillies, seeded
2" piece ginger
1½ pods garlic
1 tsp turmeric powder
1 tsp chilli powder
2 tbsp curry powder
A pinch of jaggery

Heat fat and lightly brown sliced onions. Add ground spices, cinnamon and cloves. Brown for 1-2 minutes and add meat or chicken. Sauté till brown.

Add toddy or beer and salt and simmer till meat or chicken is three-quarter done.

Add cubed onions and potatoes and cook till meat and potatoes are done.

Serve with boiled rice.

Note: The toddy must be sour. Use a little less if the dish is to be served with rotli instead of rice.

BATERO
(Meat stewed in toddy)
Serves 8

1½ kg leg or shoulder of lamb, cut into pieces with bone or
1½ kg chicken, jointed
Salt to taste
1 litre lightly fermented toddy or beer
3 tbsp ghee

Grind together:
2½" piece ginger
2 pods garlic
2 tsp turmeric powder
4 tsp chilli powder
1 tbsp cumin seeds
1 tbsp black peppercorn

Pierce meat pieces with a fork and mix with ground spices and salt. Add enough toddy to mix well and cover meat. Allow to marinate for 2-3 hours, or leave overnight in the refrigerator. Bring back to room temperature before cooking.

Heat fat in a pan and fry meat till brown. Lower heat and add remaining toddy. Cover and simmer till meat is cooked.

Serve hot with rotli.

BADAM NU GOSHT
(Savoury meat with almonds)
Serves 4-6

1 kg leg or shoulder of lamb, cut into pieces with bone

2-3 bay leaves (tej patta)
Salt to taste
A piece of fat from the meat
3 onions, chopped
6 large tomatoes, finely chopped
1 cup cream
2-3 tbsp ghee

Grind together:
100 g almonds
½" piece ginger
4 cloves garlic
6 dry red Goa chillies
1" piece cinnamon
8-10 black peppercorns
4 cloves

Boil meat with bay leaves, salt and fat from the meat in a very little water till tender. There should be one cup gravy.

Heat ghee in a pan and fry onions till brown. Add tomatoes and sauté for 2 minutes. Add ground spices and sauté for 1-2 minutes further. Add cooked meat and cream and simmer for 2-3 minutes.

Serve hot with rotli.

DHAI MA GOSHT ATHWA MURGHI

(Savoury meat or chicken with curd)

Serves 4-6

1 kg leg or shoulder of lamb, cut into pieces with bone or
1½ kg chicken, jointed
2" piece ginger, ground
1½ pods garlic, ground
1 tsp turmeric powder
Salt to taste
800 g thick curd, well beaten
1 tbsp garam masala powder
2 tbsp ghee

Chop:
4 onions

4-6 green chillies, seeded
2 tbsp coriander leaves

Heat fat and fry onion till light brown. Add a little water and simmer till onions are mushy and water has evaporated. Add ginger, garlic and turmeric powder. Sauté for a few minutes. Add meat or chicken and continue to sauté till brown, adding a little water at a time, if required. Add salt, green chillies and one cup water.

Cover pan with an inverted lid, pour water on lid and simmer, adding water to pan as and when required.

Ten minutes before meat or chicken is cooked, add curd. Simmer till meat or chicken is tender, sprinkle with garam masala and mix well.

Garnish with chopped coriander leaves and serve with hot rotli.

SURTI KHATU GOSHT
(Sour and savoury meat—Surat style)
Serves 4-6

This recipe was given to me by the staff of the Parsi Central Kitchen of Surat, where food was cooked for the Parsi dharamsala, orphanage and old peoples' home.

1 kg leg or shoulder of lamb, cut into pieces with bone
800 g thick curd, well beaten
1 tsp turmeric powder
1" piece cinnamon
4-5 cloves
6-8 black cardamoms
Salt to taste
½ coconut, ground or 1½ tbsp coconut powder
2 tbsp curry powder
A few strands saffron
50 g cashewnut powder
4 tbsp ghee

Chop:
3 onions
2" piece ginger
6-8 cloves garlic
4-6 green chillies, seeded

Heat half the fat and fry onions till light brown. Add ginger, garlic, chillies, turmeric powder, whole spices, and salt. Sauté for a few minutes. Add meat and continue to sauté till cooked, adding a little water as needed.

In another pan, heat remaining oil and sauté coconut, curry powder and saffron. Add curd and simmer till semi dry. Add cooked meat and cashew nut powder. Mix well and simmer for a few minutes further.

Remove from heat and serve with hot rotli.

PAPETA MA GOSHT ATHWA MURGHI (2)
(Savoury meat or chicken with potatoes)
Serves 4-6

This is my mother-in-law's recipe and one of my favourite ways of serving meat or chicken.

    1 kg leg or shoulder of lamb, cut into pieces with bone or
    1½ kg chicken, jointed
    2½" piece ginger, ground
    1½ pods garlic, ground
    1 tsp turmeric powder
    2 tsp cumin seeds, dry roasted and ground
    8 large potatoes, peeled and cut in half, lengthwise
    6-8 green chillies, slit
    Salt to taste
    2-3 tbsp ghee or oil
    Extra oil for shallow frying potatoes

Mix ginger, garlic and spices together and rub into meat or chicken. Leave to marinate for half an hour. Lightly fry potatoes and keep aside.

Heat 2-3 tbsp ghee or oil in a pan and fry meat or chicken till light brown. Do not overbrown.

Add green chillies, salt and a little water to pan, cover with an inverted lid, pour water on lid and let it cook till meat or chicken is half done, adding a little water to pan as and when required. Add potatoes and simmer till meat and potatoes are cooked and gravy is thick.

Note : In the original recipe there was no cumin or turmeric powder. Their addition was an improvement to the dish according to my mother-in-law.

PAPETA MA KID
(Baby lamb cooked with potatoes)
Serves 8

This is one of the classic dishes cooked at lagans and navjotes.

1½ kg baby lamb, cut into 2½" cubes, with bone
6 large onions, sliced
3" piece cinnamon
8-10 cloves
8 black cardamoms
8-10 dried red Goa or Kashmiri chillies
1½ kg large potatoes, peeled, cut in half lengthwise and lightly fried
200 g cashewnut powder
Salt to taste
2 cups coconut milk extracted from 1 coconut
4 tbsp ghee

Grind together:
3" piece ginger
12 cloves garlic
2 tsp cumin seeds

Marinate meat in ground spices for 2 hours.

Heat fat in a pan and fry onions with whole spices and red chillies, till onions are soft. Do not allow them to brown. Add one cup water and simmer till onions are mushy and water has evaporated. Add meat and sauté, turning all the time, till meat is dry. It should not be allowed to brown.

Add about 2 cups water to pan, cover with an inverted lid, place water on lid and allow meat to cook till three-quarters done.

Add potatoes, cashew nut powder, salt and coconut milk and continue cooking on low heat stirring continuously to prevent burning, till meat and potatoes are tender.

Serve with hot rotli.

VENGANA NI BURIANI
(Savoury meat and aubergine stew)
Serves 4-6

This is favourite dish with the Parsis and is served with vagharela chawal (brown rice).

> 1 kg leg of lamb cut into pieces with bone
> 800 g long aubergines (baigan), slit in ½ and cut into 3" pieces
> 5 onions, sliced
> 1 tsp turmeric powder
> 1 tbsp dhan sakh masala powder
> Salt to taste
> 4 tbsp ghee

> *Chop*:
> 3-4 green chillies, seeded
> 3 tbsp coriander leaves with tender stems
> 1 tbsp mint leaves

> *Grind together*:
> 2" piece ginger
> 6 cloves garlic

Keep aubergines soaked in salted water till required for use.

Heat ghee in a pan and fry onions till light brown. Add meat and sauté till brown. Add ginger and garlic paste, turmeric powder, dhan sakh masala powder and salt.

Cover with water and simmer till half cooked. Add aubergines and remaining ingredients. Cover pan with an inverted lid, put water on lid and continue to simmer, half covered till meat is cooked.

KHARA RUS CHAWAL
(Savoury meat or chicken with rice)
Serves 4-6

1 kg breast of meat, cut into pieces or
1½ kg chicken, jointed
4 medium onions, finely sliced
2" piece cinnamon
6-8 cloves
6-8 black cardamoms
6-8 green chillies, slit and seeded
½ cup coriander leaves with tender stems, chopped
2 tomatoes, chopped
4 large potatoes, peeled and quartered
Salt to taste
8 drumsticks, peeled and cut into 3" pieces (optional)
1 cup coconut milk extracted from ½ grated coconut (optional)
4 tbsp oil

Grind together:
2½" piece ginger
1½ large pods garlic
1-2 tsp turmeric powder
1-2 tsp chilli powder
1 tbsp cumin powder

Heat fat in a pan and fry onions with whole spices till brown. Add half cup water and simmer till onions are mushy and water has evaporated. Add ground spices and sauté for 2-4 minutes. Add meat or chicken and continue to sauté till brown, adding a little water as and when required.

Add green chillies, coriander leaves and tomatoes. Mix well and simmer till three-quarters cooked.

Add potatoes and salt, and when potatoes are half cooked add drumsticks if used. Cook till done. Add coconut milk if used, and simmer for a few minutes more.

Serve with boiled or brown rice.

VAGHARELA CHAWAL NE MURGHI

(Savoury rice with chicken)

Serves 6

1½ kg chicken, jointed
6 medium-sized onions, finely sliced
2" piece cinnamon
4-6 coves
4-6 cardamoms
5-6 green chillies, slit and seeded
2" piece ginger, chopped or ground
1 pod garlic, chopped or ground
1 tsp turmeric powder
1 tsp chilli powder
1 tsp cumin powder
Salt to taste
4 tbsp oil

For the rice:
600 g basmati rice
2 onions, sliced
2 star anise (badian)
2" piece cinnamon
4-6 cloves
4-6 black cardamoms
Salt to taste
2-3 tbsp oil
250 g sali or julienne of potatoes for garnish

To prepare chicken, heat fat in a pan and fry onions with whole spices till brown. Add 4-6 tbsp water and simmer till onions are mushy and water has evaporated. Add whole spices, green chillies, ginger, garlic, powdered spices and salt and sauté for 3-4 minutes adding water as required. Add chicken and sauté till brown, adding a little water at a time if required.

Add about 4 cups water, cover and cook till done. There should be about 2-3 cups of thick gravy.

Wash rice well till all starch has been removed. Soak in cold water for 20-30 minutes. Drain water and leave for another 20-30 minutes.

Heat fat for rice in a pan and fry onions with whole spices till brown. Add rice, sauté for a few minutes and add salt and boiling water to cover by about one-and-a-half inches over level of rice. Bring to boil then lower heat and cook without disturbing rice till small holes appear in the surface. Cover and cook till done on very low heat.

To serve, spoon rice on a platter. Place chicken on top and spoon gravy over chicken. Strew crisp potato julienne on top.

Serve with kachumber and a masala ni dar (dal) if liked.

BAFELO RUS
(Boiled lamb soup or gravy)
Serves 4-6

This is a soupy dish served from soup plates for any one who wants a light meal, and it is an excellent dish for children.

    1 kg breast of lamb cut into 1½" pieces with bone
    2 onions, quartered
    2" piece ginger, sliced
    2" piece cinnamon
    4-6 cloves
    4-6 black cardamoms
    Salt to taste
    6-8 potatoes, peeled and quartered

Put all ingredients in a pan, except potatoes. Cover with water and bring to boil. Lower heat and simmer till meat is three-quarters cooked. Add potatoes and continue to cook till meat and potatoes are tender.

Serve with boiled rice and slices of lime.

VINDALOO
(Meat cooked with spiced vinegar—Goan style)
Serves 4-6

1 kg lamb, cut into pieces with bone or
1 kg pork, cut into pieces with the fat and pressure cooked till
three-quarters done or 1½ kg chicken, jointed
4 large onions, finely chopped
1 cup vinegar
Salt to taste
4 large potatoes, half boiled, peeled and cut in half (optional)
2-3 tsp sugar
5 tbsp oil

Grind together in half cup vinegar:
3" piece ginger
2 pods garlic
20 dry red Goa or Kashmiri chillies, seeded
1 tsp turmeric powder
1 tbsp cumin seeds
1" piece cinnamon
7-8 cloves

Heat oil in a pan and fry onions till brown. Add ground spices,
sauté for 1-2 minutes and add all remaining ingredients except
sugar and potatoes. Mix well and cook till meat is nearly
tender, adding some water as and when required.

Add potatoes and sugar and complete cooking.

Boiled sweet potatoes are the usual accompaniment to this
classic Goan dish which has become part of a Parsi household.
Note : Pressure cooking helps to kill the tapeworm sometimes
found in pork. Be sure to buy your pork from a reliable and
known source.

BAFAT
(Meat cooked in spiced vinegar)
Serves 4-6

1 kg leg of lamb, cut into pieces with bone
2 onions, sliced
3" piece ginger, ground
2 pods garlic, ground
8 medium potatoes, peeled and cut in half lengthwise
4 tomatoes, chopped
Jaggery to taste
Salt to taste
2 carrots, sliced (optional)
1 cup shelled green peas (optional)
4 tbsp ghee or oil

Grind in a little vinegar:
15 dry red chillies, seeded
2 tsp cumin seeds
1½" piece cinnamon
6 cloves
6 green cardamoms
2 tsp black peppercorn

Heat half the fat and fry onions till light brown. Add ginger and garlic and sauté for 1-2 minutes. Add meat and continue to sauté till brown.

Add about one cup water and simmer till meat is three-quarters done. Add potatoes and continue to cook on low heat.

Heat remaining fat in another pan and fry ground spices. Add tomatoes, jaggery and salt and cook on low heat for 1-2 minutes. Add to meat with green peas and carrots, if used and simmer for another 10 minutes.

Serve hot with plain yellow dal and hot rotli.

This dish can be made with chicken or duck.

MASALA ROAST GOSHT

(Spiced roast leg of lamb)

Serves 8-10

2 legs of lamb, about 1 kg each
1 pod garlic, peeled and sliced
1½-2 cups thick sour curd
4 tbsp Worcestershire sauce
2 tbsp oil

Grind together in a little vinegar:
6 green chillies, seeded
3" piece ginger
1 pod garlic
2 tbsp cumin seeds
Salt to taste

Wash and dry lamb. With a sharp pointed knife, make small cuts in lamb and insert garlic slices into them. Mix all remaining ingredients and rub into lamb. Allow to marinate overnight in refrigerator.

Bring back to room temperature and roast in an oven at 175°C (350°F) for 1½ hours, basting every 15 minutes. To test if done, insert a skewer into meat. It should go through easily and juice should be clear.

Allow to cool, carve and serve with fried potatoes and a salad.

MUGHLAI MURGHI

(Mughlai chicken)

Serves 6-8

This dish is of Iranian origin. It is very popular in north India and Mughlai food has become synonymous with Muslim food. It is a great favourite at lagans and navjotes.

1½ kg chicken, jointed
6 large onions, sliced
3" piece cinnamon

10 cloves
8 black cardamoms
1 tsp saffron strands, dry roasted and soaked in ½ cup warm milk
1 cup curd
Salt to taste
1½ kg potatoes, peeled, cut lengthwise and half boiled
½-¾ cup ghee

Grind together and mix with 1 cup cream:
1 cup almonds, blanched
1 cup dried pumpkin seeds

Grind together:
3" piece ginger
2 pods garlic
16 dry red chillies, seeded
2 tsp cumin seeds

Rub ground spices onto chicken and leave to marinate for half an hour.

Heat fat in a pan and fry onions with whole spices till brown. Add one cup water and simmer till onions are mushy and water has evaporated. Add chicken and continue to sauté till brown, adding a little water as and when required.

Mix saffron mixture with curd and add to pan along with salt and almond and cream paste. Cook on very low heat, adding just enough water to prevent dish from burning.

When chicken is three-quarters done, add potatoes. Simmer till chicken and potatoes are tender.

MAI VAHALA MURGHI
(Beloved of Mother)
Serves 8-10

1½ kg chicken
2 tbsp ground ginger
1 tbsp ground garlic
100 g butter

Salt and pepper to taste
8 hard-boiled eggs, peeled and sliced in half lengthwise
8-10 green chillies, seeded and chopped
1 cup coriander leaves with tender stems, chopped
1 cup almonds, blanched, shredded and lightly fried
1 cup sultanas (kishmish), lightly fried
1 kg onions, finely sliced and fried crisp
2 cups cream
4 eggs

Rub ginger, garlic, butter, salt and pepper onto chicken and roast in oven at 175°C (350°F) for one hour, basting with a little chicken stock or water and turning it every 15 minutes so that all sides are well browned. To test if done, insert a skewer into thigh. It should go through easily and juices should be clear.

Cool and debone chicken. Reserve gravy.

Lightly grease a shallow baking dish with oil or butter. Place half the chicken pieces in dish. Put half the hard-boiled eggs over it and sprinkle with half the green chillies, coriander, almonds, sultanas, fried onions and a little salt and pepper. Beat cream with eggs and spoon over half the quantity. Repeat process, by first placing remaining chicken on top and covering with other ingredients.

Bake in a preheated oven at 175°C (350°F) for half an hour. Serve with a salad.

Note : As a variation, instead of using hard-boiled eggs, carefully break eggs on top of chicken and bake as you would for eggs cooked on any vegetables. Cook till they are set.

The method of roasting as given in this recipe is the French method and although there are many ways of roasting chicken, this is best suited to Indian chicken.

If you wish you may boil the chicken instead of roasting it. Boil with a sliced onion, a few black peppercorns, cloves, green cardamoms, 1" piece cinnamon, 2" piece ginger and salt.

BHOOJAN
(Barbecued meat)
Serves 8-12

4 kg leg of lamb, deboned and cut into 1½" pieces
2 tbsp Worcestershire sauce
1 tsp sugar
2 tsp black peppercorn, coarsely pounded
2 tbsp salt

Grind together in a little vinegar:
4" piece ginger
2 large pods garlic
6-8 dry red chillies, seeded or 2 tsp chilli powder
2 tbsp cumin seeds
6 tbsp coriander seeds
2" piece half-ripe papaya

Mix ground spices with all ingredients and rub into meat. Leave to marinate overnight in refrigerator.

Bring to room temperature and pierce pieces of meat onto well-greased skewers. Grill over a charcoal fire which is 'grey', i.e. coals must not be flaming. Keep basting with the marinade using a brush and turning skewers around so that the meat can cook on all sides. It takes about 20-25 minutes to grill.

You may use an electric grill if you must!

Serve with masala masoor dal, a salad and hot rotli or crusty French bread, or Bombay's beloved 'brun pau'. Complete meal with a fruit tart or ice cream.

Note: You will get 2½-3 kg of meat after deboning so take care.

You can also use liver and kidney. The same marinade is used, but they should be cooked on separate skewers, as cooking time differs and they cook very quickly, in about 5-8 minutes.

OOMBERIU

(Lamb with sheet beans cooked in
an earthen pot buried in the ground)

Serves 6

**1 kg lamb, cut into pieces with bone, or 4 split partridges, or
8 whole quails**
8 eggs (optional)
1 kg black sheet beans (kari papri) or green sheet beans
4 sweet potatoes, unpeeled and cut into quarters
500 g small aubergines (baigan), slit half way down
1 kg baby potatoes, unpeeled, washed and kept whole
2 pods garlic
1 small bunch green garlic, if available
2 tbsp ajwain
4 tbsp oil
Salt to taste

Grind together:
6-8 green chillies, seeded
½ cup coriander leaves with tender stems
6 spring onions with greens
2" piece ginger
1 pod garlic
1 tsp turmeric powder
1 tbsp ajwain

For cooking the oomberiu:
**1 earthen pot with a small mouth (matka), washed and
immersed in water for 2 hours**
2-3 banana leaves
Mango leaves and flowers if available
Dry twigs
1 large potato

Grind together for chutney to serve with oomberiu:
4 green chillies, seeded
3 cups coriander leaves with tender stems
1 bunch mint leaves
8 spring onions
4-6 Bombay duck, cleaned, dry roasted and pounded (optional)
Lime juice to taste
Salt to taste

Trim vegetables, wash garlic pods and green garlic. Mix ground spices with all ingredients except meat and eggs.

Line matka with banana leaves, mango leaves and flowers. Place a layer of vegetables inside. Put meat on top and then well-washed eggs. Cover with remaining vegetables. Fill matka with more banana leaves, mango leaves and flowers. Tie mouth securely with banana leaves so that nothing will come out when it is inverted.

Have a shallow hole dug in the garden and cover with twigs and hay. Set it alight. When the fire dies down, add more hay and twigs and place a potato on top. Invert matka onto hole, with mouth on potato. Cover with more hay and twigs and set it alight. Keep fire burning gently for 1-2 hours.

To check if dish is done, lift matka and test potato. If it is cooked, then it is ready.

This is a delicious dish, served with chutney during mild November evenings.

Toddy is the usual drink with this dish.

KHEEMO
(Parsi mince)
Serves 6-8

¾ kg mince meat (it tastes better hand chopped)
1 tsp turmeric powder
2 tsp cumin powder
Salt to taste
2 potatoes, peeled and diced (optional)
½ cup shelled green peas (optional)
2 tsp sugar
1 tbsp vinegar or lime juice
2 tbsp ghee

Chop:
2 onions
1" piece ginger
6 cloves garlic
2 green chillies, seeded
2 tomatoes
1 small bunch coriander leaves with tender stems

Heat fat in a pan and fry one onion till browned. Add chopped ginger, garlic, turmeric, cumin powder, salt, green chillies and remaining onion. Add mince and sauté well till browned. Mix well and remove all lumps. Add 2 cups water and simmer. When mince is half-cooked add potatoes and peas and continue to simmer till mince is cooked. Add sugar and vinegar or lime juice to taste.

The result should not be too liquidy nor too dry.

Variation:
Serve with sali (potato julienne) over the mince and you get sali ma kheema.

BAFELO KHEEMO
(Boiled mince)
Serves 6-8

Use the same ingredients as above, except oil. Do not fry onions. Place all ingredients except sugar and vinegar into a pan. Add 2 cups water and simmer till mince is cooked. Add sugar and vinegar or lime juice to taste.

KHEEMA NA CUTLETS
(Mince cutlets)
Serves 4-6

500 g mince meat
1 tsp turmeric powder
½ tsp chilli powder
2 tsp cumin powder
2 slices bread, crusts removed, soaked in water and squeezed dry
1 medium-sized potato, boiled and mashed
Salt to taste
3-4 eggs, well beaten
Breadcrumbs as required
Oil for shallow frying

Chop fine :
1 medium-sized onion
2-3 green chillies, seeded
2 tbsp coriander leaves with tender stems
1" piece ginger
6 cloves garlic

Mix all ingredients together except eggs, breadcrumbs and oil.
Add just enough beaten egg to bind.

Shape into cutlets, dip into beaten eggs and then bread
crumbs and shallow fry.

FRILL NA CUTLETS
(Frill cutlets)
Serves 4-6

Make cutlets as given above, but after covering with bread
crumbs, dip again in beaten eggs.

You will need about 6-8 eggs for this recipe.

Deep fry cutlets and spoon hot oil over them to get frills.

The secret of good crisp frills is not to beat all eggs
together—just 2-3 at a time, and fry only 2 cutlets at a time,
changing oil after frying 4-6 cutlets.

TAMATAR NI GRAVY MA CUTLETS
(Cutlets in tomato gravy)
Serves 4-6

Cutlets made as above with 500 g mince

For gravy:
2 onions, chopped
2 kg tomatoes, chopped
2 tbsp ground ginger
2 tbsp ground garlic
2 tsp chilli powder
3 tsp cumin powder

2 tbsp vinegar
2 tbsp tomato paste
Sugar to taste
Salt to taste
2 tbsp oil

To garnish:
1 cup shelled green peas, boiled
100 g wafers

Heat oil in a pan and fry onions till soft. Add remaining ingredients for gravy and simmer till thick.

Place hot cutlets on a platter, spoon over tomato gravy, sprinkle with green peas and surround dish with wafers.

KURKOOS
(Iranian mince cutlets)
Serves 4-6

This recipe was given to me by Mrs Jer Irani, a delightful lady who was a mine of information about our way of life and customs while she was alive. Her father came all the way from Iran to India by foot!

500 g mince meat
1 tbsp ginger, ground
1 tbsp garlic, ground
Salt and pepper to taste
1 tsp cumin seeds
2 eggs, beaten
Breadcrumbs as required
Oil for shallow frying

Chop:
1 onion
2 tbsp coriander leaves with tender stems
1 tbsp mint leaves
2 green chillies

Mix mince with ginger, garlic, salt, pepper and cumin seeds. Add one cup water and cook till mince is completely dry. Grind. Add all chopped ingredients and half an egg.

Mix well and shape into cutlets. Dip cutlets in beaten eggs, press into breadcrumbs and shallow fry.

CHICKEN CUTLETS
Serves 2-3

These unusual cutlets were made by my mother-in-law in Amritsar, in the days when the chicken were free-run—not broilers, but tender, fat and juicy. She used to make one large cutlet the size of a dinner plate from a large chicken breast. It was cut into wedges and served to us mid-morning with trotter jelly or chicken soup.

1 whole breast of a large chicken, skinned (i.e. wing and breast)
½ tsp turmeric powder
½ tsp cumin powder
Chilli powder to taste
Salt to taste
1 slice bread, crust removed, soaked in water and squeezed dry
4-6 eggs
Breadcrumbs as required
Oil for deep frying

Chop:
1" piece ginger
4-5 cloves garlic
1-2 green chillies, seeded
1 tbsp coriander leaves with tender stems

Chop meat on a board into a round, adding ginger, garlic, green chillies, coriander leaves, turmeric powder, cumin powder, chilli powder, salt, and bread. Chop all these ingredients into meat and form a round flat cutlet the size of a dinner plate.

Lift it off the board and carefully place it on a plate. Beat three eggs and soak them into cutlet a little at a time, by forking them into cutlet and adding more egg as it gets absorbed. Allow to soak for half an hour.

Spread breadcrumbs on a board and carefully lift cutlet off plate onto breadcrumbs, pressing it in. Spread breadcrumbs on top of cutlet and press them in.

Heat oil in a frying pan and carefully lower cutlet into hot oil. Pour remaining eggs, well beaten, on top of cutlet and spoon hot oil over it to create frills. Lower heat and let it cook through. Lift it out of pan and drain.

Place cutlet on a platter and cut into wedges. Serve with slices of lime.

MUTTON KABABS
Serves 4-6

Use same recipe as for mince cutlets and add 1 tbsp dhan sakh masala powder. Shape into rounds, dip in beaten egg and then breadcrumbs and fry.

These kababs are served with dhan sakh or with papri.

Cook papri as given in papri ma gosht but without meat. Add kababs just before serving.

CHICKEN KABABS
Serves 4-6

Use 500 g chicken mince instead of meat and cook in the same way as meat kababs.

KHEEMA NA PATTIS
(Mince patties)
Serves 8

For the mince:
¾ kg mince meat
1 tsp turmeric powder
2 tsp cumin powder
Salt to taste
1 tbsp lime juice
2 tbsp ghee

Chop for mince:
2 onion
1" piece ginger
6 cloves garlic
2 green chillies, seeded
1 small bunch coriander leaves with tender stems

For the covering:
1½ kg potatoes, boiled and mashed
50 g flour
Salt to taste
6 eggs, beaten
Breadcrumbs as required
Oil for shallow frying

Heat fat for mince in a pan and fry onions till brown. Add remaining ingredients for mince except lime juice. Sauté, adding a little water as required till mince is cooked and brown. It should be completely dry. Add lime juice. Mix well and keep aside to cool.

Mix mashed potatoes with flour and salt, wet your hands and knead well.

Wet your hands and take up a spoonful of potato mixture. Flatten and put 1½ teaspoons mince in centre. Fold over edges of potato to cover mince and shape into a ball. Flatten and shape into a small round cake. Repeat with remaining potato and mince.

Heat oil in a frying pan, dip each patti in beaten egg then press into breadcrumbs and shallow fry, turning over just once.

PARSI STYLE CRUMB CHOPS
Serves 6

Ask your butcher to make one chop out of three and to remove the side bones, leaving the middle one. Do not allow him to flatten the chops.

> 12 prepared chops
> 4 eggs, well beaten
> Breadcrumbs as required
> Oil for shallow frying

Grind together:
> 2 green chillies, seeded
> 2 tbsp coriander leaves with tender stems
> 1 tbsp ginger, chopped
> 4 cloves garlic
> 2 slices bread, crusts removed, soaked in water and squeezed dry
> Salt to taste

Clean chops and remove any sinew. Divide ground spices into 24 equal portions.

Place a chop on a chopping board. Put one portion of ground paste on top. Spread it out and with a chopper, start chopping paste into chop. It should get mixed with the meat, but the meat should not leave the bone. Turn and repeat on other side. Prepare all chops in this way.

Dip into beaten eggs and then breadcrumbs and shallow fry till crisp and cooked through.

Serve with mashed potato.

MURGHI NA FARCHA (1)

(Fried chicken)

Serves 4-6

2 small chicken weighing 750-800 g each
8 eggs, lightly beaten
Flour as required
Oil for deep frying

Grind together:
2 tbsp chopped ginger
6 cloves garlic
3 green chillies, seeded
1 tsp turmeric powder
3 tsp cumin seeds
Salt to taste

Cut chicken into four pieces by removing breast in two parts and legs and thighs into two parts. Remove skin and make light gashes in flesh. Rub ground spices into chicken and leave to marinate for half an hour.

Heat oil in a karai. Dip each piece of chicken into flour and then into beaten eggs (beat two eggs at a time so that chicken has good crisp frills) and deep fry in hot oil. Lower temperature and keep spooning oil over chicken to get frills. Fry till chicken is cooked.

Serve with slices of lime.

MURGHI NA FARCHA (2)

(Fried chicken)

Serves 4-6

Shirinbai Khambatta was our neighbour in Bombay when I was a child. We were often invited to her house to eat this speciality and they were served to us hot, as they kept coming from the kitchen—dish after dish of magnificent farcha, until we had all had our fill.

2 small chicken, skinned and cut into 4 pieces
1 tbsp ginger paste
1 tbsp garlic paste
Salt to taste
100 g fine semolina
4-5 eggs, lightly beaten
Oil for deep frying

Rub ginger and garlic paste with salt on chicken. Cover with a lid and place a weight over it. Leave for 9-10 hours.

Heat oil in a karai. Dip each piece of chicken in fine semolina and then into beaten eggs (beat 2 eggs at a time so that chicken has good crisp frills) and deep fry in hot oil, spooning oil over chicken pieces so that frills are formed. Lower temperature and fry till chicken is cooked.

Serve with slices of lime.

KHARA KHARIA
(Savoury trotters)
Serves 8

16 trotters of front legs
4 tbsp rice flour
Juice of 4 limes
2 tsp salt or to taste
8 large onions, sliced
8 tomatoes, chopped
100 g ghee

Grind together:
4-6 green chillies, seeded
50 g coriander leaves with tender stems
2" piece ginger
1 large pod garlic
4 dry red chillies, seeded
1½ tsp turmeric powder
4 tsp cumin seeds
2" piece cinnamon
8 green cardamoms, peeled

8-10 black peppercorns
4 tsp poppy seeds (khus khus)

Wash trotters well and rub with rice flour and lime juice. Wash again and cut into 2" pieces

Cover with water, add salt and bring to boil. Remove any scum that may form, lower heat and simmer for 1½-2 hours till trotters are cooked. Reserve water.

You may pressure cook them if you wish, but the texture will not be the same and the bones become rubbery. You may pressure cook them till half done and then simmer in a pan till tender.

Heat fat in a pan and fry onions till light brown. Add one cup water and simmer till mushy. Add ground spices and sauté till you get the aroma of cooked spices. Add trotters and continue to sauté on low heat for about 5 minutes.

Add tomatoes and water reserved from boiled trotters. Adjust seasoning and simmer for a further 5-10 minutes. The dish should have a thick gravy.

Serve with kachumber and hot crisp brun pau if you are lucky enough to get it, else with hot rotli.

Note : This dish can be made by adding black-eyed beans (chora).

Soak ½ kg beans in water for 15 minutes and boil till just done. Add to trotters after they have been sautéed in spices.

You will need to double all ingredients except fat and trotters.

KHARA KALEJI BOOKA
(Savoury liver, kidney and sweetbread)
Serves 8-10

10 kidneys, cleaned and cut in half lengthwise
½ kg liver, cleaned, membrane removed and cut in 1" pieces
10 sweetbread (Gurda kapura)
4 onions, sliced

Salt to taste
4 tbsp ghee or oil

Grind together:
3-4 green chillies, seeded
2" piece ginger
2 pods garlic
2 tsp turmeric powder
1-2 tsp chilli powder
1 tbsp cumin seeds

Soak sweetbread in water for one hour. Boil for 3-4 minutes and plunge into cold water. Remove membrane and peel off outer skin. Cut into one-inch pieces.

Heat fat in a pan and fry onions till brown. Add half cup water and simmer till onions are mushy and water has evaporated. Add ground spices and sauté for 2-4 minutes adding water as required. Add offals and salt and continue to sauté till done.

Take care not to overcook as they then get tough.

MASALA NI KALEJI
(Spiced fried liver)
Serves 6-8

1 kg liver, cleaned, membranes removed and cut in 1" pieces
Oil for shallow frying
Salt to taste

Grind together:
2" piece ginger
8 cloves garlic
6 dry red Goa or Kashmiri chillies
1 tsp turmeric powder
1 tbsp cumin seeds

Rub ground spices and salt into liver and shallow fry for 2-3 minutes.

Do not overfry as liver will then get tough.

MUGHLAI BOOKA
(Mughlai kidneys)
Serves 6

This recipe was given to me by Mrs Jer Irani.

12 kidneys
5 cloves, coarsely ground
5 green cardamoms, peeled and coarsely ground
6 black peppercorns, coarsely ground
2 tsp ginger, grated
2 tsp garlic, chopped
1 small tomato, chopped
2 green chillies, slit and seeded
1 onion, chopped
Salt to taste
2 cups thick curd
A large pinch of good saffron
2 hard-boiled eggs, cut into four, lengthwise
3 tbsp oil

Wash kidneys and cut into 4 pieces each. Remove membrane. Wash again. Mix all spices, ginger, garlic, tomatoes and green chillies with kidneys.

Heat oil and fry onion till lightly coloured, but not brown. Add kidney and salt and sauté for 1-2 minutes. Add one tablespoon hot water, curd and saffron. Simmer till thick and dry.

Gently add hard-boiled eggs and serve.

GURCHAN ATHWA KHURCHAN
(Spiced offals of lamb)
Serves 8

This recipe was given to me by the Parsi Central Kitchen of Surat.

1 liver
1 lung

2 hearts
1 tsp turmeric powder
1 tsp chilli powder
1 tsp garam masala powder
1 tbsp dhan sakh masala powder
2 onions, sliced
Salt to taste
1 cup toddy or beer
½ kg potatoes, peeled, cubed and sautéed in 1 tbsp ghee
2 cups shelled green peas, boiled
3-4 tbsp ghee or oil

Remove membrane from liver and cut into ½" cubes.

Wash lung and steep in cold water for one hour. Squeeze out water and cut into ½" cubes.

Slit heart and remove arteries. Wash well and cut into ¾" cubes.

Mix all spices with offals and leave to marinate for half an hour.

Heat fat in a pan and fry onions till light brown. Add offals and salt and continue to sauté till light brown.

Add toddy and simmer till done.

Add potatoes and green peas and simmer for a while till gravy is thick.

Serve with hot rotli.

TARELA BHEJA
(Fried brains)
Serves 4-6

6 sets brains
1 tbsp garlic paste
1 tbsp ginger paste
½ tsp turmeric powder
1 tsp chilli powder
Juice of 1 lime
Salt to taste
Ghee or oil for shallow frying

Clean brains and remove all membranes. Wash, dry and cut in half.

Mix all spices, lime juice and salt and spread on brains.

Shallow fry lightly on both sides.

Serve hot with rotli and slices of lime.

KHARA BHEJA
(Savoury brains)
Serves 4-6

6 sets brains
2 onions, sliced
1 tsp turmeric powder
Salt to taste
2 tbsp ghee or oil

Chop:
4 green chillies, seeded
2 tbsp coriander leaves with tender stems
2" piece ginger
1 pod garlic
2 tomatoes

Clean brains and remove all membranes. Wash, dry and cut into four pieces each.

Heat fat in a pan and fry onions till light brown. Add all ingredients except tomatoes and brains. Sauté for 2 minutes. Add tomatoes and brains and simmer for 4-5 minutes till cooked.

BHEJA NA CUTLETS
(Brain cutlets)
Serves 8

6 sets brains
½ tsp turmeric powder
½ tsp chilli powder
2 slices bread, crusts removed, soaked in water and squeezed dry

Salt to taste
2 eggs
Breadcrumbs as required
Oil for shallow frying

Chop:
1 onion
2 green chillies, seeded
1" piece ginger
6-8 cloves garlic

Clean brains and remove all membranes. Wash, dry and coarsely mash with a fork.

Add all ingredients except eggs and breadcrumbs and mix well. Add just enough beaten eggs to bind. Divide into 12 portions and shape into cutlets.

Dip into beaten eggs and spread with breadcrumbs. Shallow fry.

ALETI PALETI

(Savoury chicken liver and gizzard)
Serves 4

250 g chicken liver, washed and cut into 4 pieces each
250 g chicken gizzard, washed and cut into 8 pieces each
250 g chicken hearts, washed and kept whole
4 large onions, sliced
1½" piece ginger, chopped
1 tbsp garlic, chopped
1 tsp chilli powder
1 tsp garam masala powder
1 tbsp Worcestershire sauce
1 tbsp chopped coriander leaves with tender stems
Salt to taste
3 tbsp ghee or oil

Heat fat in a pan and fry onions till well browned. Add half cup water and simmer till onions are mushy and water has evaporated. Add ginger, garlic, powdered spices and sauté for a few minutes.

Add chicken gizzard and hearts and simmer on low heat till cooked. Add chicken liver, Worcestershire sauce, coriander leaves and salt. Simmer till cooked, adding a little water if required.

CURRIES

GOSHT NI CURRY
(Lamb curry)
Serves 6

1 kg lamb cut into pieces with bone
3 medium onions, finely sliced
4 medium potatoes, peeled and cut into four
Salt to taste
1 cup coconut milk extracted from ½ coconut or
½" slice creamed coconut
Tamarind the size of a walnut soaked in ½ cup hot water
2 tbsp ghee or oil

Grind together:
1" piece ginger
1 pod garlic
4-6 dry red Goa or Kashmiri chillies, seeded
2 tsp cumin seeds
2 tbsp coriander seeds

Or for the lazy:
Mix together into a paste with a little water:
¾ tsp ginger powder
1 tsp garlic powder
1 tsp chilli powder
1 tsp cumin powder
2 heaped tsp coriander powder

Heat oil in a pan and fry onions till brown. Add a little water and simmer till onions are mushy and water has evaporated. Add ground spices and sauté for 3-4 minutes. Add meat and continue to sauté till well browned.

Add water and simmer on low heat, half covered with a lid till three-quarters done.

Add potatoes, salt and coconut milk and continue simmering till meat and potatoes are tender. Strain tamarind juice into curry, mix well and simmer for 5-8 minutes further.

Cool curry and reheat before serving. Be sure not to allow curry to boil.

Serve with boiled rice, kachumber and papad.

ANNA'S MUTTON, BEEF OR CHICKEN GOA CURRY
Serves 6

1 kg lamb cut into pieces with bone or 1 kg chicken or 1 kg breast of beef
2 onions, finely sliced
2 tomatoes, chopped
1 cup coconut milk extracted from ½ coconut
Salt to taste
1 tbsp tamarind soaked in 1 cup hot water
2 tbsp ghee or oil

Dry roast individually and grind together not too coarsely nor too fine:

3-4 green chillies, seeded
2" piece ginger
8-10 cloves garlic
12 dry red Goa or Kashmiri chillies
1½ tsp cumin seeds
3 tbsp coriander seeds
¼ tsp aniseed (saunf)
¼ tsp nutmeg powder
½" piece cinnamon
3-4 cloves
3-4 green cardamoms, peeled
3-4 peppercorns
½ grated coconut

Heat oil in a pan and fry onions till brown. Add a little water and cook till onions are mushy and water has evaporated. Add ground spices and fry for 3-4 minutes, adding a little water if necessary. Add meat or chicken and sauté till well browned. Add tomatoes and cook for 2-3 minutes.

Add water to cover and simmer on low heat, half covered with a lid till meat is three-quarters done. Add coconut milk, salt and tamarind juice and simmer till meat is tender.

Cool curry and reheat before serving.

Serve with boiled rice, kachumber and papad.

Note : ½ kg okras cut into 1" pieces adds flavour to the curry.

½ kg quartered potatoes can also be added.

In this recipe, according to Anna, if a chicken curry is being made, use lime juice instead of tamarind and avoid cloves. If breast of beef is being used, I suggest, you pressure cook it with a sliced onion and 1 tbsp each of chopped ginger and garlic, till half done. Use stock in curry instead of water and the breast bones will be worth chewing.

BHARUCHI CURRY
Serves 6

Cooked kharu gosht made with 1 kg lamb
2 onions, sliced
2 cups coconut milk extracted from 1 coconut
Juice of 2-3 limes or 1 cup sour curd
3 tbsp oil
Salt to taste

Grind together:
1 grated coconut
3 tbsp peanuts, dry roasted
2 tbsp cashew nuts, dry roasted
3 tbsp Bengal gram (channa dal), dry roasted
12 dry red Kashmiri chillies, seeded
1 tbsp sesame seeds (til), dry roasted

1 tbsp poppy seeds (khus khus), dry roasted

Heat oil in a pan and fry onions till brown. Add ground spices and sauté well. Add meat and coconut milk. Mix well and simmer for ten minutes. Add lime juice or beaten curd. Stir well and adjust seasoning.

Variation:
This dish can be made with 1 kg fish. Grind and rub into fish:
    1 tbsp cumin seeds
    10 dry red Kashmiri chillies, seeded
    1 pod garlic
Lightly fry fish and add in place of meat

MOTHER'S ALMOND AND PISTACHIO CURRY
— Serves 6-8

I once read in my mother's cookery book, that this dish cost her Rs 4 and 9 annas (16 annas made a rupee) in 1926 and Rs 95.65 in 1970. I do not want to calculate the cost today, but it is well worth making—it is one of the finest chicken curries I have tasted.

    1¼ kg chicken left whole
    3" piece ginger, ground
    2 pods garlic, ground
    3 onions, sliced
    4 green chillies, seeded and chopped
    Salt to taste
    6 cups coconut milk extracted from 2 coconuts
    ¼ litre buffalo or full cream milk (optional)
    4-6 potatoes, peeled and quartered
    4-5 green chillies, slit (optional)
    Juice of 4 limes
    3 tbsp ghee

Dry roast individually and grind to a paste with water:
2 onions

1 tsp turmeric powder
15 dry red Goa chillies
2 tsp cumin seeds
2 tbsp coriander seeds
1 tsp black peppercorn
1 tsp garam masala powder
2 tbsp poppy seeds (khus khus)

Dry roast individually and grind to a paste with water:
250 g almonds
100 g pistachio nuts
100 g cheronji
100 g peanuts
100 g roasted gram (channa)

Rub chicken with ginger and garlic paste. Place in a pan with two sliced onions, chopped green chillies, salt and enough water to cover. Simmer for 10-15 minutes. Leave chicken in stock till required.

In another pan, heat fat and fry one onion till brown. Add ground masala and fry for 1-2 minutes. Joint chicken and add with strained stock, coconut milk and milk. Simmer for 5 minutes. Add ground nuts, potatoes, green chillies, if used and cook till chicken and potatoes are tender. Add lime juice and adjust seasoning.

Allow curry to cool and leave for at least 2-3 hours for flavour of spices and nuts to amalgamate and produce an exotic work of art!

Serve with white rice and slices of lime.

SAU BADAM NI CURRY
(Hundred almond curry)
Serves 8-10

This is one of our famous curries.

2 small chicken, kept whole

1 onion, sliced
1 tbsp black peppercorn
Salt to taste
1" piece ginger
2 cups coconut milk extracted from 1½ coconuts
Tamarind the size of a walnut, soaked in ½ cup hot water
2 tbsp ghee

Grind together:
100 almonds
1" piece ginger
7-8 cloves garlic
15 dry red Kashmiri chillies, seeded
2 tsp cumin seeds
1 tbsp coriander seeds
2 tbsp poppy seeds (khus khus)

Cook chicken with sliced onion, peppercorn, salt and ginger in 5 cups water. Allow chicken to cool in stock. Joint chicken and strain stock.

Heat fat in another pan and fry ground spices, being careful not to allow it to burn, especially as there are almonds in it. Add coconut milk and stock and simmer till curry has the consistency of cream. Add chicken and tamarind juice and simmer for another 5 minutes. Adjust seasoning.

Cool and reheat before serving.

Serve with boiled rice.

MULLIGATAWNY
Serves 6

This, as we all know is not a Parsi dish, but one that is very often eaten by us.

1 kg breast of lamb cut into small pieces
2 onions, sliced
2" piece ginger, chopped
1 tbsp black peppercorn

1" piece cinnamon
6 cloves
Salt to taste
2 onions, finely chopped
1 cup coconut milk, extracted from 1 coconut
3-4 strips curry leaves
3-4 green chillies, slit and seeded
Lime juice to taste
2 tbsp oil

Dry roast individually and grind together:
1 tbsp rice
2 tbsp roasted gram (channa)
1 tbsp peanuts
1 tsp cumin seeds
1 tbsp coriander seeds
1" piece cinnamon
3 cloves

Grind together:
4-5 green chillies
2 tbsp coriander leaves with tender leaves
2" piece ginger
6-8 cloves garlic
¼ grated coconut

Cook lamb with sliced onions, ginger, peppercorn, cinnamon, cloves, and salt. Remove from stock and strain.

Heat oil in a pan and fry chopped onions till soft, but not brown. Add both ground spices and fry for 2-3 minutes, adding a little stock as required. Add remaining stock, coconut milk, curry leaves, green chillies, salt and meat. Simmer till curry has the consistency of creamy milk.

Remove from heat and add lime juice to taste.

To serve, place in soup plates if possible (not soup bowls).

Serve with boiled rice and slices of lime to be taken separately, with this delicious soup cum main course.

14

Lentils

Dal which the Parsis call dar, means split lentils. It is also known as kathor. There are many varieties of lentils grown and prepared in India. The most commonly used dals are toover, toor, tooveram or arhar (pigeon peas), masoor (Egyptian lentils), channa (Bengal gram), urad (black beans), moong or mug (green beans), chora or lobia (black eyed beans) and lobia (kidney beans).

In Gujarat and Maharashtra, pigeon peas are the most popular. Most dals in Maharashtra and Gujarat especially pigeon peas, were rubbed with castor oil to preserve them and one can still get these in certain shops.

MORI DAR
(Plain dal)
Serves 8

This is one of the most popular and common ways Parsis eat dal. It is also quite delicious, and forms part of the dish—dhan dar ne patio (plain boiled rice, plain dal and patio), which is eaten on auspicious occasions.

Any dal can be made in this manner, but pigeon peas, husked green beans and Egyptian lentils taste the best.

1½ cups pigeon peas (toover or arhar dal), or husked green beans (moong dal) or Egyptian lentils (masoor dal)
2 onions, chopped
2 tomatoes, chopped
3-4 cloves garlic
1 tsp turmeric powder
800 ml water
Salt to taste

Vaghar (seasoning):
4 onions, finely chopped
4 tbsp ghee

Wash dal well. Place in a pan with all ingredients, except vaghar. Bring to boil, skim, lower heat and simmer till completely soft.

Pass dal through a coarse sieve, liquidize, or leave as it is, depending on taste. It tastes best if passed through a sieve. In the old days, we used a dal masher, with which it could be mashed and passed through a colander or sieve.

Heat ghee in a small frying pan and fry onions till crisp and light brown. The secret is to fry onions on low heat, so that they get crisp without getting too brown and leathery.

Pour ghee and onions into a kasio (a small tinned copper bowl) and serve with dal, boiled rice and patio.

Variations:
*   When dal is nearly done, add:
    3 onions, chopped
    2 tomatoes, chopped
    3-4 green chillies, seeded and chopped or slit
    2 tbsp chopped coriander leaves
    4-6 cloves garlic, chopped
    1 tbsp ginger, chopped
    3-4 cloves

- In 2 tbsp ghee fry:
  2 tbsp cumin seeds
  3-4 green chillies, seeded and chopped

Pour over sieved dal before serving.

- In 2 tbsp ghee fry:
  1 pod garlic, chopped
  3-4 broken red chillies

Pour over sieved dal before serving.

- Cook dal with:
  1 tsp turmeric powder
  ½ tsp sugar

When cooked, purée dal and add:
  100 g peanuts, dry roasted and skinned
  1 tbsp coriander leaves, chopped
  1 large tomato, skinned and chopped

In 2 tbsp ghee fry:
  ½ inch piece cinnamon
  3-4 cloves
  A pinch of asafoetida

Pour over dal before serving.

- In 2 tbsp ghee fry:
  2½ pods garlic, chopped

Pour over dal before serving.

MUG NI DAR
(Husked green beans)
Serves 6-8

1¼ cups husked green beans (moong dal)
1 tsp turmeric powder
Salt to taste

Chop:
2 tomatoes
4 green chillies, seeded
1 tbsp coriander leaves

Vaghar (seasoning):
2 tbsp cumin seeds
1 pod garlic, chopped
2 tbsp ghee

Wash dal and place in a pan with water to cover by one inch. Add green chillies and turmeric powder and bring to boil. Skim and simmer till done.

Mash or purée dal. Add remaining ingredients except vaghar and simmer for 10 minutes.

Heat ghee for vaghar in a small frying pan and add vaghar ingredients. Fry and pour over dal just before serving.

Serve with rotli or rice.

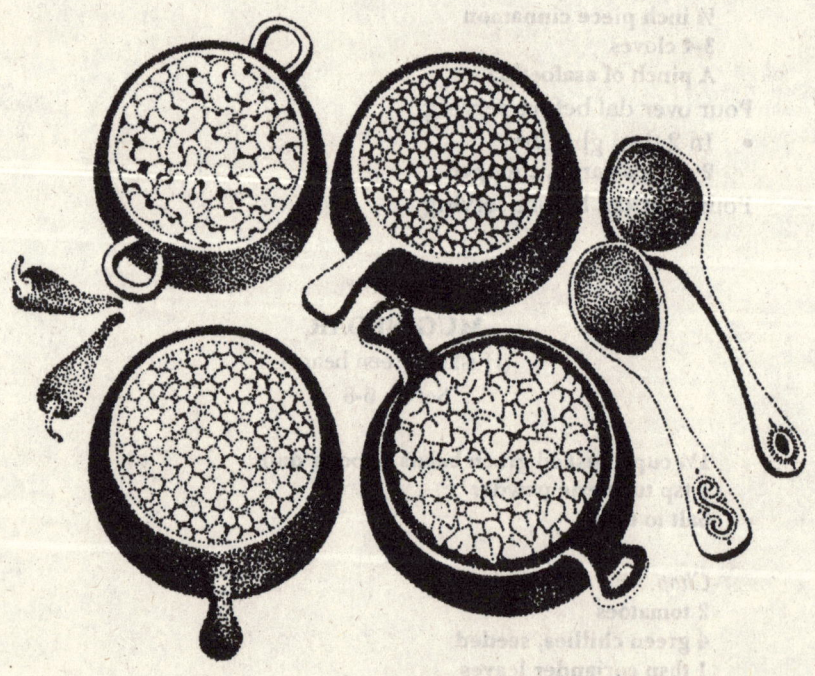

CHANNA NI DAR
(Husked Bengal gram)
Serves 6-8

1¼ cups husked Bengal gram (channa dal) washed and
soaked in water for 1 hour
1 tsp turmeric powder
Tamarind the size of a large lemon infused in ½ cup hot
water with 2 tsp jaggery
Salt to taste

Chop:
2 onions
4-5 green chillies, seeded
3" piece ginger
1 pod garlic

Vaghar (seasoning):
2-3 red chillies, broken
2-3 strips curry leaves
2 tsp cumin seeds
2 tbsp ghee

Put dal in a pan with onions, green chillies, ginger, garlic,
turmeric and enough water to cover by one inch. Place pan on
heat and bring to boil. Skim and reduce heat. Allow to simmer
till tender. The grains should not get mashed, they should
remain whole and separate and all water should be absorbed.

Strain tamarind and jaggery juice into pan and cook for a
further 5 minutes.

Heat ghee for vaghar in a small frying pan and add vaghar
ingredients. Fry and pour over dal just before serving.

Serve with rotli.

TOOVER NI DAR (1)

(Pigeon peas)

Serves 8

1¼ cups pigeon peas (toover or arhar dal)
2-3 green chillies, seeded and ground
2 strips curry leaves
1 tsp turmeric powder
1 tsp coriander powder
3-4 cocum (dried sour plums), washed well or
Juice of 1 lime
1 tsp jaggery
Salt to taste

Vaghar (seasoning):
1 tsp mustard seeds
1 tsp fenugreek seeds (methi)
A pinch of asafoetida (hing)
1 tbsp ghee

Garnish:
¼ grated coconut
2 tbsp chopped coriander leaves

Wash dal and cover with 3-4 cups water. Bring to boil and simmer till cooked. Purée, and if too thick add a little water.

Add remaining ingredients except vaghar and simmer for 5 minutes.

Heat ghee for vaghar in a small frying pan and add vaghar ingredients. Fry and pour over dal just before serving.

Garnish with grated coconut and coriander leaves and serve with rice.

TOOVER NI DAR (2)
(Pigeon peas)
Serves 8

1½ cups pigeon peas (toover or arhar dal)
Salt to taste
1 large onion, chopped
2 large tomatoes, chopped
2 tbsp ghee

Grind together:
2 green chillies, seeded
1 tbsp coriander leaves with tender stems
1" piece ginger
4-6 cloves garlic
½ tsp turmeric powder
2 tsp chilli powder
1 tsp cumin seeds or ½ tsp powder
1 tbsp coriander seeds or 1 tsp powder
½" piece cinnamon
4 cloves
2 white cardamoms, peeled
4-6 black peppercorns
1 tsp poppy seeds (khus khus)

Wash dal and cover with 3-4 cups water. Add salt and bring to boil. Lower heat and simmer till cooked. Purée, and if too thick add a little water.

Heat ghee in a small frying pan and fry onions till brown. Add ground spices and sauté for 2-4 minutes. Add tomatoes and mix well. Simmer for 2-3 minutes. Add to dal and mix well. Simmer for a further 2-3 minutes and serve with rotli or rice.

CHORA

(Black eyed beans)

Serves 6-8

2 cups black eyed beans (chora or lobia), soaked for 1 hour
Salt to taste
1 tsp turmeric powder
2 tsp chilli powder
2 tbsp cumin powder
1 tsp garam masala powder
2 tbsp lime juice
3 tbsp ghee

Chop fine:
3 large onions
1 large pod garlic
2" piece ginger
2-3 green chillies, seeded
3 tbsp coriander leaves with tender stems

Heat ghee and fry onions till light brown. Add ginger and garlic and fry for a further 2-3 minutes. Add remaining chopped ingredients and salt and continue frying for another 2 minutes. Add spices and then beans. Mix well, simmer for 1-2 minutes, add 2 cups water and cook till done.

Add lime juice before serving with hot rotli.

VAL NI DAR

(Husked field beans)

Serves 6-8

1½ cups husked field beans (val ni dar), washed and soaked in water for 1 hour
1 tbsp cumin seeds
1 tsp turmeric powder
1 tsp chilli powder
1 tbsp dhan sakh masala powder
Salt to taste

**Tamarind the size of a huge lime, soaked in ½ cup hot water
with 3 tsp jaggery**
4 tbsp sesame seed oil

Chop:
1 large onion
2 green chillies, seeded
2 colocasia leaves (arbi) with stems removed
2 tbsp coriander leaves with tender stems
2" piece ginger
10 cloves garlic
1 half-raw, half-ripe mango (optional)

Grind together:
6 green chillies, seeded
6 dried red chillies, seeded

Heat oil in a pan and fry cumin seeds. When they start
spluttering, add all other ingredients, except tamarind juice.
Mix well. Strain in tamarind and jaggery mixture.

Simmer on low heat, till tender, adding a little water from
time to time as required. When cooked, the grains should be
tender but whole, with very little gravy.

SOOKHI VAL NI DAR

(Dried field beans)
Serves 6-8

2¼ cups husked field beans (val ni dar)
4 tbsp Valsad garam masala powder
3 tbsp ghee
Salt to taste

Soak beans overnight. Dry completely on a towel. Mix masala
and salt with beans. Heat ghee in a pan and fry on low heat, till
crisp.

Serve with slices of lime and rotli.

VALSADI VADU

(Sprouted lentils—Valsad style)

Serves 4-6

1½ cups any of the following or a mixture of—whole green
beans (moong), black beans, (urad), dried green peas or
chickpeas (Kabuli channa)
2 onions, sliced
2 tbsp Valsad garam masala powder
Salt to taste
2 green chillies, seeded
1 tbsp chopped coriander leaves with tender stems
2 tbsp ghee

Soak lentils in water overnight. Drain and hang in a damp
cloth for 36 hours, or until they sprout, taking care to keep
cloth damp all the time, but not too wet.

Remove husks, if they come off easily.

Heat ghee in a pan and fry onions till brown. Add garam
masala and sauté for 2-3 minutes. Add sprouts, salt and chillies
and mix gently so that sprouts are not broken. Cook on low
heat till done, sprinkling a little water as and when required.

Add coriander leaves, mix well and serve with slices of lime
and rotli.

TEETORI

(Sprouted field beans)

Serves 8

2¼ cups field beans (val)
2 large onions, sliced
Salt to taste
2 green chillies, seeded
2 tsp garam masala powder
Pulp of 2 sour limes
2 raw mangoes, chopped
1 cup coconut milk extracted from 1 coconut
2 tbsp sesame seed oil
1 tbsp ghee

Grind together:
6 small spring onions with greens
4-6 tender white radish leaves
1 tbsp fenugreek leaves (methi)
2 tbsp coriander leaves with tender stems
6 dried red Goa or Kashmiri chillies
1 coconut

Soak beans in water overnight. Drain and hang in a damp cloth for 36 hours, or until they sprout, taking care to keep cloth damp all the while, but not wet. Remove husks.

Heat ghee and oil in a pan and fry onions till brown. Add half cup water and simmer till onions are mushy and water has evaporated.

Add sprouts and salt and sauté for a minute. Add water and cook on low heat for 3-4 minutes. Add ground spices, green chillies garam masala powder, pulp of lime and mangoes and cook till sprouts are half done, adding a little water as and when required.

When sprouts are half cooked, add coconut milk and cover pan with an inverted lid. Pour water on lid and continue cooking on low heat till done.

Serve with rotli made of rice or wheat. If a meat dish is to be served with teetori, then serve barbecued meat.

Variations

- Wash and clean ten Bombay duck, cut into 2" pieces and fry in sesame seed oil. Add to dish after coconut milk has been added.

MASOOR MA GOSHT, MURGHI ATHWA JEEB
(Meat, chicken or tongue cooked with Egyptian lentils)
Serves 8-10

1 kg leg or shoulder of lamb cut into pieces with bone or
2 small chicken, jointed or
12 small tongues, ¾ boiled, skinned and cut into two
2¼ cups unhusked, whole Egyptian lentils (masoor), cleaned and washed
5 onions, sliced
2 tbsp dhan sakh masala powder
Salt to taste
Tamarind the size of a walnut soaked in ½ cup hot water with
1 tsp jaggery
3 tbsp ghee or oil

Grind together:
3" piece ginger
2 small pods garlic
6-8 dried red Goa or Kashmiri chillies, seeded or
2-3 tsp chilli powder
3 tsp cumin seeds
2 tbsp coriander seeds

Heat fat in a pan and fry onions till pale brown. Add ground spices and dhan sakh masala powder and sauté for a few minutes.

Add meat, sauté till brown and cook with one cup water till half done. Add masoor, salt and more water if required and simmer till masoor and meat are cooked. Strain in tamarind juice and adjust seasoning.

Serve hot with slices of lime, kachumber or a whole peeled onion crushed and sprinkled with vinegar and salt and hot rotli.

This dish tastes best if cooked one day in advance.

CHANNA NI DAR MA GOSHT
(Meat cooked with Bengal gram)
Serves 8-10

This is cooked in the same way as masoor ma gosht, except that
Bengal gram (channa dal) needs to be soaked for 2 hours
before cooking.

GHAMBAR NI DAR
(Dal cooked for ghambars)
Serves 8-10

2¼ cups pigeon peas (arhar or toover dal)
4 green chillies, seeded and crushed
1 tsp turmeric powder
1 tbsp dhan sakh masala powder
Salt to taste
1-2 tsp jaggery

Chop for dal mixture:
3-4 sprigs mint leaves
2-3 tbsp fenugreek leaves (methi)
2-3 colocasia leaves (arbi)
150 g red pumpkin (kuddu)
150 g marrow (ghia)

Vaghar (seasoning):
1 tsp cumin seeds
2 tbsp ghee or oil

Chop for vaghar:
3 onions
2" piece ginger
8 cloves garlic
2 tbsp coriander leaves with tender stems
2 tbsp fenugreek leaves

Boil dal with crushed green chillies, turmeric, dhan sakh
masala powder, salt and chopped ingredients for dal and cook
till done. Purée or pass through a colander.

Heat fat for vaghar in a large pan and add cumin seeds. Fry till spluttering. Add onions and fry till light brown. Add remaining chopped ingredients for vaghar and continue to cook till moisture has evaporated. Add dal and jaggery and simmer for about 10 minutes.

Remove from heat and serve with rice.

For best results, cook one day in advance.

DHAN SAKH
Serves 8-10

No English translation for this dish!

This is the recipe from Valsad given to me by Mrs Aloo Rusi Shroff. It is one of the best dhan sakh dishes I have ever tasted.

For the dal mixture:
1 kg breast, leg, shoulder, neck or loin of lamb or any
mixture of these cuts, cut into 1" pieces
1 cup pigeon peas (toover or arhar dal)
¾ cup husked green beans (moong dal)
¾ cup husked Egyptian lentils (masoor dal)
¾ cup husked Bengal gram (channa dal)
¾ cup husked field beans (val ni dar)
2 tbsp husked black beans (urad dal)
1 tsp turmeric powder
1 tsp chilli powder
1 tbsp cumin powder
2 tbsp coriander powder
2 tbsp dhan sakh masala powder
Salt to taste

Chop for dal mixture:
2 potatoes
2 tomatoes
4-6 green chillies, seeded
2 tbsp coriander leaves with tender stems
1 tbsp mint leaves
200 g ripe pumpkin (kuddu), peeled
200 g marrow (ghia), peeled
1 medium-sized aubergine (baigan)

**8 bunches of the small variety of fenugreek leaves (methi), or
¼ bunch of the larger variety
4-6 green garlic with leaves (if available)
2-3 spring onions with greens
2" piece ginger
1 pod garlic**

Spices (1):
**3 large onions, sliced
1" piece cinnamon
4-6 broken cloves
4-6 peeled black cardamom
2 star anise (badian)
50 g ghee or fat from kidney for frying**

Spices (2):
Mix together to form a thick paste:
**1 tsp turmeric powder
Chilli powder to taste
1 tbsp cumin powder
2 tbsp coriander powder
2 tbsp dhan sakh masala powder
1 tbsp ginger paste
1 tbsp garlic paste
1 tbsp sambhar masala powder (optional)**

Chop very fine:
**2-3 tomatoes
1 tbsp coriander leaves with tender stems
2-3 sprigs mint leaves
3-4 strips curry leaves
4 bunches of the small variety of fenugreek leaves, or
3 tbsp of the larger variety**

Doru:
**Tamarind the size of a large lime, soaked in ½ cup hot water
with 1 tbsp jaggery
Juice of 1-2 limes**

Mix fenugreek leaves with half tsp salt and leave for twenty
minutes. Squeeze out water to remove bitterness from leaves.
Wash dals well and mix with meat and all ingredients for

dal mixture. Put into a pan with water to cover by one inch. Bring to boil and reduce heat. Simmer till meat is tender. Remove meat from mixture and press mixture through colander. Put meat back into the coarse purée.

Heat ghee in a large pan and fry spices (1) till onions are brown. Add spices (2) and fry for 1-2 minutes, adding a little water if required. Add chopped ingredients and sauté for 1-2 minutes.

Add dal mixture, and mix well to incorporate all ingredients. Simmer on low heat for 10-15 minutes, adding a little water if too thick.

Mix ingredients for doru, strain and add to dal mixture.

Serve with brown rice (vagharela chawal), kabab and gor amli nu kachumber.

MAMAIJI'S DHAN SAKH
Serves 10

For the dal mixture:
1 kg lamb cut into 1" pieces with the bone
1 cup pigeon peas (toover or arhar dal)
½ cup husked green beans (moong dal)
¼ cup husked Egyptian lentils (masoor dal)
¼ cup husked Bengal gram (channa dal)
2 tbsp ginger paste
2 tbsp garlic paste
Salt to taste

Chop for dal mixture:
2-3 green chillies, seeded
2 tbsp coriander leaves with tender stems
100 g ripe pumpkin (kaddu), peeled
1 medium sized aubergine (baigan)
6 bunches of the small variety of fenugreek leaves (methi), or
2 tbsp of the larger variety
100 g cholai bhaji
6 spring onions with greens

Spices:
1 large onion, finely chopped
½ tsp turmeric powder
6-8 red chillies, finely ground
2 tbsp dhan sakh masala powder
2 tbsp sambhar masala powder (optional)
2-3 tbsp ghee for frying

Doru:
Tamarind the size of a large lime, soaked in ½ cup hot water with 1 tbsp jaggery

Mix fenugreek leaves with half teaspoon salt and leave for 20 minutes. Squeeze out water to remove bitterness from leaves.

Rub ginger and garlic paste into meat pieces, place in a pan, add salt and water to cover. Bring to boil and lower heat. Simmer till meat is tender and some gravy is left.

Wash dals well and mix with other ingredients for dal mixture. Put into a pan with water to cover by one inch. Bring to boil and reduce heat. Simmer till dal is cooked. Strain mixture through a colander. Add meat and gravy.

Heat ghee in a large pan and fry onions till pink. Add remaining spices and fry for 1-2 minutes, adding a little water if required. Add dal mixture, and mix well to incorporate all ingredients. Simmer on low heat for 10-15 minutes, adding a little water if too thick.

Mix ingredients for doru and add to dal.

Serve with brown rice (vagharela chawal), kababs and a kachumber.

15

Rice

We have an infinite variety of rice in India. There is no doubt that basmati is the king of rice, but there are many other varieties that are just as popular and good. Depending on the rice grown in the area where one lives, these other types of rice are usually cooked on a daily basis and basmati rice is reserved mainly for pulaos, biryani or fried rice. There was a time when a variety of rice called jeerasal was popular in Bombay.

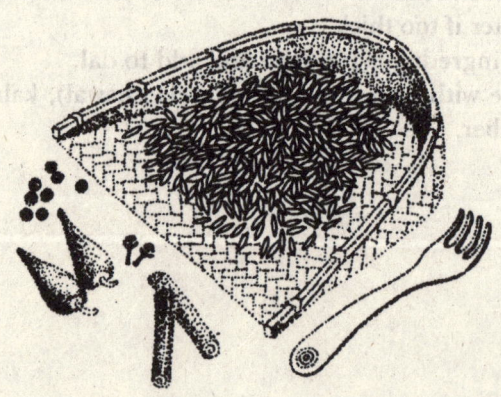

Good rice should preferably be about a year old. New rice when cooked breaks up very quickly and becomes gooey. Old rice is usually off-white in colour, whereas new rice is white.

In olden days in homes with large store rooms new rice was bought for the year rubbed with castor oil and stored in large earthenware jars and left to mature for a year. Hence one automatically got old rice for the household.

Today one can still do this by storing less quantities—the ratio of castor oil to rice being about 2-3 tbsp castor oil to 1 kg of rice.

BAFELA CHAWAL
(Boiled rice)
Serves 8-10

2½ cups rice
1 tsp salt

There are two ways to cook rice, so that every grain is separate.

First method:

Wash rice well several times in cold water to remove all starch. Soak in cold water for 20 minutes. Drain in a sieve and leave for 20 minutes. Boil three times the quantity of water and add rice and salt to boiling water. Bring back to boil, lower heat and simmer till rice is just tender. Drain out water, swirl some cold water into rice and drain it out again. This does not make it cold, but separates the grains.

The drained water is called rice conji and is a strengthening drink, often given to people who have an upset stomach, as it also helps in binding the stomach.

Second method:

Wash rice and soak for 20 minutes in cold water. Discard water and put rice into a pan with salt and enough cold water to come about one inch over level of rice. Bring to boil, lower heat and simmer with pan half covered. Cook till holes appear in the surface. Check rice to see it is done, toss with a fork and add a little more water if required. Cover pan and cook till done.

In this method, each variety of rice requires a different quantity of water to cook and the quantity given above is just an indication. Once you have cooked a particular variety of rice you will know how much water should be put in at the start of cooking and there should be no need to add more water halfway through. Here starch is not removed from the rice which makes it a more nourishing way of serving it.

Always toss rice with a fork in the pan, before serving.

CONJI
Serves 2

This is a dish which is semi liquid, with rice water and rice in it.

    2 tbsp rice
    4 cups cold water
    1 tsp black peppercorn
    1 tsp salt
    Lime juice to taste

Wash rice well but do not remove all starch. Place in a pan with water, salt and black peppercorns. Bring to boil and lower heat. Simmer till rice is overcooked. Remove from heat and add lime juice. Serve in soup bowls.

This is the original conji and is a good dish on a cold day when one is feeling hungry.

Chopped coriander leaves, green chillies, onions and even small pieces of meat can be added as variations. The famous pish pash has evolved from this dish—created by the Goan cooks for the Parsis.

PISH PASH
Serves 6-8

1 kg breast of lamb cut into pieces or
1¼ kg chicken, jointed
3 onions, sliced
3" piece ginger
2" piece cinnamon
6-8 cloves
6-8 black cardamoms
1 tbsp black peppercorn
Salt to taste
1½ litre water
2 cups rice, washed and drained
500 g potatoes, peeled and quartered
1 cup milk
2 tbsp butter
Lime juice to taste

Place all ingredients except rice, potatoes, butter, milk and lime juice in a large pan and bring to boil. Lower heat and simmer till meat is three-quarters done. Add rice and potatoes. Continue cooking till meat and potatoes are tender, removing scum.

Add milk, butter and lime juice to taste. Serve in soup plates, if you are lucky enough to own some in this day of soup bowls! An excellent dish to serve children and people convalescing from illness.

VAGHARELA CHAWAL

(Brown rice)

Serves 8

2¼ cups rice
2 onions, sliced
2" piece cinnamon
6-8 cloves
6-8 black cardamoms
Salt to taste
2 tbsp ghee or oil

Wash rice and soak for 20 minutes. Drain and keep in a strainer for another 20 minutes.

Heat ghee or oil in a pan and fry onions with whole spices, till onions are brown. Add rice and salt and sauté for 2-3 minutes.

Add boiling water to cover rice by one inch. Bring to boil, lower heat and simmer, with pan half covered. Cook till holes appear in the surface. Check rice to see if it is done, toss with a fork, adding a little more water, if required. Cook covered till done.

Toss with a fork in the pan, before serving.

BAFELI KHICHDI

(Yellow rice with dal—boiled)

Serves 8

2 cups rice
¾ cup dal—husked green beans (moong dal), Egyptian lentils (masoor dal) or pigeon peas (arhar or toover dal)
2 onions, sliced
1 tsp turmeric powder
2" piece cinnamon
6-8 cloves
6-8 black cardamoms
Salt to taste
3-4 tbsp butter (optional)

Wash rice and dal. If pigeon peas are used, soak for half an hour, or half-boil.

Place all ingredients except butter in a pan and add water to cover by one inch above level of rice and dal.

Bring to boil, lower heat and simmer, with pan half covered. Cook till holes appear in the surface. Check rice to see if it is done, toss with a fork, adding a little more water if required. Cook covered till done. Add butter if desired.

A second method of cooking this is to fry onions and whole spices in 1-2 tablespoons ghee or oil till onions are brown. Add rice and dal, sauté for 1-2 minutes then add water and cook in the usual way.

Toss khichdi with a fork in the pan, before serving.

POCHI OR MALIDAR KHICHDI
(Soft khichdi)
Serves 8

Use same ingredients and method as above, but less water. When khichdi is half cooked, add one cup coconut milk extracted from half a coconut or one cup milk and 2-3 tbsp butter or ghee. Cover and cook till done.

CHE DAR NI KHICHDI
(Khichdi with six dals)
Serves 6-8

1½ cup rice
¼ cup husked green beans (moong dal)
¼ cup husked Egyptian lentils (masoor dal)
¼ cup pigeon peas (arhar or toover dal)
¼ cup husked Bengal gram (channa dal)
¼ cup husked black beans (urad dal)
¼ cup husked field beans (val ni dar)
2 onions, sliced
2" piece cinnamon

6-8 cloves
6-8 black cardamoms
1 tsp turmeric powder
Salt to taste
3 tbsp ghee

Wash rice and all dals separately. Half-boil pigeon peas, Bengal gram, black beans and field beans. Soak rice and remaining dals for 20 minutes.

Heat ghee in a pan and fry onions and whole spices till onions are brown. Add dals and rice, sauté for 3-4 minutes. Add turmeric, salt and enough hot water to cover by one inch.

Bring to boil, lower heat and simmer, with pan half covered. Cook till holes appear in the surface. Check khichdi to see if it is done, toss with a fork, adding a little more water, if required. Cover pan and cook covered till done.

Toss with a fork in the pan, before serving.

Serve with a raitu, plain thick curds or a doru and papads.

VAGHARELI KHICHDI
(Savoury khichdi)
Serves 8-12

2 cups rice
½ cup husked green beans (moong dal)
½ cup husked Egyptian lentils (masoor dal)
½ cup pigeon peas (arhar or toover dal)
½ cup husked Bengal gram (channa dal)
3 onions, sliced
1 tbsp mixed whole garam masala
Salt to taste
4 tbsp ghee or oil
2 medium-sized carrots, peeled and cubed
8-10 French beans, trimmed and cut into 2" pieces
1 cup shelled green peas
2 capsicums, cut into cubes, with seeds and pith removed
2 turnips (shalgum), peeled and cubed

150 g cauliflower, cut into flowerets
2 medium sized long aubergines (baigan), cubed
200 g sali or fine potato julienne (optional)
Kharu gosht made with 1 kg lamb

Grind together.
4 green chillies, seeded
2 tbsp coriander leaves with tender stems
1 tbsp mint leaves
3" piece ginger
1½ pods garlic
1 tsp turmeric powder
3 tsp chilli powder
3 tsp cumin seeds

Wash rice and all dals separately. Half-boil pigeon peas and Bengal gram. Soak rice and remaining dals for 20 minutes.

Heat ghee in a pan and fry onions and whole spices till onions are brown. Add half a cup water and simmer till onions are mushy and water has evaporated. Add ground spices and sauté for 2-3 minutes.

Add dals and rice, sauté for 3-4 minutes longer. Add salt and hot water to cover by one inch.

Bring to boil, lower heat and simmer for 3-4 minutes. Add vegetables. Simmer on low heat, with pan half covered. Cook till holes appear in the surface. Check khichdi to see if it is cooked, toss with a fork, adding a little more water, if required. Cook covered till done.

Mix meat with khichdi and serve, or place khichdi on a platter and spoon meat over it.

Strew sali (potato julienne) over dish and serve.

This is a meal in itself and quite delicious. A light egg dish could precede it and a fruity dessert to complete the meal.

BHARUCHI VAGHARELI KHICHDI

(Savoury khichdi—Bharuch style)

Serves 12

2½ cups rice
1 cup pigeon peas (arhar or toover dal)
½ cup husked Bengal gram (channa dal)
½ cup husked Egyptian lentils (masoor dal)
½ cup husked green beans (moong dal)
24 Bombay duck
2 onions, sliced
1 tbsp mixed whole garam masala
1 tsp turmeric powder
Salt to taste
4 tbsp oil

Grind together for khichdi:
1 pod garlic
3" piece ginger
6 green chillies, seeded
2 tsp turmeric powder
1 tbsp cumin seeds

Grind together in a little vinegar, for Bombay duck:
2 green chillies, seeded
2 tbsp coriander leaves with tender stems
1 tbsp mint leaves
2 pods garlic
½ tsp turmeric powder
2 tsp chilli powder
1 tbsp cumin seeds
1 tsp garam masala powder

Wash Bombay duck well and cut in half. Rub with oil and spices ground for Bombay duck, and fry lightly. Keep aside.

Wash and half-boil pigeon peas and Bengal gram together. Wash and soak rice and other dals.

Heat oil and sauté onions and whole garam masala till onions are brown. Add spices for khichdi and sauté for 2-3 minutes. Add rice, dals, turmeric powder, salt and enough hot water to cover by one inch.

Bring to boil, lower heat and simmer, with pan half covered. Add Bombay duck when rice is half cooked and press into khichdi. Continue cooking till holes appear in the surface. Check khichdi to see if it is done, toss with a fork, adding a little more water, if required. Cover pan and cook till done.

MASALA NI KHICHDI
(Spiced khichdi)
Serves 8-10

2 cups rice
¾ cup husked green beans (moong dal)
¾ cup husked Egyptian lentils (masoor dal)
3 onions, sliced
2" piece cinnamon
4-6 cloves
4-6 black cardamoms
Salt to taste
2 tbsp butter
2 tbsp ghee

Grind together:
4 green chillies
2 tbsp coriander leaves with tender stems
1 tbsp mint leaves
3" piece ginger
1 pod garlic
1 tsp turmeric powder
1-2 tsp chilli powder
2 tsp cumin seeds
2 tbsp coriander seeds
2 tsp fenugreek seeds (methi)

Wash rice and dals and soak for 20 minutes.

Heat ghee in a pan and fry onions and whole spices till onions are brown. Add half cup water and simmer till onions are mushy and water has evaporated. Add ground spices and sauté for 3-4 minutes.

Add dals and rice, sauté for 3-4 minutes longer. Add salt and hot water to cover by one inch.

Bring to boil, lower heat and simmer, with pan half covered. Cook till holes appear in the surface. Check khichdi to see if it is done, toss with a fork, adding a little more water, if required. Cook till done. Stir in butter.

Toss with a fork in the pan, before serving.

Serve with bafena and papad.

EEDA NE PANEER NI KHICHDI
(Khichdi with eggs and cream cheese)
Serves 12

2 cups rice
2 cups husked green beans (moong dal)
400 g Surti salt paneer (ordinary homemade paneer will do)
6 medium onions, finely sliced
2" piece cinnamon (optional)
6-8 cloves (optional)
6-8 black cardamoms (optional)
1 tbsp black peppercorn
Salt to taste
1 tsp turmeric powder
8 eggs, well beaten
4 tbsp ghee

Wash rice and dal and soak for 20 minutes. Cut paneer into medium-sized pieces.

Heat ghee in a pan and fry onions and whole spices, if used, till onions are brown. Add one cup water and simmer till onions turn mushy and water has evaporated. Add dal, rice, salt and turmeric, and sauté for 2-3 minutes. Add water to cover by one inch.

Bring to boil, lower heat and simmer, with pan half covered. Cook till holes appear in the surface. Add paneer and mix with rice using a fork. Check khichdi to see if it is done, toss with a fork adding a little more water, if required. Cook till tender.

Remove pan from heat and add eggs. Toss with a fork to incorporate eggs. The heat of the rice will cook the eggs. If required, you may put it on very low heat for 3-4 minutes.

This is a soft khichdi and quite delicious. Serve it plain or with kachumber and a light lime pickle made without spices.

COLMI NI KHICHDI
(Khichdi with prawns)
Serves 8-10

2½ cups rice
1¼ cup husked green beans (moong dal)
250 g medium-sized prawns, shelled, cleaned and deveined
4 onions, sliced
2" piece cinnamon (optional)
6-8 cloves (optional)
4-6 green chillies, slit and seeded
Salt to taste
1 tsp turmeric powder
6-8 cups coconut milk extracted from 2 coconuts
4 tbsp ghee

Wash rice and dal and soak for 20 minutes. If prawns are large, cut in half. Blanch prawns and reserve water.

Heat ghee in a pan and fry onions and whole spices, till onions are brown. Add one cup water and simmer till onions turn mushy and water has evaporated. Add dal, rice, green chillies, salt and turmeric, and sauté for 2-3 minutes. Add coconut milk to cover by one inch. Bring to boil and add prawns.

Lower heat and cook till holes appear in the surface. Check khichdi to see if it is done, toss with a fork, adding a little more coconut milk or water in which the prawns were blanched, if required. Cover and cook till done.

Toss with a fork in the pan, before serving.

AEK TAPELI MA KHICHDI NE PATIO

(Khichdi and patio cooked in one pan)

Serves 6-8

For khichdi:

2 cups rice
¾ cup husked green beans (moong dal)
2 onions, sliced
1 tsp turmeric powder
2" piece cinnamon
6-8 cloves
6-8 black cardamoms
Salt to taste

Grind in a little vinegar to make a thick paste for patio:

1 large pod garlic
1 tsp turmeric powder
1-2 tsp chilli powder or
6 dried red chillies, seeded
2 tsp cumin seeds
2 tsp sugar
50 g tamarind without seeds or strings
Salt to taste

250 g Bombay duck or small dried shrimps
2 large banana leaves
Cotton string
Oil for shallow frying Bombay duck
2 tbsp sesame seed oil

Wash and clean Bombay duck and cut into 2-inch pieces. Shallow fry till crisp and mix with paste for patio along with 2 tablespoons sesame seed oil.

Carefully remove centre veins of banana leaves and soften by holding about 6 inches above a fire. Place them one on top of the other on a board.

Place patio mixture on leaves and wrap leaves around it to make a parcel, taking care not to leave any opening through which patio can leak out. Tie parcel with cotton thread.

Wash rice and dal. Mix all ingredients for khichdi and place half in a large pan, put banana leaf parcel on top and cover with remaining half of khichdi ingredients. Add hot water to cover rice and dal by one inch.

Bring to boil, lower heat and simmer, with pan half covered. Cook till holes appear in the surface. Check khichdi to see if it is done, toss with a fork, adding a little more hot water, if required. Cook covered till done.

When rice and dal are cooked, remove banana leaf parcel.

Serve khichdi in a platter and pour patio over it or serve separately.

Note : If you are at all unsure of the quantity of water to be used, add less water to start with so that khichdi does not become too wet.

PARSI PULAO
(Savoury rice cooked with meat or chicken)
Serves 12-16

This recipe was given to me by my cousin Bapsy Jemi Mehta and is one of best Parsi pulaos I have ever tasted.

Kharu gosht made with 1 kg meat or chicken, and ½ kg potatoes
1 kg basmati rice
Salt to taste
1 tsp saffron soaked in 2 tbsp warm milk
2 cups curd
4 large onions, sliced, fried crisp and drained
Ghee as needed
Milk as needed
Wheat flour as needed

Garnish:
2 onions, sliced, fried crisp and drained
2 tbsp almonds, blanched, slivered, fried and drained
2 tbsp sultanas (kishmish), fried and drained

Wash rice well several times in cold water to remove all starch. Soak in cold water for 20 minutes. Drain in a sieve and leave for 20 minutes longer.

Divide rice in two. Cook one half of rice with hot water, salt and saffron in usual way till three-quarters done.

Cook second half in plain water and salt till three-quarters done. Mix with curd and fried onions, using a fork.

Place meat mixture in a large pan, cover with rice and curd mixture and put rice and saffron mixture on top. Sprinkle with melted ghee, cover with an old cloth or handkerchief and sprinkle some milk on it. Cover pan with lid.

Make a paste of wheat flour and water and seal lid onto pan. Cook on dum, i.e. on low heat with a few pieces of hot coal on top of lid or put in an oven at 175°C (350°F) for about twenty minutes. Spoon onto a platter. Add garnish.

Serve with ghambir ni dar or dar made for dhan sakh and kachumber.

Note : A vegetable pulao can be made in the same way, using mixed vegetables instead of meat or chicken.

16
Breads

The traditional rotli of the Parsis are ghau ni rotli made from wheat flour and chokha ni rotli made from very fine rice flour.

The nan which is of Iranian origin, now absorbed in north Indian tandoori and Muslim cuisine, was dropped by the Parsis when they landed in India on the western coast. They adopted the rotli of Gujarat as they were lighter to digest in the local climate. Five or six of these light rotli can easily be eaten and digested in the course of one meal.

Parsis have also adopted the rotla of Gujarat and Maharashtra, made from jowar (milo) and bajra (millet). These are much thicker than rotli and each has its own distinctive flavour and is delicious in its own way, accompanied with garlic or Bombay duck chutneys. No oil or fat is used in making rotla. They are supposed to be excellent for people with high cholesterol levels. No wheat four is used either, except when patting them out. They are not rolled out with a rolling pin as they are too thick, but are patted out on a table by hand, in a circle, then slowly cooked on a tava or griddle.

There is a special art in making each of these varieties of breads. The chokha ni rotli are the most difficult to make as they need a very good quality of very fine rice flour. Few people can make them correctly as one needs a good deal of practice. One way to test the quality of chokha ni rotli is to make a pile of a hundred rotli and place a silver rupee coin on top. It should sink right down to the last one in the pile—that is how soft and pliable they should be!

The Parsis do take other types of breads such as the paratha, shirmal and kulcha from different parts of the country, but the traditional rotli of the Parsis are the ghau ni rotli and chokha ni rotli.

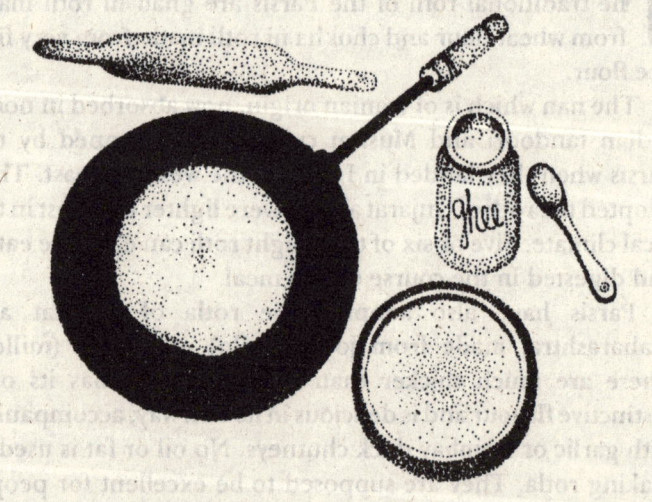

GHAU NI ROTLI
(Wheat flour rotli)
Makes 15-18

The secret of making these rotli lies in using boiling water, and not cold water as is commonly done.

 2½ cups whole wheat flour (atta)
 ½ tsp salt
 1 tbsp ghee or oil
 Boiling water as required
 Extra flour for rolling
 Extra ghee or oil for brushing on top

Sieve flour with salt in a thali. Make a well in the centre and pour in fat. Add enough boiling water to bind. Mix using a wooden spoon, till dough cools down. Knead with your hands, adding more water if required to make a pliable dough.

Another method is to beat dough on surface of table about 10-12 times as Italians do with their pasta. This makes a superb dough and saves a lot of kneading.

Roll out into a long sausage and cut into 15-18 pieces.

Place tava on heat. Do not make it too hot as this produces brown blisters on the surface and makes the rotli hard.

Roll out one rotli at a time and place on tava. As soon as bubbles appear on the surface, flip over and press surface with a folded cloth, kept specially for this purpose. The rotli will start puffing up. Keeping pressing it all over till entire surface has puffed up. Make sure the tava is not too hot and no brown spots appear. Do not overcook as then they will become tough. Remove from tava and brush with melted ghee or butter. Fold in half and keep in an air-tight container till ready to serve.

They will remain soft for about 24 hours. If using leftovers the next day, heat on a tava lightly or keep rolled in a napkin and heat in an oven for 15 minutes at 150°C (300°F).

Note : There is another way of rolling rotli. After it has been rolled to about 3 inches in diameter, dust your hands and flap it between your palms, to enlarge it. (Not like roomali roti which is flung into the air and stretched by the fingers—what an art that is! We in India take it so much for granted, but I wonder what would happen to one of our dhaba boys if he were to make them in a restaurant abroad. People would probably stop eating, stare in amazement and give him a standing ovation!)

CHOKHA NI ROTLI
(Rice flour rotli)
Makes 15-18

Again, the secret of making these rotli is in using boiling water.

2½ cups fine rice flour
½ tsp salt
Boiling water as required
Extra flour for rolling

Sieve flour with salt in a thali. Make a well in the centre and pour in 4-5 tablespoons boiling water. Mix using a wooden spoon, till dough cools down. Knead and beat to make a pliable dough.

Continue as for wheat flour rotli, making dough as pliable as possible and rolling out as thin as possible.

Extra care is needed while roasting them, as rice is apt to get scorched quicker than wheat flour.

DOODH MA GHAU ATHWA CHOKHA NI ROTLI
(Wheat or rice flour rotli made with milk)
Makes 15-20

Use boiling milk instead of water and proceed as given in recipes above. These rotli will stay softer longer than those made with water.

TARI NI ROTLI
(Rotli made with toddy)

Use toddy or beer instead of water, let dough rest for half an hour and proceed as given in recipes for ghau ni rotli and chokha ni rotli.

POORI
Makes 15-20

2½ cups whole wheat flour (atta) or a mixture of whole wheat and refined flour (maida)
½ tsp salt
Oil for deep frying

Sift flour with salt. Add water to bind. Knead into a pliable dough. Roll out into a sausage and cut into half-inch pieces. Roll each piece into 4-inch rounds.

Heat oil in a karai and deep fry poori, stroking or pressing poori with a flat perforated spoon, to puff up. Flip over after a minute and cook till light brown and crisp. Remove from oil and drain in a colander.

Serve hot.

Variations:
- Add to dough:
  2 tbsp ghee, butter or oil

- Add to dough:
  ¼ tsp turmeric powder
  ½ tsp chilli powder
  3 tsp cumin seeds, dry roasted
- Add to dough:
  2 tbsp sour curd and less water

Traditionally Parsis eat poori with doodh pakh, which is a delightful sweet, cooked with rice.

Poori is also eaten with savoury potatoes and as part of a meal instead of rotli, with any other vegetables.

BAJRA NA ROTLA
(Millet flour rotla)
Makes 2 large rotla

1 kg millet flour (bajra)
½ tsp salt
Whole wheat flour (atta) for rolling
1 tbsp butter or ghee (optional)

Divide flour into 2 portions. Mix one portion with quarter teaspoon salt and enough water to bind. Knead well. Dust hands with flour and shape into a large flat cake about quarter-inch thick, pressing and turning it on a board. (This method is called 'thappo' in Gujarati).

Cook gently on a hot tava, till done, turning once only.

Spread with ghee or butter if desired.

Repeat with second portion of flour.

This rotla is eaten by Maharashtrians with a garlic or Bombay duck chutney.

JOWAR NA ROTLA

(Milo flour rotla)

Makes 2 large rotla

Cook in same way as bajra na rotla.

DHEBRA

(Thick rotla)

Makes 10-12

500 g whole wheat flour (atta)
2 tsp chilli powder
3 tsp cumin seeds, dry roasted
2 tsp salt
2 tbsp hot ghee
Extra ghee or oil as needed

Mix all dry ingredients together. Make a well in the centre and add hot ghee slowly. Incorporate into flour. Add warm water to bind.

Knead well. Roll into a sausage and cut into 10-12 portions, about one-inch thick. Roll out into 4-inch rounds, about quarter-inch thick.

Heat a little oil on a tava and cook carefully on gentle heat, turning on both sides till cooked through.

METHI NA DHEBRA

(Fenugreek leaf rotla)

Makes 10-12

½ cup whole wheat flour (atta)
½ cup milo flour (jowar)
½ cup millet flour (bajra)
½ cup gram flour (besan)
1½ tsp salt
1 tsp chilli powder

1 tbsp ghee
2 tbsp sesame seed or peanut oil

Chop:
1 tbsp fenugreek leaves (methi)
4-6 green chillies, seeded
3 tbsp coriander leaves
1 tbsp mint leaves

Grind together:
2" piece ginger
3-4 cloves garlic
2 tsp cumin seeds

Mix fenugreek leaves with salt and leave for half an hour. Squeeze out water to remove bitter juice from leaves.

Mix all flours, salt and chilli powder together. Add chopped greens and ground spices. Melt ghee and add to mixture. Mix well and add enough warm water to bind.

Knead well. Roll into a sausage and cut into 10-12 portions, about one inch thick. Sprinkle some wheat flour on a board, dust hands with flour and start pressing dough on board turning it around all the while into a 4-inch round (about half to three-quarter inch thick).

Heat a little oil on a tava and roast carefully on gentle heat, turning on both sides, till cooked through.

These rotla are delicious eaten hot with melted butter on top. You can serve them with lassi or a curry.

17

Tea-time Snacks

Parsis have no boundaries when it comes to good food and will accept any dish that their palates fancy. Their tea-time snacks are a delightful mixture of Gujarati, Maharashtrian and European dishes, as well as their own typical ones.

In Bombay, baking and selling cakes is a flourishing business among Parsi ladies.

The cities of Surat, Navsari and Pune are famous for their biscuits. A visit to Pune is incomplete without buying the famous Shrewsbury, ginger and butter biscuits and batata chevda to take back home.

From Surat we get the khari pur ni biscot (light flaky salt biscuits), batasa (crisp round biscuits—sweet or salted with a cumin flavour), nankhatai (a rich shortbread) and macaroons with almonds and cashew nuts which are small, round and delightfully crisp. There are of course those gastronomical delights like the buglu, topli na paneer and malai na khaja.

A number of snacks are also made at home. Patrel is made with stuffed, steamed colocasia leaves. Chapat is a nutty pancake, and popatji are small yeast cakes fried in a pan called popatji nu panu. Bhakra are delicious small doughnuts made with toddy and sadhna are another delicious speciality made with rice flour and toddy. Hariso is a sweet made with cracked wheat and nuts while khaman na larva are dumplings stuffed with grated coconut. There are ghari and dar ni pori which are stuffed cakes, kervai made of bananas and kerkaria made with sweet potatoes.

While most of these dishes are typically Parsi, they have borrowed from Gujarat and Maharashtra the famous bhajia or pakora (batter-fried potatoes, spinach, chillies, okras, etc.), served with a mint or sweet and sour chutney.

Bhel poori made famous by Vithal, and sometimes called Vithal nu bhatu is a favourite of every Parsi. Pani poori—small puffed poori stuffed with sprouted green beans, dipped in jeera pani and a sweet and sour chutney or dhai batata poori—flat poori sprinkled over with potatoes, beaten curd and chat masala served on dhuna leaves are the other roadside favourites. All these have to be eaten on the spot.

These are also made at home, but eating with a spoon out of a plate, is not the same, as strolling down Chowpatty, Juhu or Varsova beach or sitting on the rocks of Scandal Point of my youth, feeling the spray of the sea on your face, eating bhel poori from the dhuna leaves with your fingers and washing it all down with cool coconut water drunk straight from the coconut (Nowadays we are even given straws to drink the water—one misses out on the full flavour of the drink!)

A favourite haunt of the Parsis for tea or morning coffee or a quick lunch used to be a restaurant called Mongini's, near Flora Fountain in Bombay. Their speciality was patties stuffed with mince, chicken, or vegetables. Patties, tarts, and macaroons from Star Bakery and others were often bought and served at home at tea-time. Unfortunately these shops have closed down and restaurants with no particular speciality of their own have taken their place.

Samosa have their origin in Iran and the Middle East and

are prepared and served all over India, but the stuffing of those we get in Bombay and Hyderabad is quite different. These are stuffed with vegetables or minced lamb, but then leave it to the Parsis to add all sorts of ingredients, including a thick rich Mornay sauce—delicious all the same!

Poori are not a common item eaten by Parsis with their meals, but stuffed poori are always present in Parsi homes, to be taken at tea-time, or after lunch, or by school-going children, after breakfast.

Two other specialities that are always available in Parsi homes are chevda, a pressed rice speciality and sev ghatia, a crisp gram flour snack typical of Gujarat and Maharashtra.

Many of these snacks are bought and rarely made at home,

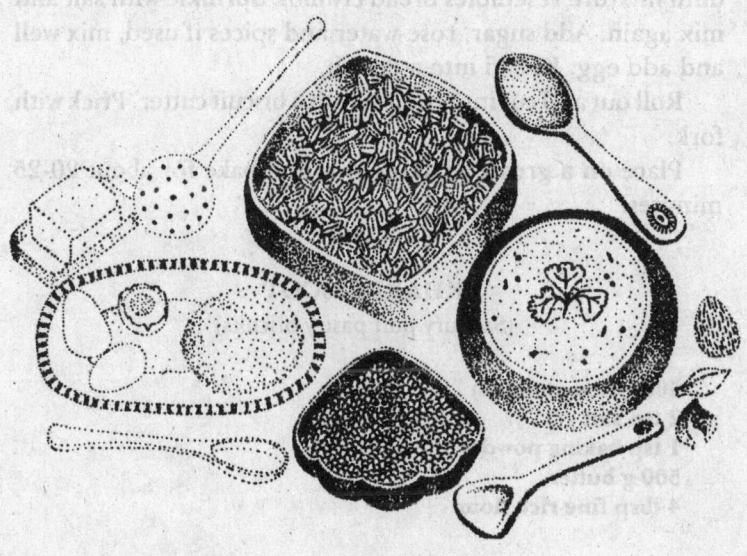

but for those who want to make their own, here are some of the recipes.

SHREWSBURY BISCUITS

250 g flour (maida)
125 g butter
A pinch of salt
125 g castor sugar
Rose-water to taste (optional)
½ tsp powdered cinnamon or cumin and coriander powder mixture (optional)
1 large egg

Set oven to 175°C (350°F).

Sift flour into bowl. Add butter and work with finger-tips until mixture resembles bread crumbs. Sprinkle with salt and mix again. Add sugar, rose-water and spices if used, mix well and add egg. Knead into a dough.

Roll out and cut into rounds with a biscuit cutter. Prick with fork.

Place on a greased baking tray and bake for about 20-25 minutes.

KHARI BISCOT
(Savoury puff pastry biscuits)

500 g flour (maida)
2 tsp salt
1 tsp baking powder
500 g butter
4 tbsp fine rice flour

Set oven to 175°C (350°F).

Mix wheat flour, salt, baking powder and enough water to bind. Knead well and beat on a table or board for 10-15 minutes. The dough must be soft and pliable. It is important to get the right consistency. Cover with damp cloth or cling wrap film and leave for 20-30 minutes.

Soften butter to a spreadable consistency.

Roll out one half of dough as thin as paper into a 12-inch square. Spread softened butter on it very carefully and evenly. Cut square into 6 equal strips and divide each into three, so that there are 18 pieces altogether. Place each of these pieces one on top of the other. The first piece will have the buttered side facing up, but the remaining should be placed with buttered side facing downwards. Sprinkle with rice flour and very carefully roll out lengthwise into a one-inch thick layer. Cut into 2-inch long pieces.

Repeat with second half of dough.

Place on a wet baking tray and bake for about 20-25 minutes.

Note : At the Cordon Bleu School of Cookery I was taught to 'knock back' cut edges of each piece lightly with the back of a knife so that the dough would rise during baking in case edges got stuck in the cutting. Pricking the dough on top with a needle helps in even rising.

KHARA BATASA

2½ kg whole wheat flour (atta)
600 ml toddy or beer or
75 g fresh yeast mixed with 1 tbsp water and kept till it froths
2 tsp salt
500 g ghee
350 g butter
1¼ cup sugar
1 tbsp caraway seeds (shahi jeera)
1 tsp crushed seeds of white cardamom
Halved cashew nuts for decoration, as required

Set oven to 175°C (350°F).

Mix wheat flour and salt with toddy, beer or yeast and set

aside for 1-2 hours to rise.

Beat ghee and butter with sugar till light and fluffy. Add caraway seeds and crushed cardamoms. Fold in wheat flour mixture and mix well.

Using 2 wet spoons, put small rounds of mixture on a greased baking tray. Cover lightly with damp cloth or wet cling wrap film and allow to rise for about 1-2 hours.

Make a cross mark on biscuits, with a sharp knife and put halved cashew nuts on top.

Place in oven and bake for about 20-25 minutes.

NANKHATAI
(Shortbread biscuits)

> 5½ cups flour (maida)
> A pinch of salt
> 1 tsp crushed seeds of green cardamom
> 2 tsp bicarbonate of soda
> 2½ cups castor sugar
> 50 g ghee or butter
> 6-8 tbsp curd, beaten till smooth
> Cashew nut halves for decoration

Set oven to 175°C (350°F).

Sift flour with salt, crushed cardamom and bicarbonate of soda.

Beat ghee or butter with sugar till light and fluffy. Add curd and mix well. Add flour and mix to a stiff dough. Rest dough for half an hour.

Place one teaspoon mixture on a greased baking tray for each biscuit, leaving a space of 2 inches between each. Place a cashew nut on top of each biscuit.

Place in oven and bake for about 20-25 minutes.

BHAKRA
(Parsi doughnuts)
Makes about 10

2 cups whole wheat flour (atta)
1¾-2 cups fine semolina
½ tsp baking powder
1 tbsp crushed nutmeg and seeds of green cardamom
½ tsp salt
¾ cup castor sugar
4 eggs, beaten
1 tbsp ghee
1 cup thick curd, beaten till smooth
2 tbsp rose-water
Oil for deep frying

Sift flour, semolina, baking powder, spices and salt together.

Mix sugar and eggs together and beat well. Add flour mixture and ghee. Fold in curd and rose-water and mix well to form a smooth dough.

Cover with cling film or damp cloth and keep in a warm place for about 1-2 hours, till dough has risen.

Roll out about quarter-inch thick and cut into one-and-a-half-inch rounds with a biscuit cutter.

Deep fry and drain. Cool and store in an airtight glass jar.

BHAKRA WITH TODDY
(Parsi doughnuts)
Makes 5-6

This recipe was given to me by Mrs Mehroo Meherjirana K Dastur.

¾ cup whole wheat flour (atta)
1 cup flour (maida)
½ cup fine semolina
1 tsp crushed nutmeg and seeds of green cardamom

½ tsp salt
½ cup sugar
½ cup ghee
1 egg, beaten
125 ml toddy or beer or 1 tsp fresh yeast mixed with 1 tsp
sugar and 125 ml warm water
Oil for deep frying

Sift flour, semolina, spices and salt together.

Beat sugar and ghee together. Add egg and mix well. Add flour mixture, mix well and add toddy. Beat to a stiff dough, adding water if necessary.

Cover with cling film or damp cloth and keep in a warm place for about 2-3 hours, till dough has risen.

Roll out about quarter-inch thick and cut into one-and-a-half-inch rounds with a biscuit cutter.

Deep fry and drain. Cool and store in an airtight glass jar.

CHAPAT
(Parsi pancake)

2 cups flour (maida)
½ tsp crushed nutmeg and seeds of green cardamom
A pinch of salt
6 eggs, beaten
8 tbsp castor sugar
2 cups coconut milk extracted from ¾ grated coconut
2 tbsp rose-water
2 tbsp almonds, blanched and sliced
2 tbsp cheronji
1 tbsp ghee or melted butter

Sift flour, spices and salt into a large mixing bowl. Make a well in the centre. Add beaten eggs, sugar and coconut milk. Incorporate flour slowly into this and keep mixing till dough is smooth.

Add rose-water, almonds and cheronji and mix again. Allow dough to rest for one hour.

Just before cooking chapats beat dough well, once again.

Heat a small frying pan 5-6 inches in diameter and coat base with ghee or butter. Allow it to melt and pour in enough batter to cover base of pan. Cook on low heat till light brown at the bottom. Flip over and cook other side. Flip onto a plate.

Sprinkle with a little flour and continue cooking all chapats. Place chapats, one on top of the other, sprinkling a little flour in between to prevent them from sticking to each other.

KUMAS
(Semolina cake)

This recipe was given to me by Mrs Mehroo Meherjirana K Dastur.

    2 cups fine semolina
    1 cup whole wheat flour (atta)
    1 tsp crushed nutmeg and seeds of green cardamom
    A pinch of salt
    1 cup sugar
    2 tsp ghee
    5 eggs, beaten till frothy
    2 tbsp flour (maida)
    1 cup coconut water (water from a fresh coconut—not
    extracted milk)

Mix semolina, whole wheat flour, spices and salt.

Add sugar and ghee to eggs and beat well. Add semolina mixture and mix well. Add refined flour and coconut water to make a batter of dropping consistency (like that of an ordinary cake). Keep aside in a warm place for 24 hours to rise.

Set oven to 175°C (350°F).

Prepare a one-kg cake tin and spoon in mixture. Bake for 25-30 minutes. You will know it is done when a skewer pierced into the cake comes out clean.

SADHNA
(Steamed cakes made with toddy)

This recipe has been given to me by Mrs Pervis P Dhunbura.

800 g fine rice flour
1 tbsp ghee
½ litre milk
1 large grated coconut
600 g castor sugar
½ litre strong toddy or 1 tsp dry yeast mixed with ½ tsp
sugar in ½ cup lukewarm water or ½ litre beer
3-4 tbsp rose-water or 1 tsp rose essence

Garnish:
4 tbsp cheronji
4 tbsp sultanas (kishmish)
4 tbsp poppy seeds (khus khus), dry roasted

Mix 100 g rice flour with ghee and a little milk. Mix well and cook till thick and gluey.

Heat remaining milk and add to grated coconut. Purée well, or liquidize and strain into remaining rice flour. Add sugar and cooked mixture, stirring continuously until sugar has dissolved.

Add toddy, beer or yeast and rose-water. Mix well. The consistency should be that of a thick sauce. Keep covered overnight in a warm place.

Grease small thalis 4-5 inches in diameter and pour in mixture. Sprinkle with garnish ingredients and steam in sadhna nu vaasan till done. To test, press with your finger. The sadhna should not stick to it and should spring back.

If you do not have a sadhna nu vaasan, there are many other ways of steaming them. One simple way is to use an idli pan and steam them in that.

You may set up a steamer. Place a small pan inside a large broad-based one. Put water inside the broad-based pan. Place a large lid on the small pan and place thali of sadhna on it. Cover the large pan and steam.

You may also steam in a pressure cooker, by cooking without pressure weight for 15-20 minutes.

Serve by themselves or with cream, milk, thick coconut milk or hariso (see recipe below).

HARISO

    2 cups broken wheat (dalia)
    2 tbsp ghee or butter
    2 cups water
    1½ cup sugar
    4 cups milk
    ½ cup rose-water
    1 tsp crushed nutmeg and seeds of green cardamom
    A pinch of salt

Garnish:
    3 tbsp almonds, blanched and slivered
    3 tbsp sultanas (kishmish)

Heat ghee or butter in a pan and fry broken wheat for 1-2 minutes. Add water, sugar and milk and continue cooking till it reaches the consistency of a thick custard.

Remove from fire, add rose-water, salt and spices. Pour into a bowl and sprinkle with garnish ingredients.

Serve with sadhna.

POPATJI
(Yeast or toddy batter-fried fritters)

    ½ kg whole wheat flour (atta)
    50 g ghee or butter

5 eggs
400 ml milk
3 tbsp almonds, blanched and chopped (optional)
3 tbsp black currants
100 g orange peel, finely chopped
1 tbsp caraway seeds (shahi jeera)
1 cup toddy or beer or 2 tsp fresh yeast mixed with 1 tsp
sugar and ½ cup warm water
Oil as needed
Icing sugar as needed

Beat ghee or butter until soft and smooth. Add one egg at a
time, beating constantly. Gradually add flour and milk
alternately, and keep mixing. Add almonds, if used, black
currants, peel and caraway seeds. Mix and add toddy or beer or
prepared yeast. Mix well, cover with cling wrap film or damp
cloth and keep in a warm place for about 1-2 hours, till well
risen.

Heat a popatji nu panu. Half fill the depressions with oil
and allow to get hot. Spoon in enough batter to fill the
depressions three-quarters full. When base is cooked and
crisp. Turn over with a skewer and cook other side. When
brown and crisp on both sides remove from oil with a pair of
tongs or a skewer and drain well in a colander. Repeat till all
the batter is finished.

Dredge with icing sugar and serve.

KARVAI
(Banana fritters)
Makes 5-6

2½ cups ripe banana pulp
2 tbsp cornflour
½ tsp crushed nutmeg and seeds of green cardamom
5 tbsp almonds, blanched and chopped
3 tbsp cashew nuts, chopped
6 tbsp sultanas (kishmish)

A pinch of salt
Castor sugar to taste
Poppy seeds (khus khus) as needed
Oil for deep frying

Mix cornflour, spices and banana pulp. Fry nuts lightly, drain and add to pulp. Add sultanas, salt and sugar to taste. Take 2 tablespoon of mixture at a time and form into a ball. Roll fritters in poppy seeds to coat and deep fry. Deep fry one fritter first. If it breaks add a little more cornflour to the mixture.

For easier frying shape into round discs and shallow fry. Serve hot.

KERKERIA
(Fritters)

1¼ cup fine semolina
¾ cup whole wheat flour (atta)
½ cup icing sugar
2 tbsp ghee
6 eggs, beaten
300-350 ml toddy or beer
3 tbsp rose-water
1 tsp crushed nutmeg and seeds of green cardamom
½ cup milk or as required
Ghee or oil for deep frying

Mix flour, icing sugar and semolina together. Add 2 tablespoons ghee and eggs. Mix and beat well. Gradually add toddy, rose-water and spices. Add enough milk to reach the consistency of a thick batter. Allow it to rise for about half an hour.

Heat ghee or oil in a karai and drop in spoonfuls of batter. Deep fry till crisp. When done, they will rise to the top.

Remove from oil, drain and serve hot.

KERA NA KERKERIA
(Banana fritters)

6 large completely ripe bananas preferably Vasai variety or
'any other breed of a lesser kind'
3 tbsp almonds, blanched and chopped
1 tsp crushed nutmeg and seeds of green cardamom
1 tsp rose-water
Sugar to taste
Fine semolina as required
Ghee or oil for deep frying

Peel and slit bananas. Remove central vein and mash to make
up abut 250 g of pulp. Add almonds, spices, rose-water and
sugar to taste. Mix to make a paste that holds its shape. If too
thin, add some fine semolina.

Heat oil or ghee in a karai and drop in spoonfuls of
mixture. Deep fry till crisp, remove from fat, drain and serve
hot.

KHAMAN NA LARVA
(Rice dumplings with grated coconut)
Makes about 25

This is a delightful sweet, typically Parsi and this recipe has
been given to me by Mrs Pervis P Dhunbura.

Covering:
1 cup cornflour
1 cup + 1 tbsp rice flour
6 tbsp castor sugar
A pinch of salt
4 cups milk
4 cups water
½ cup rose-water
5 tsp melted ghee

Filling:
2 fresh coconuts, grated

2 cups sugar
8 tbsp water
1 tsp rose-water or vanilla
1½ tbsp melted ghee
1 tsp crushed nutmeg and seeds of green cardamom

Place dry ingredients for covering into a pan and mix well. Add liquid ingredients slowly, mixing all the while to make a smooth dough. Cook on medium heat till mixture becomes thick, stirring all the time, so that it does not burn. Cool.

Place all ingredients for filling, except spices, into a karai. Mix well and cook till thick. Cool and add spices.

Divide dough into 25 small rounds. Grease your hands. Take one portion, make a depression in the centre and place one tablespoon filling in it. Cover filling and shape into a smooth round ball. Repeat for remaining portions.

Place a few larva at a time into a steamer and steam for 15-20 minutes till cooked and firm. Allow to cool in steamer. If you try to remove them while hot, they will break.

DAR NI PORI
(Cakes stuffed with lentils)
Makes 1

Filling:
2 cups pigeon peas (arhar or toover dal)
2 tbsp ghee
6 tbsp sugar
3 tbsp almonds, blanched and chopped
3 tbsp cheronji
3 tbsp sultanas (kishmish)
2 tsp crushed nutmeg and seeds of green cardamom
2 tbsp rose-water

Dough:
4 tbsp flour (maida)
2 tbsp fine semolina

½ tsp salt
3 tbsp butter or ghee

Maan (Lining):
4 tbsp flour (maida)
4 tbsp ghee or butter

Clean and wash dal. Place in a pan, cover with water and cook till soft and dry. Mash thoroughly to a smooth paste. Add sugar and ghee and simmer, mixing all the while, until sugar has dissolved and mixture is thick. Cool and add remaining ingredients for filling. Mix and keep aside.

To make dough, mix flour, salt and semolina. Add butter and rub to resemble breadcrumbs. Add water and mix to make a soft dough.

To prepare lining, heat ghee and add flour. Mix well into a paste and remove from heat.

Divide dough and lining into 4 portions. Roll out each dough portion into a round the size of a half plate. Spread lining on top of each round. Place rounds one on top of the other and roll out to the size of a dinner plate. Spread filling in the centre, pick up sides and cover filling completely, shaping into a round cake. Dampen edges so that they do not open out.

Classically pori is cooked on a griddle, on medium heat, till evenly cooked on both sides. This is done by lightly pressing top of pori with a folded cloth. It can also be cooked in a frying pan or baked in a preheated oven at 190°C (375°F) for about 25-30 minutes.

Dar ni pori can stay in the refrigerator for at least a week.

KHAJOOR NI GHARI
(Date filled pastry)
Makes 2

Pastry:
2¼ cups flour (maida)
2¼ cups fine rice flour

2 tsp baking powder
½ tsp salt
250 g butter
2-3 tbsp each of butter and oil for shallow frying

Filling:
500 g dates, stoned and minced
2-3 tbsp butter
4-6 tbsp milk
1 tbsp rose-water
A pinch of salt

To make pastry, sift flours, baking powder and salt together. Beat half the butter till soft. Add flour and mix to a soft dough. Roll into a large round. Spread remaining butter over round and sprinkle a little extra flour over it. Roll up the dough into a sausage. Divide into two pieces.

To make filling, heat butter in a pan and add dates. Fry for a few minutes and add remaining ingredients. Cook gently until it becomes a soft paste. Remove from heat and cool.

Roll out each piece of dough into a round the size of a half plate. Divide filling into 2 and spread onto centre of each round. Pull up dough on all sides, to completely cover filling, dampen edges so that they do not open out and shape into a round cake on a floured board.

Heat tava or lohri and put a little butter and oil on it. Gently fry gharis till crisp and light brown on both sides.

Cut into wedges and serve warm or at room temperature.

MEHERBAI GORANI NO MALIDO

1 egg, beaten
1 tbsp ghee
2 cups whole wheat flour (atta)
A pinch of salt
½ cup sugar
1 tsp crushed nutmeg and seeds of green cardamom
Rose-water to taste
2 tsp almonds, blanched and slivered

2 tsp sultanas (kishmish)

Mix egg and ghee together. Add half the flour and salt and make a thick rotli. Cook on a tava till cooked through. Cool and break into very small pieces.

Make a sugar syrup with a little water and cook to a single thread consistency. Add broken rotli and keep stirring till mixture is thick. Add remaining flour and powdered spices and simmer till malido is a thick paste and cooked. Remove from heat.

Add rose-water to taste, mix well, sprinkle with almonds and sultanas and serve with papri.

MEVA NO MALIDO

8½ cups whole wheat flour (atta)
1 tsp salt
1 cup milk
1¼ kg ghee
1 kg 350 g castor sugar
7 eggs, beaten
550 g mavo (dried unsweetened condensed milk)
Rose-water to taste
1 cup pistachio nuts, coarsely chopped
1 cup almonds, blanched and slivered
1 cup sultanas (kishmish)
2-3 tsp crushed nutmeg and seeds of green cardamom

Mix flour, salt, milk and 3-4 tbsp ghee and bind. Knead and roll into rotli.

Shallow fry in a little of the measured ghee. Cool and break into fine pieces, like rough semolina.

Make a thin syrup with sugar and a little water. Cool and add eggs, mavo and broken pieces of fried rotli. Add remaining ghee and cook on low heat, till ghee rises to top.

Remove this ghee if desired. I would!

Cool and add rose-water. Sprinkle with nuts, sultanas, cardamom and nutmeg mixture, and serve with papri.

PAPRI

2 cups whole wheat flour (atta)
1 cup flour (maida)
½ cup fine semolina
4 tbsp ghee
Salt to taste
Oil for frying

Mix all ingredients together except oil, adding water if needed to make a stiff dough. Knead well and roll out into a long sausage. Cut off pieces about a quarter of an inch thick and roll out into circles about 3-4 inches in diameter. Prick with a fork so that it does not puff up while frying.

Shallow or deep fry and drain. Cool to room temperature. Serve with malido.

PANEER
(Cream cheese)

¼ litre curd
¼ litre cream
Juice of ½ lime
1 litre warm full cream milk
1 tsp salt
1 large paneer pan
A piece of cotton cloth to line paneer pan

Beat curd with cream and lime juice. Add to milk with salt and mix well, pouring mixture from one pan to another, 3-4 times.

Place on low heat stirring constantly, to turn milk. Wait till whey is transparent and remove from heat immediately.

Line paneer pan with wet cloth and pour turned milk into it. Allow to drain. Cover pan with its lid.

Leave for half an hour. Invert onto a plate and serve.

TOPLI NA PANEER

(Cottage cheese made in small baskets)

2 litres full cream milk
2-3 dried linings of chicken stomach (choosdo) soaked in
vinegar or
8-10 rennet tablets, crushed
2 tsp salt
12-14 small cane baskets, 2" in diameter and 1½" deep
12-14 pieces of muslin cloth to line baskets

Warm milk to body temperature. Do not boil. Pour into a pottery or glass dish and add rennet tablets or linings of chicken stomach. Allow milk to set. This will take about 3-4 hours depending on the weather—it sets best in a warm moist atmosphere.

Line baskets with wet muslin cloth pieces and spoon junket into baskets. Sprinkle with salt. Place baskets on top of glasses to hold whey. When paneer sinks down, carefully turn each to drain other side. When whey has completely drained out, carefully remove from baskets and place in cold water with a pinch of salt.

Serve with crackers or on their own. Delicious!

Note : If Saltless paneer is required, then do not add salt.

PATREL

Makes 6

3 cups gram flour (besan)
1 cup whole wheat flour (atta)
1 cup flour (maida)
6 ripe bananas, mashed
2 onions, finely chopped with their moisture squeezed out
3 tbsp chopped coriander leaves with tender stems
1 tsp turmeric powder
2 tsp chilli powder
2 tbsp dhan sakh masala powder

1 tbsp sambhar powder
100 g tamarind infused in 2 cups hot water with 50 g jaggery
Salt to taste
Oil for shallow frying
18 medium-sized colocasia leaves (arbi patta)
Cotton thread

Grind together:
4-6 green chillies
1 large pod garlic
2 tsp cumin seeds
2 tbsp mustard seeds
1 tbsp fenugreek seeds (methi)

Mix all ingredients except colocasia leaves and oil with ground spices and strained tamarind and jaggery mixture.

Wash and dry colocasia leaves. Carefully remove protruding central vein from back of leaves.

Place three leaves upside down on a board, and spread some mixture on each of them. Place each leaf one on top of the other and fold in sides. Roll, starting from tip of leaves going towards base. Tie down with cotton thread.

Repeat with remaining leaves and mixture.

Heat oil in a large frying pan and fry rolls lightly till leaves turn dark green. Steam for about 10-15 minutes and then lightly fry again.

Cool and store.

Patrel can stay in a refrigerator for a fortnight and over a month in a deep freezer.

To serve, bring to room temperature, slice about half inch thick and fry slices. Serve with lime.

Note : Patrel may be served without frying.

BHAJIA
(Batter fried vegetables)
Serves 2-4

These bhajias are of the type made by famous Bombay bhajiawallas.

Batter:
1 cup gram flour made from roasted husked Bengal gram (channa dal)
1 tsp cumin powder
½ tsp pepper
½ tsp bicarbonate of soda
½ tsp salt
Sesame seed oil for deep frying

Grind together:
1 medium-sized onion
½" piece ginger
4-5 cloves garlic
3-4 green chillies
1 tbsp coriander leaves with tender stems

Sieve all dry ingredients together and add ground spices. Mix together with a little water to make a stiff paste.

Hear oil till very hot. Lower heat and drop spoonfuls of batter into oil, using 2 wet spoons. Keep turning them around with a fish slice until crisp and golden.

Remove from heat and drain well. Serve hot with a coconut chutney.

Note : If you want to make bhajias with vegetables, thin down batter with a little water to consistency of thin cream. Dip slices of vegetables—potatoes, bananas, aubergines, onions, whole tender okras, green chillies, cottage cheese, phuee bhaji (a special type of spinach leaf used for these bhajias) etc., in batter and fry.

KOOTO ATHWA COLMI NA BHAJIA
(Batter fried small shrimps)
Serves 4-6

**350 g kooto, (very small shrimps) washed and cleaned or
shrimps, shelled, cleaned, deveined and coarsely chopped
1 tsp turmeric powder
Salt to taste
1-2 tbsp gram flour (besan)
1 cup ghee
1 cup sesame seed oil**

Grind together:
**1 onion
1 tbsp coriander leaves with tender stems
6 cloves garlic
1 tsp cumin seeds
5-7 dry red chillies**

Mix shrimps with salt, turmeric and ground spices. Add
enough gram flour to make a stiff paste.

Heat oil and ghee till hot and drop in spoonfuls of mixture.
Fry till crisp and golden, turning them with a fish slice.

Serve hot with a coconut chutney

TARKARI NA BHAJIA
(Batter fried vegetables)
Serves 4-6'

**2 large potatoes
2 onions
2 bananas
Oil for deep frying**

Batter:
**1 cup gram flour (besan)
½ tsp bicarbonate of soda
½ tsp turmeric powder**

½ tsp salt
Tamarind the size of a lime infused in 3 tbsp hot water

Grind together:
3 green chillies
1 tbsp coriander leaves with tender stems
6 cloves garlic
4 dried red chillies

Peel and dice potatoes. Boil one and fry the other lightly. Peel and chop onions. Fry one onion lightly. Peel and mash bananas.

Sieve dry ingredients for batter together. Add ground spices, vegetables, bananas and strained tamarind juice. Mix well to make a stiff paste.

Heat oil and drop in spoonfuls of mixture. Fry till crisp and golden, turning them with a fish slice.

Serve hot with a coconut chutney.

BHEL POORI

There is no English translation to this magnificent snack which the rich and poor consume with relish.

Poori:
1½ cup whole wheat flour (atta)
½ cup fine rice flour
3 tbsp gram flour (besan)
A pinch of salt
2 tbsp hot sesame seed oil
Sesame seed oil for deep frying

Sweet chutney:
2 tbsp jaggery
1 pod garlic, finely ground
1" piece ginger, finely ground
Salt to taste
100 g tamarind infused in 2 cups hot water

Hot coconut chutney:
1 grated coconut
1 onion
4-6 green chillies
4 tbsp coriander leaves with tender stems
1 tbsp mint leaves
Juice of 2 limes
A pinch of sugar
½ tsp salt

Gram chutney:
6 tbsp husked Bengal gram (channa dal), dry roasted and ground
1 small onion
1 small pod garlic
2 tsp cumin seeds
1 tsp chilli powder
½ tsp salt
50 g tamarind infused in 1 cup hot water

Bhel:
4 cups puffed rice (murmura)
1½ cups sev (savoury gram flour crisps)
½ tsp chilli powder, or to taste
Salt to taste
4 large onions, chopped
400 g boiled, peeled and diced potatoes
2-3 green chillies, seeded and chopped
2 tbsp chopped coriander leaves
1 green mango, chopped

To make poori, sift flours with salt into a thali. Make a well in the centre and add hot sesame seed oil. Mix and add enough water to make a stiff dough. Knead well. Roll out thin and cut into one-and-a-half-inch rounds with a biscuit cutter and prick surface with a fork.

Heat oil in a karai and deep fry till crisp. Drain and cool.

To make sweet chutney, mix all ingredients with strained tamarind juice and add enough water to make a thick pouring consistency.

To make coconut chutney, grind all ingredients with a little water. Add enough water to make a thick pouring consistency.

To make gram chutney, grind all ingredients with strained tamarind juice.

To serve bhel poori, break poori, mix with puffed rice, and sev and place in a large bowl. Mix salt and chilli powder and place in a small bowl. Place all other ingredients and chutneys in individual bowls.

Have small bowls and teaspoons for your guests to serve themselves with the items and chutneys according to their own tastes.

Do not mix bhel ingredients together with vegetables or chutneys, as it becomes soggy very quickly.

Note: Dry ingredients of the mixture can be kept in an airtight glass jar for weeks.

Poori can also be bought readymade in most cities and towns of India.

BATATA POORI
(Flat poori with potato topping)
Serves 6-8

Poori:
3 cups whole wheat flour (atta)
1 tsp salt
3 tbsp hot sesame seed oil
Sesame seed oil for deep frying

Date chutney:
100 g dates, seeded and finely chopped
1 tsp turmeric powder
2 tbsp coriander leaves
3 green chillies, seeded and chopped
75 g tamarind, seedless, infused in 1 cup hot water
Salt to taste

Coconut chutney:
As for bhel poori

Topping:
4 potatoes, boiled, peeled and diced
150 g sev (savoury gram flour crisps)
2 onions, finely chopped
2 green chillies, chopped and seeded
2 tbsp coriander leaves, chopped
50 g sprouted green beans (moong)

Garnish:
1 tsp chilli powder
1 tsp cumin powder
1 tsp coarsely ground black pepper
1 tsp dry mango powder
1 tsp salt

To make poori sift flour and salt in a thali. Make a well in the centre and pour in a hot oil. Incorporate with flour and add water to make a pliable dough. Knead well and roll out into a thin circle. Cut 2 inch rounds with a biscuit cutter and prick all over with a fork to prevent puffing.

Fry in hot sesame oil till crisp. Drain and keep aside.

To make date chutney, soak dates in water for 10 minutes. Mash and add remaining ingredients. Purée or grind with water to make a chutney of thick pouring consistency.

Make coconut chutney as for bhel poori.

To serve, place some poori on a flat platter. Sprinkle with a teaspoon of each chutney. Mix ingredients of topping and spoon on top of poori. Mix ingredients for garnish and sprinkle over potatoes. Add more chutney if desired and serve. You may spoon the topping items separately instead of mixing them.

Note : If curd is also sprinkled on the poori, the dish is called dhai batata poori.

KHARO RAVO
(Savoury semolina)
Serves 4-6

This is a simple yet delicious dish, given to me by my friend Amy Adenwalla.

2 cups semolina
4 tbsp butter
1 tsp oil
1 large onions, sliced
2 tbsp cumin seeds, crushed
Salt to taste

Brown semolina on a tava, lohri or frying pan, stirring all the time so that it browns evenly.

Melt butter in a pan with oil. Brown onion and add cumin seeds, salt and semolina. Mix well. Cover mixture with hot water and cook on low heat till all water is absorbed and semolina is dry.

CHOORA
(Savoury pressed rice)

500 g pressed rice (poha)
2 cups peanuts, peeled
1½ cups cashew nuts
1 cup sultanas (kishmish), washed and dried
1 cup hushed green beans (moong dal), soaked for 1 hour, drained and dried
8-10 green chillies, seeded and chopped
4 strips curry leaves, with stems removed
1 tsp turmeric powder
2 tsp chilli powder
1 tsp citric acid crystals
2 tsp sugar
2 tsp salt
Oil for deep frying

Heat oil in a deep karai. Place 4 tablespoons pressed rice in a steel strainer and lower strainer into oil. Allow to fry on low heat, so that rice does not get brown. As rice gets crisp, it will automatically rise to the top. Remove strainer from oil, let oil drain out. Put rice into a colander to drain thoroughly. Repeat till all rice has been fried. Place in brown paper and wrap so that all oil is absorbed.

Fry nuts individually using strainer, then sultanas, green beans, chillies and curry leaves.

Using a strainer to fry helps to cook ingredients evenly, and they do not burn, as they might if using a slotted spoon to remove them from oil.

Drain each ingredient in a colander and wrap them separately in brown paper to absorb oil. Leave for half an hour, changing paper if necessary.

Spread out all fried ingredients on a large tray and add remaining ingredients. Mix well, cool and store in an airtight glass jar.

Note: One may add almonds and pistachio to choora, if desired.

GANTHIA
(Thick savoury gram flour strips)

2½ cups gram flour (besan)
2½ cups fine rice flour
1 tsp turmeric powder
2 tsp chilli powder
2 tsp ajwain, dry roasted and crushed
1 tsp black salt
½-1 tsp salt
Oil for deep frying

Mix all ingredients together except oil. Add one tablespoon very hot oil. Mix well and add enough water to make a stiff dough. Knead well.

Heat oil in a karai or deep frying pan.

Put mixture into an icing tube with a star-shaped nozzle and press out one-inch strips into hot oil. Deep fry till crisp taking care not to let it brown.

Drain, cool and store in an airtight glass jar. It will stay crisp for about one week.

Note : There is a brass vessel available in the market especially used for pressing out ganthia and sev. In the latter case holes through which mixture is pressed out are very fine.

SARIA
(Rice crackers)

2 cups old basmati rice, washed, dried and ground
½ tsp bicarbonate of soda
1 tsp cumin powder
1 tsp salt
½ tsp black salt
A white cotton sheet
A long piece of muslin cloth
Straw matting

Mix all dry ingredients together. Add enough water to make a paste of thick dropping consistency. Put mixture in a pan and place it on medium heat. Slowly bring to boil, stirring continuously to prevent it burning at the base. Once the mixture is bubbling remove from heat.

Spread a straw matting in the sun, place a wet sheet over it and with 2 wet spoons or a large star-shaped piping nozzle, place about one tablespoon of mixture at a time on sheet. Cover with muslin cloth to protect sarias from dust and insects and allow to dry completely. This can take 3-4 days, depending on the weather.

Dampen sheet from back to soften saria slightly and peel off sheet. Turn them over to allow dampened part to dry and store in an airtight glass jar.

Deep fry when required. They will double in size and rise to

the top when crisp. Remove from oil, before they brown.
Note : Saria may be dried out in a cool oven by placing them on
a floured baking sheet.

VARAD VARA
(Parsi wedding cakes)

1½ cup castor sugar
½ cup ghee
5 eggs, beaten
3¼ cups fine semolina
1 cup flour (maida)
Salt to taste
1 tsp crushed seeds of green cardamom
¼-½ tsp grated nutmeg
1¼ cup curd, well beaten
2-4 tbsp rose-water
1½ tbsp almonds, blanched and slivered
1½ tbsp cheronji
Oil for deep frying

Beat sugar and ghee together till light and fluffy. Add eggs one
at a time and beat again. Mix together semolina, flour, salt,
cardamom and nutmeg. Add to ghee mixture, alternately with
curd and rose-water. Beat well for about 5 minutes. Cover with
cling film or damp cloth and leave to rise for 12 hours.

Divide dough into 3 portions, roll out into circles, 8 inches
in diameter and one inch thick. Sprinkle with nuts. Leave for
½-¾ hour and deep fry till cooked through.

Cool and serve.

18

Sweets

Ravo, sev and meethu dhai are the three sweets that are always present on every auspicious occasion of the Parsis. All these, I believe, have their roots in Iran. Malai na khaja is a typical example of the Indo-Iranian combination and it is very similar to the baklava of Iran. (I know many non-Iranians, especially the Greeks, will not agree with me regarding the origin of this sweet). Both these dishes are made in a similar manner and while the baklava is filled with walnuts, the Indian version is filled with rose-flavoured cream. The malai na khaja are deep fried and quickly dipped into a sugar syrup and removed to preserve their crispness. It is a speciality of Surat and has to be ordered from special sweet shops.

Kulfi, I firmly believe, is one of the best frozen desserts of the world. It has come down to us from the Mughal days. One of the best kulfis to be had today is made by an old man who sits on the pavements of Daryaganj in Delhi, with his large matka filled with ice and kulfi cones, gently moving the matka to set the kulfi. There are many corner shops in Bombay now that serve excellent kulfi, but in the old days it was always the Parsi Dairy, on Princess Street, and of course, the caterers for our wedding and navjote feasts.

Gorpapri was a great favourite of the children when we were young, and they were specially made for us to '*jarakh mithu monu karvo*' (to sweeten one's mouth) after a meal. Chikee is another favourite and eaten all over India, but a trip from Bombay to Pune was never complete without buying chikee from Lonavala (supposed to be the best).

Doodh pakh, adapted from Gujarat is another favourite sweet served after meals. The recipe given here is that of my sister-in-law, Villie Mehta and it makes the most delicious doodh pakh I have tasted.

Kheer is somewhat similar to doodh pakh and made all over India, with each community having its own special form. The Parsis and the Gujaratis make the same type.

Doodh pava is eaten by Parsis and Gujaratis and always served on full moon nights with hot poori.

Custer is copied from the traditional baked custard and has put the original dish to shame with its richness and flavour.

Goolkand, a conserve made from red rose petals is mostly eaten to soothe an upset stomach, but Freny Billimoria, one of the best cooks and hostesses in Delhi serves it after a heavy meat dish like bafat, to counteract the heavy feeling at the end of the meal.

Some of the sweets that the Parsis love are available all over India. Barfi, for example, made from dry condensed milk, is ordered by the Parsis in the shape of fish for their auspicious occasions. Damoria are small bundi (tiny balls of gram flour, soaked in sugar syrup) from which the agherni no larvo is made.

Sootherfani is typically Gujarati and is a speciality of Bharuch. It looks like soft vermicelli and is made with flour, rice flour, ghee, sugar and rose-water. It is professionally made. If it gets stale, mix it with hot milk, cool and freeze to make a delicious ice cream.

Jalebis are also eaten all over India, but the favourite of the Parsis is a large crisp juicy one, the size of a dinner plate, available in Bombay. Other parts of the country prefer the small ones, which are about three inches in diameter. The jalebiwallah at the street corner of Dariba lane in Chandni Chowk in Delhi is famous all over north India for his delicious hot jalebis, which must be eaten then and there.

Audh is a delicate sweet made with coconut milk, and there is of course the famous baglu from Surat, made of layers of puff pastry so light that they resemble the soft down of the cygnet which is called baglu.

Some of the favourite halvas are Mahim no halvo made from a sweet flour paste into paper-thin flakes; sohan no halvo, a hard brittle sweet made with sugar, ghee and flour and a speciality of Delhi; chikat halvo, a chewy, sticky sweet in a variety of flavours—difficult to chew and cut—which needs strong teeth and a sharp knife.

Rasgulla, ras malai and gulab jamuns the 'immortals' of Bengal are much appreciated by the Parsis as also the shrikand of Maharashtra.

Ice creams, water ices, hot and cold souffles, parfaits, flans, gateaux of all kinds are made and perfected by the enthusiastic Parsi housewives in their quest for different tastes and flavours.

These sweets that I have mentioned are a mere drop in the ocean of the sweets of India.

I am going to start the recipes with the most auspicious of sweets—the ravo, but before I give the recipe I must relate the story of how my daughter Sherna made the ravo for our silver wedding anniversary.

We were in Bangalore at the time and on the day of our anniversary we had a jashan followed by tea. The menu included ravo, sev, dhai, tareli machhi, chicken sandwiches, chocolate gateau, vol au vent and a few other dishes.

I asked Sherna, whether she would like to make the ravo or go to the market to buy the fish. Not being a great enthusiast in such matters, she reluctantly opted for the ravo. When I returned, I found her stirring the ravo. She was using a metal spoon (first mistake), but I said nothing, it being a saro sapar no daro (an auspicious day). Then I noticed some black spots in the ravo (second mistake) and asked her what they were. She said she thought that it had got a little burnt. I said not a word, it being a saro sapar no daro. Then I noticed some lumps (third mistake) and asked her what they were. She answered that it had got a bit lumpy. Again not a word from me. Then she made the fatal mistake of asking me whether it mattered! And all hell broke loose—'How many times have I told you the importance of correct utensils and gadgets! Why are you using a metal spoon instead of the flat-based wooden spoon? Don't you know that is why the ravo has got stuck to the base and turned lumpy and burnt? I though a first-class student of science would have better sense! Now strain the stuff and set it!' There was complete silence from the other side and I felt sorry, but still being furious did not say anything further.

When the Jashan was over our guests were invited to the table. Not a word about my excellent vol au vent or chocolate gateau, in fact not a word about anything except the excellent ravo and a gentle voice whispered in my ear, 'Who is the Cordon Bleu and who is the science student who does not know anything?' I can never make this dish without thinking of her!

Well, here come the recipes. Many do not have an English translation as it is difficult to find a correct one for them.

RAVO

(Semolina pudding)
Serves 4-6

Actually it is anything but a pudding!

3 tbsp butter
3 tbsp fine semolina
A pinch of salt
1 cup water
4 tbsp sugar
1 litre full cream milk
1 cup cream
2 tbsp rose-water
1 tsp crushed nutmeg and seeds of green cardamom

Garnish:
2 tbsp almonds, blanched and slivered
2 tbsp sultana (kishmish)

2 tbsp butter for frying almonds and sultanas
1 tsp crushed nutmeg and seeds of green cardamom
Pale pink rose petals

Melt butter in a pan and add semolina. Sauté for one minute. Add water, salt and sugar and simmer, stirring continuously till thick. Please use a flat-based wooden spoon, so that you can scrape the entire surface of the base of the pan. In this way no lumps will form nor will it burn. Add milk and continue simmering and stirring till it starts thickening. Add cream and continue cooking till it reaches the consistency of pourable porridge. Keep stirring while it cools so that it does not form a layer of skin.

Add spices and rose-water. Pour into a glass dish and garnish with lightly fried almonds and sultanas, powdered spices and rose petals.

Serve at room temperature or chilled.

Variations:

Add 4 egg yolks, ½ tsp vanilla essence and ½ tin condensed milk instead of cream. Reduce quantity of sugar if condensed milk is sweet.

SEV
(Vermicelli)
Serves 4-6

125 g fine vermicelli
2-3 tbsp butter
1 cup sugar
¼ cup water
¼ cup milk
2 tbsp cream (optional)
1 tbsp rose-water
2 tbsp almonds, blanched and slivered
2 tbsp sultanas (kishmish)
1 tsp crushed nutmeg and seeds of green cardamom

Melt butter in a pan with a dash of oil and lightly fry vermicelli, till light brown. Keep aside.

Make sugar syrup with sugar, water and milk. Add vermicelli and gently simmer till all liquid has evaporated. Add cream and rose-water and mix well.

Spoon onto a platter and garnish with almonds, sultanas and powdered spices.

MEETHU DHAI
(Sweet curds)
Serves 4-6

1 litre full cream milk
5-6 tbsp sugar
1 tbsp sour curd, well beaten

The milk should be of excellent quality.

Bring milk to boil, lower heat and simmer slowly till it is reduced by a quarter. Add sugar and continue to simmer for 10 minutes, till it is further reduced stirring all the while.

Remove from heat and allow to reach room temperature. Brush surface of bowl in which you are going to set curd, with some beaten curd. Add remaining curd to milk and mix well. Pour milk from one pan into another 5-6 times, keeping pans as far away from each other as possible while you are pouring the milk.

Pour milk into bowl lined with curd, cover with a plate, cover whole with a towel and leave overnight in a warm place to set. It should be firm enough to cut with a knife.

Chill and serve.

Note: The setting of curd depends very much on the weather. If it is very cold, it will not set well and you may need to warm an oven very slightly, switch it off and leave curd inside to set. If it is very hot, you may need to set curd in the morning for a few hours only and place in refrigerator, else it will turn sour.

DOODH PAVA
(Pressed rice pudding)
Serves 8-10

1½ litre full cream milk
2 cups sugar
1 cup cream
350 g pressed rice (poha), cleaned, washed and drained
2 tsp crushed nutmeg and seeds of green cardamom
Rose-water to taste or
Vanilla essence (though this is not traditionally used)

Bring milk to boil, lower heat and simmer gently till reduced by a quarter. Add sugar and continue reducing, stirring continuously for about 10 minutes more. Add cream and cook for 3-5 minutes. Add pressed rice and cook gently till mixture thickens a little.

Remove from heat, add spices and rose-water. Mix well, chill and serve in small glass bowls or ice cream cups.
Note: The texture should be of milky porridge and not dry. If it gets dry, add a little more milk.

VANILLA ICE CREAM

1½ cups sugar or to taste
6 egg yolks, beaten till frothy
1 litre hot full cream milk
250 g cream, lightly whipped
A pinch of salt
1-2 tsp vanilla essence
1-2 tsp brandy (optional)

Add sugar to egg yolks and beat till thick. Gradually add hot milk, beating continuously. Cook on low heat stirring with a wooden spoon, till mixture coats back of spoon. Remove from heat and strain.

Cool, add cream, salt and flavourings. Chill and freeze.

Serve with:
- Praline
- Chocolate sauce
- Gooseberry, plum or peach preserve
- Fresh strawberries

KULFI
Serves 4-6

This sweet is rather akin to the French bombé, except that kulfi moulds are smaller and conical in shape, with tight fitting lids.

1 litre full cream milk
4-6 tbsp sugar or to taste
2-3 tbsp rose-water
6 tbsp ground almonds
6 tbsp chopped pistachio nuts

Heat milk gently and cook, stirring constantly till reduced by half. Add sugar and continue simmering and stirring till dissolved. Cook for another 3-5 minutes.

Remove from heat, cool and add remaining ingredients.

Semi-freeze in a freezer. Spoon into kulfi moulds and freeze overnight.

To serve, dip moulds into hot water for a second, remove lid and push kulfi out onto quarter plates.

MANGO KULFI
Serves 6-8

12 large ripe alphonso mangoes
150 g cream
Sugar to taste
Lime juice to taste
A pinch of salt

Peel and purée mango. Combine all ingredients. Mix well, semi-freeze in a freezer, spoon into kulfi moulds and freeze overnight.

To serve, unmould as given above.

MANGO SOUFFLE
Serves 8-10

No recipe book written by me can be complete without this dish. Amongst my friends are Group Captain Peter Lewis and his wife Liza. It was Liza who had helped me when I was writing my first book, typing and re-typing the recipes.

This dish was created for Peter on one of the occasions when they came to our home for dinner. My husband wanted a Continental sweet and I wanted an Indian one, so I took the Indian mango and made a souffle!

      850 g thick mango pulp
      6 eggs, separated
      1½ cup castor sugar
      1 cup hot milk
      3 tbsp gelatine powder dissolved in ½ cup water
      A pinch of salt
      1 cup whipped cream
      Juice of 1-2 limes
      Varaq (silver leaf) for decoration (optional)

Prepare a two-pint souffle mould with paper and tie down.

Beat egg yolks with sugar and gradually add hot milk, beating continuously till well mixed. Cook on low heat, stirring with a wooden spoon to form a custard which coats the back of the spoon.

Remove from heat, strain into a bowl and cool. Add mango pulp, gelatine and salt. Semi-set on ice, stirring occasionally.

Fold in whipped cream, lime juice and stiffly beaten egg whites. Semi-set over ice and spoon into prepared souffle mould. The mixture should come ¾-1 inch above the rim of the mould. Chill to set.

To serve, carefully remove paper lining and cover top with varaq.

JOHN'S BYCULLA SOUFFLE
Serves 4

Byculla was once a very prestigious place in Bombay as Government House was located there, before it was shifted to Walkeshwar. It was such an important place that the Deccan Queen, that famous train (now reduced to a very ordinary one) actually stopped there for 5 minutes to allow distinguished travellers from Pune to disembark. Byculla Club was also an extremely prestigious club and not everyone could become a member. The food was superb and the Byculla Souffle a closely guarded secret.

We had a cook called John, famous for his paper-thin slices of pickled hump, fried oysters and chicken curry, but most envied because he was able to produce the Byculla Souffle which is actually a mousse. The recipe was given to him by his friend who was the cook who produced this souffle at the club.

4 egg yolks
½ cup castor sugar
1 tbsp gelatine dissolved in ¾ cup water
½ liqueur glass each of kummel, curacao, chartreuse and benedictine
¾ cup burnt crushed sugar or crushed macaroons
½ cup cream

Prepare a one-pint souffle mould with paper, and chill while making souffle.

Chill liqueurs and cream.

Whip yolks with sugar over low heat till thick. Add gelatine and liqueurs. If you are using burnt sugar, fold in half the sugar. Whip cream and fold it in. Semi-set over ice. Spoon into souffle mould. The mixture should come ¾-1 inch above the rim of souffle dish. Chill to set.

To serve, remove paper lining carefully, press remaining burnt sugar or macaroons onto sides and sprinkle rest on top.

CUSTER
(Parsi baked custard)
Serves 10-12

1 litre full cream milk
200 g sugar
200 g cream
8 large eggs, well beaten
4 tbsp blanched and ground almonds
1 tsp crushed seeds of green cardamom
½ tsp grated nutmeg
2 tbsp cheronji
2-4 drops vanilla essence
2 tbsp rose-water or to taste
A pinch of salt.

Set oven to 300°F (150°C).

Bring milk to boil, lower heat and simmer till reduced to roughly half Add sugar and simmer, stirring continuously for 3-5 minutes. Remove from heat, add remaining ingredients and mix well.

Pour mixture into baking dish, place in pan of hot water and bake for one hour.

Serve at room temperature or chilled.

ARISO
Serves 6

A cool refreshing milk and nut sweet.

> ¾ litre milk
> 1½-2 cups sugar
> 100 g cream
> A pinch of salt
> 300 g almonds, blanched, slivered and lightly fried
> 300 g shelled pistachio nuts, dry roasted and coarsely
> chopped
> 2 tsp crushed nutmeg and seeds of green cardamom

Mix milk with sugar and cook on low heat till reduced by two-thirds. Add remaining ingredients and continue cooking gently for 2-3 minutes further.

Cool, chill and serve in small bowls with hot poori.

GOOLKUND

This recipe was given to me by Freny Russi Billimoria.

> ½ kg red rose petals
> ¾ litre water
> Juice of 1 lime
> 2 kg sugar
> 2 tsp crushed seeds of green cardamom
> ½ cup rose-water

Pressure cook rose petals with water for half an hour. Strain. Add lime juice and sugar to rose petal water. Heat to dissolve sugar. Boil rapidly to candy consistency.

Remove from heat. Add rose petals, cardamom and rose-water. Allow to stand till cool. Pour into clean jars and store.

KHEER

(Rice pudding)

Serves 8-10

1¼ cup rice, washed and drained
3 tbsp ghee
2" stick cinnamon
8-10 white cardamoms
3½ litre full cream milk
1 tsp salt
2½ cups sugar
1 cup sultanas (kishmish), washed and dried
1 tbsp rose-water
3 tbsp almonds, blanched and slivered

Heat ghee and add cardamom and cinnamon. Add rice and half litre water. Cook on gentle heat till water is absorbed. Add milk and cook for 15 minutes. Stir vigorously, add salt and sugar and continue cooking, stirring continuously till sugar is dissolved. Add sultanas and remove from heat.

Cool, add rose-water and serve in individual bowls, sprinkled with almonds.

SANTRA NI KHEER

(Milk pudding with oranges)

Serves 4

1 litre full cream milk
4 oranges
6 heaped tbsp castor sugar
A pinch of salt

Cook milk till reduced by half and cool.

Peel and flake oranges, collecting any juice that may run out.

Dissolve sugar in orange juice over low heat and cool.

Add salt, sugar and orange flakes to cooled milk. Chill and serve.

A delightfully refreshing sweet for summer.

DOODH PAKH
Serves 6-8

This recipe was given to me by my sister-in-law, Villie Furdoon Mehta, and makes the most delicious doodh pakh.

    10 cups milk
    3 tbsp coarsely ground rice
    ¾ tin condensed milk
    2½ cups sugar
    A pinch of salt
    1 cup almonds, finely ground
    1 cup shelled pistachio nuts, finely ground
    1 tsp crushed seeds of green cardamom
    ½ tsp grated nutmeg

Mix rice with one cup cold water. Add to milk and cook, stirring continuously till it comes to boil. Lower heat and simmer till reduced to about seven cups. Add condensed milk, sugar and salt and continue cooking till it thickens a little more. Add remaining ingredients and remove from heat.

Do not cook after nuts have been added.

Serve cold with hot poori.

BADAM NI BARFI

    1 litre full cream milk
    2 cups sugar
    550 g almonds, blanched and ground
    Green food colouring
    Varaq (silver leaf), optional

Simmer milk with sugar, stirring continuously till thick and practically solid, Add almonds and a pinch of green colouring. Continue cooking and stirring for 3-4 minutes further or until it is no longer sticky.

Pour mixture onto a greased tray and allow to cool. Cover with varaq. Cut into diamond shapes.

JALEBI

Batter:
500 g flour
2 tsp baking powder
1¼ cup curd, well beaten
Water as required
¼ tsp saffron, dry roasted, crushed and infused in 1 tbsp water
2-3 drops yellow food colouring

Syrup:
1¾ kg sugar
Juice of 2 limes
Peel of ½ lime
2-3 drops yellow food colouring
2 tbsp rose-water

Garnish:
1 tbsp shelled pistachio nuts, chopped
2 tsp crushed nutmeg and seeds of green cardamom
Rose petals

Oil for deep frying

To make batter, mix all ingredients with a little water to get the consistency of thick cream. Allow to stand for one hour.

To make sugar syrup, add 3 cups water to sugar. Allow sugar to dissolve on low heat. Keep brushing sides of pan with a wet brush, to prevent sugar granules forming. Bring to boil, add lime juice, peel and yellow colouring. Boil rapidly to make a one thread syrup. Cool to body temperature and add rose-water.

Heat oil in a karai or deep frying pan. Put batter in a forcing bag fitted with a plain quarter-inch nozzle. Force out mixture into oil, making spiral rounds about 2-3 inches in diameter. Fry till crisp on both sides. Drain and dip into sugar syrup. Leave for one minute and remove. Place in a colander to drain.

Continue cooking till all the batter is used up.

Place on a platter and garnish with nuts, spices and rose petals. Serve hot if possible.

Note : If you are daring enough, make one large jalebi 10-12 inches in diameter, using a half-inch icing nozzle.

LARVA

Mixture:
250 g gram flour (besan)
1 tbsp ghee
A pinch of salt

Syrup:
500 g sugar
2 cups water
½ tsp saffron, dry roasted, crushed and infused in
2 tbsp rose-water
1½ tsp vanilla essence (optional)

Garnish:
1 tbsp almonds, blanched and slivered
1 tbsp shelled pistachio nuts, chopped
2 tsp crushed seeds of green cardamom
1 nutmeg, grated

Oil for deep frying

To make mixture, sieve gram flour with salt and rub in ghee.

Add a little water to make a stiff paste. Keep aside.

To make syrup, dissolve sugar in water. Boil to make a medium, two-thread syrup. Leave on low heat for a few minutes. Add saffron-coloured rose-water and vanilla essence if used. Remove from heat and keep aside three-quarter cup of syrup.

Heat oil in a deep karai or frying pan. Press gram flour paste through a colander into oil, so that small drops of mixture fall in. Fry till light golden brown.

Remove from oil and drain in a colander. Put into syrup and mix well. If all the syrup has been absorbed add reserved three-quarter cup.

When all the mixture has been fried and soaked in syrup, pass through a coarse mincer. Spread onto a flat Swiss roll tin, sprinkle garnish ingredients on top and press into mixture, firmly. Cut into small rectangular shapes and serve.

To make agherni no larvo, shape into a large cone.

MEHSOOR

1 kg husked Bengal gram (channa dal) ground and sieved
1 kg sugar
1 kg ghee
A pinch of salt

Make a strong sugar syrup with three cups water.

Cook gram flour in half the ghee till well done and orange or almost red in colour. Add sugar syrup and salt and mix well. Keep mixing, taking care it does not burn, until mixture starts to froth at top.

In another pan heat remaining ghee till very hot. Add gram flour mixture carefully taking care not to burn yourself. Continue stirring and cooking till holes appear in mixture.

Pour into well greased trays, cut into diamond shapes and place at a slight incline to allow excess ghee to drain out.

Cool and store

Note: Cover your arm and hand with a towel while cooking this sweet, as it splutters while cooking and you may get burnt if not careful. Cook in a large pan as the mixture tends to froth and rise.

COPRA NI CHICKEE
(Coconut toffee)

1 tbsp butter
½ cup sugar
1 coconut, grated
A pinch of salt

Grease a marble slab or Swiss roll tin with butter.
Caramelize sugar with 3 tbsp water and boil to 'crack'. Add
coconut and salt and mix well. Continue cooking till mixture
leaves sides of pan. Pour onto tin or marble slab and flatten out
with back of a greased wooden spoon.

Cool and cut into diamond shapes, before it is completely
set.

COPRA PAKH

This recipe was given to me by Mrs Mehroo Meherji Rana K
Dastur of Navsari.

1 kg well-formed coconut, not completely dry (weighed after
the hard outer shell is removed)
1 kg mavo or khoya (dried unsweetened condensed milk)
700 ml rose-water
1 kg sugar

Garnish:
2 tbsp almonds, blanched and slivered

Grate coconut. Break up mavo so that there are no lumps.
Make a syrup with rose-water and sugar and cook to a
two-thread consistency. Add coconut and simmer for a few
minutes till thick.

Remove from heat, add mavo and mix well.

Sprinkle half the almonds onto a greased tray, spoon pakh
over it and smooth out surface with a greased wooden spoon or

greased hand. Sprinkle remaining almonds over pakh and press them in lightly with a greased hand.

Allow to set, turn out on a marble slab and cut into diamond shapes. Store in a glass jar.

AUDH

1¼ cup fine rice flour
2 cups icing sugar
3½ cups hot water
A pinch of salt
225 g ghee
2 cups coconut milk extracted from 1 large coconut
1½ cup rose-water
1 tbsp almonds, blanched and slivered
1 tbsp crushed seeds of green cardamom

Boil water, add rice flour and sugar gradually, stirring continuously.

Add salt and one-third of the ghee. Cook on medium heat and stir till ghee is absorbed. Add coconut milk, rose-water and remaining ghee alternately till all are absorbed. Keep stirring and cooking till mixture forms a ball and leaves sides of pan.

Sprinkle half the almonds on a greased tray and spread mixture over it. Smooth out with a greased wooden spoon or greased hand and cover with cardamom and remaining almonds. Press into mixture. Cool, cut into diamond shapes and serve.

Note : While making this dish, it is important to stir continuously to get a smooth paste and to cook on low to medium heat to prevent burning.

SWEET POORI
Makes 30

This recipe was given to me by Mrs Mehroo Meherji Rana K
Dastur of Navsari.

2 tbsp fine semolina
1 heaped cup flour (maida)
1 tsp salt
6 tbsp castor sugar
7 tbsp ghee
Water as required
Oil for deep frying

Mix semolina, flour, salt and sugar. Rub in ghee and add
enough water to make a pliable dough. Knead well. Roll into a
sausage and divide into 30 small portions. Roll out each
portion into a poori and deep fry in a karai, in hot oil.

MALAI NA KHAJA
(Cream-filled pastry)
Makes 3

Pastry:
3 cups flour (maida)
½ cup fine rice flour
1 tbsp butter
Rose-water to mix

Maan (lining):
½ cup softened butter
2 tbsp fine rice flour
1 tbsp flour
1 tsp baking powder

Filling:
500-600 ml thick cream without any moisture
2 tbsp rose-water or
½ tsp rose essence

Sugar syrup:
1½ cup sugar
¼ cup rose-water
¾ cup water

Extra flour for sprinkling
Oil for deep frying

To make pastry, mix flour with rice flour. Rub in butter and add rose-water to mix to a stiff dough.

To make lining, mix all ingredients till well blended.

Mix ingredients for filling till well blended.

Roll out pastry about ¼ inch thick. Spread with lining, fold pastry over, roll up into a sausage shape and twist it like a rope. Cut into six portions. Flatten each portion into a round and roll out about one-eighth inch thick. Place a spoonful of filling on 3 of the rounds, Wet edges with rose-water and cover each with remaining 3 rounds. Press edges firmly together, twist pastry edges into any pattern and chill.

Make a sugar syrup and keep warm. Deep fry pastries and plunge into syrup for 1-2 minutes. Remove and drain well. Cool and serve.

PAKHS

Pakhs are usually eaten in winter and are supposed to be strengthening. Usually one dessertspoon is taken daily.

BADAM PAKH

1 litre milk
125 g cream
1 kg almonds, blanched
350 g butter
½ litre rose-water
4 cups sugar
2 tsp crushed nutmeg and seeds of green cardamom
A pinch of salt

Cook milk on low heat till reduced by half. Cool and add cream.

Fry almonds lightly in butter till golden. Cool and mince coarsely with a little chilled rose-water. This prevents the oil oozing out of almonds.

Make a syrup with remaining rose-water and sugar. Boil to a thread. Remove from fire, add almonds, milk and butter in which almonds were fried. Mix well and cook on low heat, till mixture reaches consistency of a thick batter. Add spices and salt, mix well and pour into a serving dish, or store in a glass jar.

Note: This is semi solid and can be kept for weeks in a refrigerator. It is given to women after childbirth, to strengthen the back.

In the old days, a mother would give her children 5 blanched almonds soaked overnight and crushed with 1 tsp sugar crystals and ½ tsp butter, 2-3 weeks before school examinations. It is supposed to improve one's memory.

PASTA PAKH

This is made in the same way as Badam pakh using pistachio nuts in place of almonds.

EEDA PAKH

1½ kg sugar
25 egg yolks, well beaten
1½ kg ghee for frying remaining ingredients

Chop and lightly fry, individually in the measured ghee:
1 cup almonds, blanched and slivered
1 cup pistachio nuts
1 cup cheronji
1 cup char magaz
1 cup pinenuts (chilgoza)

Lightly fry individually in the measured ghee and grind to a powder:

- 125 g ghau nu doodh or cream of wheat
- 125 g dry water chestnut (singora)
- 125 g dry lotus roots (kamal kakri)
- ½ cup husked black beans (urad dal)
- ½ cup Bengal gram (channa dal)

Grind to a powder:

- 1 tsp white pepper
- 20 white cardamoms, peeled
- 3 nutmegs
- ¼ tsp mace
- ½ tsp pipri mooth na gath

Make a syrup with sugar and half litre water. Boil to a one-thread consistency. Keep syrup on low heat and add fried nuts and fried and ground ingredients. Add egg yolks, and keep stirring on low heat till thickened.

Remove from heat and add ground spices. Mix well and cool.

Store in a glass jar and keep in refrigerator. A spoonful is eaten at a time.

Note : Char magaz is a mixture of water melon marsh melon, cucumber and marrow seeds.

SOONTH

- ½ kg ghau nu doodh or cream of wheat
- 150 g baval nu goonder (resin of baval tree)
- ½ kg almonds, blanched
- ½ kg pistachio nuts, blanched and peeled
- ½ kg cheronji, blanched and peeled
- 200 g poppy seeds (khus khus)
- 4 kg dry ginger (soonth)
- 1 kg icing sugar
- ¼ kg jaggery
- 1 egg
- 10 white cardamoms, peeled
- 1 nutmeg powdered
- A pinch of salt
- 3 kg ghee for frying ingredients

Heat a little ghee and fry individually cream of wheat and resin. Cool, powder and keep aside.

Chop nuts coarsely and fry individually. Mix and keep aside.

Heat some ghee and fry poppy seeds. Cool, powder and keep aside.

In a flat frying pan add a little ghee. Add ginger, a little at a time, turning with two fish slices, so that it does not get burnt. Cool, powder and keep aside.

In a large pan, mix jaggery, icing sugar, egg with crushed shell and half a litre water. Dissolve jaggery and bring to boil. Remove scum and cook to a one-thread consistency. Using a slotted spoon remove egg shells and as much scum as possible.

Strain through a cloth, put into a large pan and add all ingredients except nuts, cardamoms and nutmeg. Simmer for 4-5 minutes, stirring continuously so that ginger does not burn.

Add fried nuts and remove from heat. Add nutmeg and cardamoms. Mix well, cool and store in a cool place.

SUVA PAKH

2½ kg sugar
3½ litres full cream milk
350 g dill seeds, coarsely pounded
A pinch of salt
1½ kg ghee

Chop individually and fry in the measured ghee:
225 g ghau nu doodh or cream of wheat
450 g dry water chestnuts (singora)
225 g baval nu goonder (resin of baval tree)
100 g lotus roots (kamal kakri)

Powder individually:
20 g pipri mooth na gath
1 tsp black peppercorn
20 white cardamoms, peeled
2 nutmegs

Make a sugar syrup with one cup water and boil till it is of a one-thread consistency.

Heat milk and bring to boil 2-3 times. Remove from heat each time it comes to boil. Add dill and cook on low heat till thick. Add ghee and sauté slowly till mixture is fried. Add sugar syrup and mix well. Add all remaining ingredients except nuts, cardamom and nutmeg. Sauté for 2-3 minutes on low heat.

Remove from heat, add nuts, cardamom and nutmeg and mix well.

Cool and store in refrigerator.

VASANU

½ kg char magaz
50 g baval nu goonder (resin of the baval tree)
2¼ kg sugar
1 litre milk
750 g mavo (dry condensed milk)
1½ kg ghee for frying ingredients

Soak overnight in hot water, peel and chop:
½ kg almonds
½ kg pistachio nuts, shelled
250 g cheronji

Powder individually:
250 g dill seeds (sua)
½ kg dried water chestnuts (singora)
450 g dried lotus roots (kamal kakri)
50 g dholi musri
10 g Punjabi salan

20 g pipri mooth na gath
25 g white pepper
100 g gokhru
25 g kali musri

Coarsely crush:
30 g white cardamoms, peeled
3 nutmegs
25 g vai varan
350 g dry ginger (soonth)

Fry individually all peeled and chopped nuts, char magaz and resin. Grind resin.

Make a sugar syrup of one-thread consistency, using enough water just to cover sugar. Add fried ingredients, keeping aside ½ cup mixed chopped nuts for garnish.

In another pan, cook dill with milk till thick. Add about two cups water if needed. Pour dil mixture into sugar syrup with mavo and resin.

Heat a little ghee in a shallow frying pan and fry all powdered ingredients, individually, a little at a time, adding them to the mixture with ghee, as they are fried. Mix well, place on low heat and cook, stirring continuously, to prevent burning.

When thick, add crushed spices, mix well and remove from heat.

Pour into a tray or pyrex dish, sprinkle over reserved nuts and store in a cool place.

This recipe has been evolved from a number of recipes for vasanu, and is excellent even if I may say so!

Note : Ingredients for this recipe and other pakhs are available in specialized shops selling spices, and from Motilal Masalawalla Grant Road, Mumbai 400 007.

19

Achars, Chutneys, Murumbas

The Parsis developed a taste for pickles after their arrival in India. Some Parsis eat very hot food, but most prefer savoury food with pickles and chutneys as accompaniments.

During the centuries that they have been in India, the Parsis have evolved some delicious pickles which are typically their own, like bafena made from whole ripe mangoes and lagan athwa meva nu achar, which are served at wedding and navjote feasts. There is a gajar nu achar (a light and refreshing pickle) and gor keri nu achar, which has ripe mangoes in it. Colmi, machhi ne gharub nu achar (prawn, fish and fish roe pickles) are also typically Parsi. I have also tasted a delicious pickle made with fresh sardines.

Pani nu achar (small raw mangoes pickled in salt), the lime pickles, the methia nu achar (mangoes pickled with fenugreek) are all of Gujarati and Maharashtrian origin, while a number of brine-based pickles have their origin in the West.

Each family has its own recipe for making these favourite pickles and there are no hard and fast rules about them.

The mango chutney is by far the most popular of all chutneys. Even the colonial Englishman would never dream of eating his curry and rice without the mango chutney, and we have a Colonel Grey's Mango Chutney! There are at least fifteen different ways of making this delicious chutney. The tomato and lime chutney follow closely in popularity, and there is also gooseberry, rossella. and cocum chutney.

The favourite of all fresh chutneys is the coconut and coriander one, popular throughout India, eaten with bhajias and bhel poori. There is also one made from courgette skin.

The mango reigns supreme as far as murumbas are concerned. The mango murumba was made using a variety called Cavasji Patel mangoes. They were huge—the size of small watermelons and had been originally cultivated by a gentleman of that name. One can still find these mangoes, in the mango season, in the Grant Road or Crawford markets of Bombay.

Closely following the mango murumba is the one made with koru (ash gourd). I have also eaten a delicious murumba from whole naspati—a type of hard pear—made by my mother-in-law. We would have it for breakfast with lashings of fresh cream on hot toast! In the old days, every Parsi home had large jars of murumba made in season, that would last the whole year round. Today, most homes have a couple of jam jars bought off the market.

Ambakalio is a preserve made of half raw, half ripe mangoes and usually eaten with dhan sakh. I still remember the days when the Parsi cricket team played in the pentagonal contests in Bombay, they would do brilliantly till lunch time. Lunch consisted of dodhi ma gosht, followed by dhan sakh, kababs and ambakalio, all washed down with chilled beer! No wonder they could not keep up their performance after lunch!

Today there are some excellent sherbets made commercially, but in the old days, when the housewife had more leisure and servants, these were made at home. The most popular was rose. Even today, while health conscious people prefer the cooling limbu pani, the rose sherbet is a great favourite.

I have to say a word about vinegars. The cities of Navsari and Valsad are renowned for their vinegars, made from sugarcane, dates or toddy. Parsi pickles, chutneys, patias and vindaloos have a completely different taste when made with these vinegars and cannot really compare with those made from the synthetic ones. I would most strongly urge that the Navsari or Valsad vinegar be used for these dishes. The Goans, by the way make their own date vinegar, which they use in their classical dishes.

ACHARS

LEEBU NU ACHAR—NAVSARI STYLE
(Lime pickle from Navsari)

This recipe has been given by Mrs Mehroo Meherji Rana K Dastur of Navsari.

1 kg thick-skinned limes
250 g salt (sea salt if possible)
1 kg sugar
2 tsp chilli powder

Wash and completely dry limes. Slit into 4 sections three-quarters down lime, leaving them whole. Stuff with salt and put into a glass jar for one month shaking bottle every day.

After one month, drain out liquid. Put sugar in a pan and gently mix limes with it. Leave for 2 hours. After sugar has dissolved, put pan on low heat for half an hour, stirring occasionally

Remove from fire and cool completely. Mix with chilli powder and bottle. It will keep for over a year.

PANI NU ACHAR
(Raw mango pickle in brine)

5 kg small raw mangoes with soft kernels
10-15 g powdered alum
¾ kg to 1 kg sea salt or rock salt, crushed

Wash and dry mangoes. Mix with alum and some salt. In a large jar, place a layer of salt and alternate layers of mango and salt till jar is full, making sure it is tightly packed. After a week, open jar, remove water and discard any mangoes that may have gone bad, replacing with fresh mangoes and more salt, if required. Keep for one and half months, shaking jar every 2-3 days and turning the mangoes over.

Variation

- In the Gujarati version, 3 tbsp turmeric powder, 3 tbsp chilli powder and 1 tsp asafoetida are also added. Sometimes only the asafoetida is added. Do not keep for more than a year as the mangoes will become soft.

LAGAN ATHWA MEVA NU ACHAR
(Wedding or dry fruit pickle)

1 kg carrots, grated and kept in the sun for 3 days to dry, covered with cotton net
600 g dried apricots
600 g dried dates, seeded
600 g dried figs, chopped
300 g sultanas (kishmish)
300 g raisins (munakka), seeded
Vinegar as required to wash dry fruit
¾ litre Navsari vinegar
500 g jaggery
5 pieces cinnamon, 1" each, crushed
15 green cardamoms, peeled and crushed
15 cloves, crushed
1 tbsp cumin seeds, crushed
7 tbsp chilli powder
500 g ripe mango pulp, preferably tinned, (optional)
Salt to taste
250 g mustard powder

Wash all dry fruit in a little vinegar. Soak apricots overnight in 1½-2 cups of the measured vinegar.

Cook jaggery in half the remaining vinegar till dissolved. Strain into another pan. Add crushed spices and chilli powder and bring to boil. Add all fruit, carrots, mango pulp if used and salt, while vinegar is still boiling. Reduce heat and cook till fruit is tender. Remove from heat and cool.

Beat mustard and remaining vinegar together for about 5 minutes or till strong enough to sting eyes and nose when sniffed. Add to cooled pickle and mix well.

Keep for one week before using.

It will keep for one year.

METHIA NU ACHAR
(Mango pickle with fenugreek)

20 large hard-seeded raw mangoes
150 gm sea or rock salt
1 pod garlic, ground without water
¾ kg fenugreek seeds (methi), dry roasted and coarsely crushed
3 tbsp turmeric powder
300 g chilli powder, or to taste
2 tsp asafoetida (hing)
¾ litre sesame seed oil
¾ litre mustard oil
1 lime
2 tbsp mustard seeds, coarsely crushed

Wash, dry completely and cut mangoes through the seed into medium-sized pieces. Discard seeds. Rub with salt and keep aside for 2 hours. Drain out water, mix with garlic and all spices except mustard seeds. Leave for 4 hours.

Heat both oils in a large pan, with lime cut in half. When hot, remove from heat.

Remove lime and cool oil. Add mangoes and mustard seeds. Allow to cool completely and store in glass jars.

This pickle will stay for one year.

GAJER NU ACHAR
(Carrot pickle)

> 500 g dried dates, seeded
> 1 litre Navsari vinegar
> 3 tbsp mustard powder
> 3 kg young carrots, peeled and sliced lengthwise in 8 pieces
> 500 g fresh ginger, peeled and cut into julienne
> 3 tbsp chilli powder
> 300-350 g granulated sugar
> 1 tbsp salt

Wash dates in a little vinegar and soak overnight in one cup vinegar. Remove seeds.

Beat mustard in a little vinegar for 15 minutes, till strong enough to sting eyes and nose when sniffed.

Mix all ingredients and keep for one week before using. This pickle will keep for more than a year.

GOR KERI NU ACHAR
(Mango and jaggery pickle)

> 4 kg half-ripe mangoes
> 250-300 g sea salt or rock salt
> 500 g dried figs
> 500 g dried apricots, seeded
> 200 g black currants
> Vinegar as required to wash fruit
> 2 cups dried orange peel, cut into julienne
> 1 large pod garlic, ground in vinegar
> 2½" piece ginger, peeled and cut into julienne
> 25 g turmeric powder
> Chilli powder to taste
> 2-3 pieces cinnamon, 1" each
> 1 tbsp cloves
> ½-¾ litre Navsari vinegar
> 2 tbsp mustard powder
> 2 kg jaggery

Peel and cut mangoes into small pieces. Rub with salt and dry in sun, covered with a thin muslin cloth for two days.

Wash dry fruit in extra vinegar and cut figs into small pieces.

Mix all ingredients except jaggery, mustard and half cup vinegar. Add enough vinegar to keep mixture moist. Keep for 2 days.

Beat mustard powder with vinegar till strong enough to sting eyes and nose when sniffed. Crush jaggery, add to pickle with mustard and mix well.

Store in a glass jar for one week before use.

This pickle will keep for more than a year.

BAFFENA
(Mango pickle with mustard)

12 ripe alphonso mangoes
1 tsp turmeric powder
1 litre sesame seed oil
1 pod garlic (optional)
1¼ cup mustard powder
2 cups Navsari vinegar
125 g chilli powder or to taste
2 tbsp salt
12 cloves
1¼ cup crushed jaggery

Wash and wipe mangoes. Heat oil with turmeric in a large patio or flat bottomed pan. Add mangoes and cook on medium heat for about 30 minutes. Keep pan covered with an inverted lid with water on it. Remove lid occasionally to turn mangoes so that they do not stick to pan. Take care that water from lid does not fall into pan.

Remove mangoes from pan and place in a tray overnight. They should be dull in colour and skin should be soft and shrivelled.

Clean garlic, cut each cloves in half and smash.

Beat mustard with vinegar for 15 minutes till strong enough to sting eyes and nose when sniffed. Add chilli powder, salt, cloves and crushed jaggery and beat for another 15 minutes.

Line an opaque jar with mustard mixture, and with a clean hand, dip mangoes one by one in remaining mixture and place in jar. Pour any remaining paste on top.

Cover jar securely, wrap a cloth around lid and store for one month before use.

This pickle will keep for one year and is delicious with khichdi and kheemo.

GHARAB NU ACHAR
(Fish roe pickle)

This recipe was given by Mrs Dhunmai Khushru Cama at an unforgettable breakfast of Bharuchi akoori, fried prawns, gharab nu achar and hot ghau ni rotli.

15 large fresh fish roe, preferably of grey mullet (boi)
100 g mixed whole cinnamon, cloves and cardamoms
1½ kg sesame seed oil
1½ litre Navsari vinegar
1 kg husked mustard seeds, ground
1½ cup cumin seeds, dry roasted and ground
500 g garlic, ground with vinegar
500 g sugar
1½ cup chilli powder
Salt to taste

Wash and dry fish roe.

Peel cardamoms and crush with cinnamon, and cloves.

Heat oil and 400 ml vinegar together. Add roe and fry. Remove, cool and cut into one-inch pieces.

Beat mustard and vinegar till strong enough to sting eyes and nose when sniffed.

Reheat oil and add all ingredients except chilli powder, salt and roe. Fry lightly.

Add chilli powder and remove from fire. Add roe and salt to taste. Cool and bottle.

The pickle must be covered in oil. Keep for 2-4 days before using. This pickle will stay for a year.

TAJI SARDINE NU ACHAR
(Fresh sardine pickle)

This pickle was made famous by my kaki (aunt) Khorshed Gustad Mehta—who would literally make it by the gallon and distribute to all her relations in India from Karachi.

> **1 kg fresh sardines**
> **2-3 tbsp salt**
> **¾ litre sesame seed oil**
> **2 heaped tbsp mustard powder**
> **1½ cup Navsari vinegar**
> **1½ pods garlic**
> **1 tbsp cumin seeds**
> **2 tbsp chilli powder**
> **Salt to taste**

Clean and gut fish. Pat dry. Rub with a little salt and shallow fry in a little of the measured oil. Leave in oil to cool.

Beat mustard with a little vinegar for 15 minutes, till strong enough to sting eyes and nose when sniffed.

Coarsely grind garlic and cumin seeds in remaining vinegar. Add chilli powder to make a paste. Heat remaining oil and fry ground spices, adding salt to taste. When oil rises to top, remove pan from heat. Cool and mix in mustard paste.

Cover base of a glass jar with mixture. Dip cooked sardines, one by one into remaining mixture and place in jar. Pour in any remaining spices on top of fish in jar.

Keep for 1-2 days before use. It will keep for 6-8 months.

COLMI NU ACHAR

(Prawn pickle)

2 kg prawns, shelled, cleaned and deveined
4 tbsp salt
3 pods garlic, peeled and coarsely ground in a little vinegar
2 tbsp chilli powder
2 tbsp cumin seeds, dry roasted and ground
1½ cup Navsari vinegar
500 g sesame seed oil
2 tbsp mustard powder

Rub prawns with salt and keep aside.

Mix garlic, chilli powder, cumin powder and salt to a paste with a little vinegar. Put prawns in half this mixture and keep aside for half an hour.

Heat half the oil and fry remaining paste lightly. In another pan, heat remaining oil and fry prawns. Add fried spices and oil and sauté lightly for a few minutes till moisture from prawns evaporates. Cool.

Beat mustard with remaining vinegar for 15 minutes, till strong enough to sting eyes and nose when sniffed. Mix with cooled prawns.

When completely cold, place in a glass jar. Keep for 2-3 days before using. The pickle must be covered with oil

MASALA NI SUKHI MACHHI NO ACHAR

(Dried fish pickle)

25 small fresh pomfret, sole, plaice or fillet of any fish
Banana leaves
Salt solution made with 3 litre water and 3 tbsp salt

Grind together in 1½ cups Navsari vinegar and leave for 48 hours:

2½ cups cumin seeds
1¼ cup mustard seeds
250 g dried red chillies
250 g garlic
250 g cleaned tamarind

Slice fish through bone about three-quarter inch thick and rub with salt. Put fish on banana leaves and place on a platter. Cover with more leaves and leave overnight.

The next day wash fish in salt solution, Grease fish with a little oil, place on a platter, cover with thin muslin cloth and leave in the sun to dry completely. This may take one or two days.

Cover dried fish with ground spices and fry each piece gently before serving.

SUKHI GHARUB NU ACHHAR
(Dry fish roe pickle)

- 1½ kg dry fish roe
- 125 g garlic
- ½ cup cumin seeds
- 1 cup chilli powder
- ¾ litre Navsari vinegar
- 250 g sesame seed oil
- 250 g mustard oil
- Salt to taste

Wash, dry and cut fish roe into 2-inch pieces. Peel garlic and keep one pod aside. Grind remaining garlic with cumin seeds and chilli powder in a little vinegar.

Fry fish roe in a little mixed sesame seed and mustard oil. Remove from pan and drain. Add remaining mixed oil to pan and fry ground spices and salt for 1-2 minutes. Add remaining vinegar and garlic and cook till oil floats on top. Add fish roe and bring gently to boil 2-3 times. Leave pickle in pan for 24 hours to cool completely.

Place in a glass jar, making sure that it is completely covered with oil. The oil preserves the pickle and if more is required, boil some, cool and pour over.

Note : You can prepare Bombay duck pickle in the same way, making sure to clean fish well before use.

GOSHT NU ACHAR
(Lamb pickle)

2 kg lamb or game meat, washed, dried, deboned and cut into
2" pieces with fat removed
3 pieces cinnamon (1" each)
2 tbsp cloves
10-12 green cardamoms
Sugar to taste
Salt to taste
¾ litre Navsari vinegar
400 g oil

Grind with a little vinegar to a thick paste:
3" piece ginger
3 large pods garlic
1 tbsp cumin seeds
½ cup coriander seeds
10 black peppercorns
10 dried red chillies

Rub some salt into meat pieces and fry in oil with whole spices till well browned and cooked. Add ground spices, sugar, vinegar and salt. Simmer gently till spices and meat are well amalgamated and cooked through.

Cool and bottle, keeping pickle covered with oil. Keep in a cool place. Allow to mature for about 15 days:

Nice to take on picnics. It will keep for 6-12 months.

CHUTNEYS

Please remember that all chutneys will thicken further after cooking.

LEEBU NI CHUTNEY
(Lime chutney from Navsari)

24 limes with thin skins
2-4 tbsp sea or rock salt, or to taste
1 kg sugar
250 g ginger
125 g garlic
1¼ cup chilli powder
500 g dates, seeded

Wash and dry limes, cut into four pieces each. Mix with salt and place in a glass jar for 3 days, shaking the jar 2-3 times a day. Remove from jar and place in a tray, cover with a fine muslin cloth and leave in the sun for 3 days.

Mince limes coarsely with remaining ingredients and store in a glass jar. Keep for a week to mature before use. Keep in a cool place and use within 6 months.

KERI NI CHUTNEY
(Mango chutney from Navsari)

This recipe and the next one have been given to me by Mrs Mehroo Meherji Rana K Dastur of Navsari.

1 kg half-ripe half-raw Rajapuri mangoes (or any other good variety)
500 g sugar
500 g jaggery
500 g ginger, peeled and sliced
300 g garlic, peeled and chopped
Salt to taste
Navsari vinegar as needed

Peel and grate mangoes. Mix all ingredients with vinegar to make a loose mixture. Leave for 2 hours. Place in a pan and cook gently on low heat stirring continuously till you get a three-thread syrup.

Cool and store in glass jars. Keep for 2 weeks for chutney to mature before use. It will keep for over a year.

MEETHI KERI NI KATRI NI CHUTNEY
(Sweet sliced mango chutney)

4 kg half-ripe mangoes
5-6 kg sugar, depending on sourness of mangoes
1 litre Navsari vinegar
700 g sultanas (kishmish)
Salt to taste

Grind in a little of the measured vinegar:
150 g garlic
100 ginger
30 g dry red chillies or
1 tbsp chilli powder

Peel and slice mangoes. Dissolve sugar in some vinegar to make a syrup. Add sliced mangoes and bring to boil. Add ground spices and half the sultanas and simmer till mixture thickens, stirring continuously. Add salt and remove from heat.

Cool, add remaining sultanas and vinegar and replace on heat. Simmer for 10 minutes, cool and bottle in glass jars. It will keep for over a year.

Note : You will have to judge the amount of sugar by tasting a little of the mango. Juice of two limes improves the flavour.

GOOSEBERRY CHUTNEY

3 kg gooseberry, peeled, washed and dried
2 kg sugar
2-3 tbsp chilli powder
½ litre vinegar
Salt to taste

Grind with a little vinegar:
3 pods garlic
100 g ginger

Crush gooseberries slightly with sugar and simmer till sugar has dissolved. Add remaining ingredients and simmer till it has reached the consistency of a chutney.

FRESH CHUTNEYS

COCONUT CHUTNEY

There are many ways in which this chutney is made. Try my way!

1 large ripe coconut, grated
100 g coriander leaves with tender stems
4 green chillies, seeded
1 bunch mint leaves
1" piece ginger
6-8 cloves garlic
1 tsp cumin powder
½ tsp sugar
Juice of 2 limes
Salt to taste

Grind all ingredients together. Mix well and serve.

POORANVATI'S CHUTNEY

Pooranvati was my children's ayah and my daughter Erna would spend many hours with her in her room, while she was cooking her food. While I was doing the course at the Cordon Bleu School of Cookery, we were taught how to cut onions the French way. I was most impressed and returned home to show Erna this new method of chopping onions, when she informed me that Pooranvati always chopped her onions that way!

Here is her chutney, which I think is quite delicious.

1 large onion
2 green chillies
2 tbsp coriander leaves with tender stems
8-10 mint leaves
2 tomatoes
4-6 cloves garlic
A pinch of sugar
Salt to taste

Grind all ingredients together.
Serve with bhajias or plain dal and rice.

SOOKHA BOOMLA NI CHUTNEY (1)
(Bombay duck chutney)

25 Bombay duck
Juice of 1 lime
Salt to taste
3 tbsp sesame seed oil

Grind together:
10 dried red chillies
2 pods garlic
2½" piece ginger

Remove head, clean out stomach and wash Bombay duck. Dry and remove backbone. Fry in hot oil till crisp, but not burnt. Cool and grind.

Fry ground spices in oil and mix with Bombay duck. Add lime juice and salt to taste.

Cool and store in glass jars.

It will keep in the refrigerator for one month. If you grind spices in vinegar, the chutney will keep for 6-8 months.

SOOKHA BOOMLA NI CHUTNEY (2)
(Bombay duck chutney)

25 Bombay duck
3 tbsp sesame seed oil
Juice of 1 lime
Salt to taste

Grind together:
6-8 green chillies
4 tbsp coriander leaves with tender stems
2½" piece ginger
2 pods garlic
½ grated fresh coconut

Remove head and clean stomach of Bombay duck. Wash well and dry. Remove backbone. Heat oil and fry fish till crisp. Cool and grind. Mix with ground spices and fry again. Add salt and lime juice to taste.

This will stay in the refrigerator for one week.

Note : Both the above chutneys can be converted into garlic chutney by not adding the Bombay duck. These chutneys can be served with a dal or rotla.

SOOKHA KOOTO NO POWDER
(Dried shrimp powder)

250 g dried kooto (very tiny shrimps), cleaned of all other small fish which is usually mixed with them
2 tbsp cumin powder

Sesame seed oil for shallow drying
Chilli powder to taste
Salt to taste

Wash kooto in a sieve under running water to remove all sand, spread on a tray covered with a muslin or net cloth and dry completely in the sun.

Fry kooto with cumin till crisp. Cool and powder coarsely. Add chilli powder and salt to taste. Bottle.

This can stay for about 4-6 months and is delicious with plain dal and rice.

COCUM CHUTNEY
(Dry sour plum chutney)

3 tbsp cocum (dry sour plums)
6 dried red chillies
⅓ cup jaggery
1 tbsp poppy seeds (khus khus)
2 tbsp coriander seeds
1 tbsp cumin seeds
Navsari vinegar as needed
Salt to taste

Wash cocum in a little vinegar. Soak chillies in vinegar. Grate jaggery and dry roast remaining ingredients.

Grind all ingredients together, adding a little vinegar as required to make a paste.

This will stay in the refrigerator for about one month.

KANDA NI CHUTNEY
(Onion chutney)

200 g white onions
1-2 tbsp ghee
Salt to taste

Grind together:
6 dried red chillies
5-6 dried dates, seeded

Peel and chop onions. Heat ghee and fry onions till light brown. Mix with ground spices and salt.

This will stay in the refrigerator for 2-3 days.

PRESERVES (MURUMBAS)

BAELFRUIT MURUMBO
(Woodapple preserve)

5 kg ripe woodapples (baelfruit)
2½ kg sugar
Juice of 2-3 limes
1 tsp salt
2 tsp crushed seeds of green cardamom

Break open fruit. Lightly oil your hands and remove all seeds and stringy part of fruit. Spoon out the fruit from the shell, cut into 2-inch pieces and pierce with a fork.

Make a sugar syrup with half litre water, lime juice and sugar to a one-thread consistency. Add fruit and continue cooking till syrup thickens. Add salt and remove fruit from syrup. Continue cooking till syrup begins to set. Add crushed cardamom and gently mix in fruit. Cool and bottle.

KAPELI KERI NO MURAMBO
(Sliced mango preserve)

10 kg half-raw, half-ripe mangoes
125 g chemical lime (choonam)
1 litre water for lime solution

    7½ kg sugar
    6 litres water for syrup
    2 limes
    3-4 pieces cinnamon, 1" each
    2 tbsp pounded seeds of green cardamom
    2 tsp salt

Peel and cut mango into 1½-inch chunks. Pierce with a fork. Mix chemical lime with water and allow lime to settle. Gently strain water and mix with mango pieces. Leave for 8-10 hours. Wash mangoes in fresh water.

Make sugar syrup. Squeeze in lime juice along with cut limes. Bring to boil. Remove scum and strain.

Add mangoes and cinnamon. Simmer till mangoes are cooked and syrup is thickened. Add salt and cardamom. Cool completely and bottle.

The original recipe uses double the quantity, as this preserve will stay for over a year.

KORA NO MURAMBO (1)
(Ash gourd preserve)

The recipe was given to me by Mrs Mulmul Pochaji Billimoria in Pune.

    1 kg ash gourd (petha)
    Peel of 2 oranges
    50 g chemical lime (choonam)
    750 g sugar
    Juice of 5 limes
    Rind of 1 lime
    1 tsp salt
    6-8 peeled and crushed green cardamoms

Peel and discard soft part of gourd. Cut into 1½-inch slices. Remove pith from orange peel and slice thinly as for marmalade. Blanch and dry. Soak chemical lime in enough water to cover gourd. Allow lime to settle and strain. Soak gourd in strained water for 1-2 hours.

Dissolve sugar in one cup water and bring to boil. Add rind and juice of one lime, boil and strain.

Squeeze out water from gourd and add gourd to syrup. Cook rapidly till most of the liquid is absorbed. Lower heat, add orange peel, remaining lime juice and salt. Continue cooking till syrup is thick. Add cardamoms, cool completely and bottle.

This preserve should set like a thick jam.

KORA NO MURAMBO (2)
(Ash gourd preserve)

3 kg ash gourd (petha)
2½ kg sugar
Juice of 2 limes
A pinch of salt
2-3 tbsp rose-water
6-8 green cardamoms, peeled and crushed

Peel and grate hard part of gourd. Discard soft part.

Squeeze out excess water from gourd. Mix gourd with sugar, lime juice and a pinch of salt and simmer gently, stirring continuously till soft, and light brown in colour. Remove from fire, cool, add rose-water and cardamoms and bottle.

A preserve can also be made with the soft part of the gourd, using equal parts of sugar, but this does not stay longer than a month, and must be eaten first.

KACHI KERI NO MURAMBO
(Raw mango preserve)

4 kg raw mangoes, peeled and grated
4½ kg sugar
2 litres water
Juice and peel of 2 limes

Pinch of salt
3 tbsp pounded green cardamoms with skin

Soak mangoes with enough water to cover for 2 hours. Strain through a colander.

Caramelize 3 tbsp sugar by placing in a pan on gentle heat and cooking till it melts and turns brown. Add remaining sugar and 2 litres water and bring to boil. Add lime juice and peel and continue boiling for 2-3 minutes. Strain through a wet muslin cloth and continue cooking till thick.

Add mangoes and salt and cook further on low heart, stirring continuously till mangoes are cooked and mixture is semi-set. It will thicken further when cool.

Sprinkle with cardamoms, mix well and bottle.

NASPATI NO MURAMBO
(Naspati pear preserve)

This recipe was my mother-in-law's speciality.

2 kg small naspati pears, with stems if possible
Juice of 3 limes
2 cups water
1 kg sugar
6 green cardamoms, peeled and crushed
Pinch of salt

Peel pears thinly, leaving a half-inch circle on top with stem. With an apple-corer or pointed knife, scoop out core from base of pear. Gently pierce pears with a fork, without breaking them.

Make sugar syrup with sugar, water, lime juice, cardamoms and salt. Add pears and simmer gently till fruit is cooked and has a golden hue and syrup is thick. Cool and bottle.

If you have small pears of even size, you could serve halved pears with icecream or whipped cream for dessert.

PEACH NO MURAMBO
(Peach preserve)

2 kg firm ripe peaches, peeled and halved
2 kg sugar
2-3 tbsp water
2" piece cinnamon
Juice of 1 lime
Pinch of salt

Place peaches with all ingredients and peach stones in a large flat bottomed pan, where all peach pieces can fit in one layer.

Cook gently till sugar has dissolved and peaches have turned light brown at the bottom. Carefully turn over peaches and continue cooking gently till all of them are browned. Allow syrup to thicken. Cool, remove stones carefully and bottle.

A peg of brandy added while peaches are still warm would greatly enhance the flavour.

SHERBETS

GULAB NO SHERBET
(Rose sherbet)

1 kg fresh red rose petals
½ kg sugar
Juice of 1 lime
1 tsp rose essence
1-2 drops red food colouring
A pinch of salt

Dry rose petals for two days and chop. Combine with one litre water and pressure cook for 20 minutes. Strain and squeeze out juice from petals. Add sugar to water and cook on low heat till dissolved. Bring to boil and cook rapidly till syrup is slightly thick. Remove from heat, and add remaining ingredients.

Cool and bottle.

BAELFRUIT SHERBET

(Woodapple sherbet)

4 large woodapples (baelfruit)
Sugar equal to weight of woodapple pulp
1 litre water
Juice of 1-2 limes
A pinch of salt

Break open fruit. Lightly oil your hands and remove all seeds and stringy part of fruit. Mash fruit and weigh. Weigh an equal amount of sugar. Pass fruit through a sieve, adding a little water to facilitate straining .

Mix purée with water and sugar. Cook till thick. Add lime juice and salt.

Cool, bottle and store in refrigerator. Excellent for a weak stomach.

To serve, add 2 tablespoons in a glass of cold water. Mix well and serve.

DRY MIXTURES

SUVA

½ kg dill seeds (sua)
1 cup almonds
1 cup char magaz (cucumber, marsh melon, pumpkin and water melon seeds)
½ cup aniseed (saunf)

Dry roast each ingredient, mix and bottle.

Excellent for a nursing mother.

DHANA DAL MIXTURE

500 g husked coriander (dhania ka dal)
250 g char magaz

200 g red pumpkin seeds
250 g aniseed (saunf)
1 cup white sesame seeds (til)
4 tbsp poppy seeds (khus khus)
1 tsp salt

Dry roast each ingredient separately. Cool, mix with salt and bottle.

A good after-meal muncher

Note : Coriander dal is made by removing outer crust of coriander seeds. It is available in shops where condiments are bought.

20

Kitchen Medicine

Here are some grandmother's remedies. My husband, a doctor, insists tongue in cheek, that Parsi women will overthrow medical science! But do try them out.

HOT COMPRESS OF AJWAIN—AJMA NO SEK

This is excellent for infants, babies, children and even adults who have colds and coughs.

Heat some ajwain on a griddle and put it into a piece of flannel cloth or large folded handkerchief. Apply it on the chest, temples, forehead and back for a few minutes, lightly pressing these areas. Then apply any balm or a paste of nutmeg. This is made by mixing nutmeg powder with water and heating it.

HOT COMPRESS OF PAAN—PAAN NO SEK

In the olden days, when an infant developed a colic, the mother would rub castor oil on a paan leaf and heat it over an oil lamp. She would then place it on the baby's navel and tie it down with a bandage to keep it in place. It is a remarkable cure. Before applying paan on baby's stomach make sure it is not too hot.

PURE TURMERIC POWDER

It must be pure and has remarkable healing powers. If put on small cuts it helps to stop the bleeding. One teaspoon of pure turmeric powder mixed with half a cup of milk and 1-2 teaspoons crushed, large crystals of sugar, if drunk by any person suspected of having sustained an internal injury, will help to stop any haemorrhage that may have started.

MANGO TURMERIC—AMA HURAD

This is a type of turmeric which has a flavour of raw mango. It makes a delicious pickle mixed with lime juice, salt and slit green chillies. Dried, it has excellent medicinal value. If ground in water and then heated and applied on bruises, swelling, sprains or a twisted ankle, it helps in faster healing.

SANDALWOOD PASTE

Sandalwood rubbed on a clean dry curry stone or pure sandalwood, powdered and made into a paste with rose-water when applied to pimples will help them disappear.

PEACH STONE

Peach stones scraped with rose-water, made into a paste and applied to pimples also help them disappear.

WOOD APPLE SYRUP—BAELFRUIT SYRUP

The syrup or muramba made with this fruit helps to soothe an upset stomach. Fresh baelfruit made into a drink is very refreshing, soothing and cooling. The recipes for these have been given earlier.

LIMBU PANI

The humble limbu pani drunk at the height of summer with a pinch of salt before going out will reduce exhaustion and help to prevent sunstroke.

TO KEEP SUNSTROKE AT BAY

Boil or dry roast on the fire two raw mangoes. Peel and extract the pulp. Sieve. Add chopped mint, sugar, salt, roasted crushed cumin seeds to taste. Serve as a chutney or as a drink by adding one tablespoon to a glass of a cold water. It is a very cooling drink.

SAGO KANJI—SABUDANA KANJI

Soak sago seeds in water for 15 minutes. Cook with water and sugar. Sprinkle with a little nutmeg and cardamom powder. This helps to soothe an upset stomach as well as bind it.

ROSE PETAL JAM—GOOLKAND

This is a jam made from red rose petals and is good for weak stomachs. The recipe for this has been given earlier.

ROCK SALT

Coarsely powdered rock salt, heated on a griddle, wrapped in a cloth and applied to rheumatic joints helps to relieve pain.

KAVO

Kavo is a medicinal drink useful in curing colds and coughs. In one cup of water boil 3-4 cloves, a small piece of cinnamon, 4-5 black peppercorns, a blade of lemon grass, half teaspoon ajwain and a small piece of fresh ginger. Simmer and reduce to half. Strain and add half teaspoon honey with a squeeze of lime and a dash of brandy. This should be sipped as hot as possible the last thing at night. It helps in relieving colds and coughs and gives a really good night's sleep. One can have it 2-3 times in the daytime as well.

When my husband was in the Air Force, all the young pilots would come to me for their treatment of colds and coughs and I would give them this kavo—with an extra dash of brandy of course!

RICE PASTE

This is very good for small burns. Apply a paste made with rice flour and cold water immediately to the burn.

DOODH SODA

This is a refreshing light drink to give someone who has fever. It is not too heavy on the stomach and is very soothing. Mix half a cup of milk with half a cup of chilled soda water. Add sugar to taste and a drop of vanilla.

EYE WASH TO IMPROVE EYE SIGHT

Rinse out in running water one teaspoon whole harar, one teaspoon whole bhera and one teaspoon whole amla. Soak it overnight in one cup water. The next day strain and use it as an eye wash. It can bring down the number of your glasses.

FOR BROKEN BONES AND SPRAINS

Cook 25 g dried ama harad, 15 g chotseji, 20 g durd maida, 25 g haad jor in 50 g mustard oil and store. When required heat and apply. Wrap with Arand ka putta (castor oil leaves) or cotton wool and a bandage. It helps in the healing process. All these ingredients are available at herbal medicine shops.

FOR EXCELLENT COMPLEXIONS

For your daughter, apply fresh milk or cream on the face, leave till dry and wash off. During the bath rub her body with bread soaked in milk and then wash off with soap. If this is done from babyhood till the age of six or seven, she will have a beautiful complexion and skin.

AN EXCELLENT FACE PACK

Make a paste with 2 tablespoons Fuller's earth or kaolin powder, two drops Savalon antiseptic lotion, ¼ teaspoon lacto calamine, one teaspoon Milk of Magnesia, two drops of a light cologne. Add 4 teaspoon skin tonic and 2 teaspoons almond oil or fresh cream and rose-water. Apply onto a clean skin and allow to dry. Wash off. The result is stunning even on a 72 year-old!

FOR PRICKLY HEAT

Mix multani mitti, sesame seed oil and rose-water to a paste. Apply and leave for half an hour.

Boil some neem leaves with their stems in water for about half an hour. Pour the water into a bucket of hot water and bathe.

21

Chalo Jamva Avoji

About thirty to fifty years ago, lagans and navjotes were held at Albless Bagh, Cama Bagh, Colaba ni Agiari, or in the grounds of the palatial homes of the richer Parsis of Bombay. Soon after the ceremony, a call would be heard—'*Chalo jamva avoji*'—come to eat. It was not a statement, but a beautifully sung call—most pleasing to the ear, in the soft and genteel atmosphere of the times, and in anticipation of the banquet to follow.

On hearing the call, the guests would approach the row upon row of neatly arranged tables, covered with spotless white tablecloths (changed for every sitting), and laid out with shining clean banana leaves, glasses, napkins, and nowadays, spoons and forks. They would wind their way amongst the tables, greeting each other, sometimes stopping to chat a moment with an acquaintance they had not met earlier in the evening and selecting their seats to sit with friends.

No one would think of being so ill-mannered as to go to the tables before this call was heard. There was no jostling or pushing or hasty reserving of chairs. Nowadays, there is hardly any need for the call. No sooner is the ceremony over, and there is a mad rush for the tables! Hardly has one completed the meal, sometimes even before the dessert is served, and you will find someone standing behind you, to take your place! And if he is too hungry he may even take a couple of wafers off your banana leaf!

But in the old days, that was the call everyone waited for as the food served on these occasions was and still is superlative.

Many years ago the wedding feast was a vegetarian one, in deference to our Hindu friends' beliefs. Nowadays a paraji no bhonu (a vegetarian meal) is served separately for vegetarians and there are special caterers who prepare this food apart from those who prepare the traditional non-vegetarian meals.

Parsi navjote and lagan feasts are another legend, prepared by people who specialize in cooking for these occasions. When all the guests are seated, and at a given signal, men dressed in spotless white start serving from large thalis.

The lagan or meva nu achar comes first. It is placed on the top left-hand corner of the leaf. Next come the rotli, which are placed next to the achar. We used to get a wheat and a rice rotli, but now we only get the wheat ones—maybe the art is lost or no one is inclined to take the trouble to prepare the rice ones.

Fine yellow crisp wafers arrive next, in large thals and served with a karchi or tavato. It is a wonder how a man can support a huge tray one-and-a-half-feet in diameter on his left hand and serve with his right, without dropping a single wafer! Connoisseurs of these meals can tell at this stage, whether the food is going to be good or mediocre.

If a paneer is on the menu it is served now. This is usually the topli nu paneer ordered from Surat or made locally.

Fish comes next. It can be tareli machi, patra ni machi or machi no sas.

Hardly has one completed the fish, when the chicken dish

arrives. Traditional chicken dishes are sali ma murghi, murghi na farcha, mughlai murghi or masala ni murghi. If a murambo is ordered, it is served at this stage.

Now comes any of the following meat dishes—sali ma boti, tamatar ni gravy ma cutlets, kid gosht (if made correctly it is one of the finest ways in the world of serving lamb) jerdaloo ma gosht, or meva ma gosht.

The eggs arrive next. The method by which fried eggs are prepared is quite an art. A little water is placed in the base of large greased thals, and eggs are carefully broken in the thals. They are cooked till just set. Papeta per eeda and tamatar per eeda are the most popular, but sometimes akoori is also served. With the eggs is served the custer and khatu meethu estew if either are ordered and then the aleti paleti, which is usually served in the last panth or sitting, when the host family dine.

All the while, the achar, rotli and soft drinks are offered and in the old days, before prohibition struck Bombay, the finest of Scotch whiskies, brandies, sherries and port were also served.

Now each dish, from wafers onwards is repeated for a second helping. Then comes the piece de resistance—the pulao and dal. The white and yellow rice with succulent pieces of meat, scented with saffron is so delicious that one could eat it plain without any accompaniment. This too is offered a second time.

When one has finished eating, one folds the patru or banana leaf in three and puts the spoon and fork on top. These are removed with great dexterity, without a drop of food falling on the cloth. Now comes the man with the karasio of hot water and a basin to wash the hands. One usually drops in a coin for the man. My mother, after washing her hands would rinse them in Hennesey brandy (which cost Rs. 5 per bottle in those days)!

Kulfi rounds off the meal and it used to be served with a

small plate of delicious crisp macaroons, a few almonds, pistachios, paan and sopari on the side.

Salamatis (toasts) would traditionally be offered to the King (even though foreign!) and then later to our own country's President, bride and groom, and their parents.

If the function was held in the morning the menu would be slightly different. It would start with meethu dhai and sev, a small yellow banana and some sugar in case one needed it. Instead of the pulao dar there would be dhan dar ne patio.

Some Parsis are doing away with the entire concept of the traditional patra no bhonu (meal on the banana leaf) and hold receptions in five star hotels. It is sad that not only are we losing a great tradition, but an excellent art—that of cooking the lagan nu bhonu (the wedding feast) will be lost forever!

The delightful ambience of a garden or bagh, with the food served on a banana leaf is so different from the food served on a plate in a hall. It is like the difference between drinking champagne from a fine glass or a thick cup! A beautiful way of life and these delightful customs are gradually dying out, and with them, the grand caterers, who have served the community for generations by producing food fit for the gods!

Glossary

ENGLISH	HINDI	PARSI GUJARATI
Condiments	**Masala**	**Masalo**
Allspice	Kabab cheeni	Kabab cheeni
Aniseed	Saunf	Variali
Asafoetida	Hing	Hing
Caraway	Shahi Jeera	Shah jeeru
Cardamom		
- white/green	Elychi	Elchi
- black	Bari elychi	Elcho
Chilli		
- green	Hari mirchi	Leela murcha
- red	Lal mirchi	Lal murcha
Cinnamon	Dalchini	Tuj
Clove	Laung	Lavang
Coriander seeds		
- whole	Dhania	Sookha dhana
- husked	Dhania ka dal	Dhana ni dar

Cumin seeds	Jeera	Jheeru
- black	Shahi jeera	Shah jheru
Curry leaves	Curry patta	Curry patta
Dill	Sua	Suva
Fenugreek	Methi	Methi
Mace	Javitri	Javitri
Mango powder		
- dried	Amchur	Amchur
Mustard powder	Peesi hui rai	Peeseli rai
Musard seeds		
- whole	Rai	Rai
- split	Rai ka dal	Rai ni dar
Nutmeg	Jaiphul	Jaiphul
Onion seeds	Kalaunji	Kalaunji
Pepper		
- black	Kali mirch	Kari mari
- long	Peeper	Peeper
Pomegranate seeds		
- dried	Sooké Anaar dana	Sooka daram na dana
Poppy seeds	Khus khus	Khus khus
Saffron	Kesar	Kesar
Star anise	Badian	Badian
Turmeric	Haldi	Hurd
Whole garam masala	Sabut garam masala	Akho garam masalo
- black pepper	Kali mirch	Kari mari
- clove	Laung	Lavang
- cardamom	Elychi	Elchi
- cinnamon	Dalchini	Taj
- bay leaves	Tej patta	Tej patta

Dry fruit	**Meva**	**Mevo**
Apricot	Khurmani	Jurdaloo
Chinese date	Unaf	Unaf
Currant		
- black	Kala angur	Kari darak
Fig	Anjeer	Anjeer
Indian black		
sour plum	Cocum	Cocum
Raisin	Munakka	Munakka
Sultana	Kishmish	Kismis

Fish	**Machhi**	**Machhi**
Bombay duck	Sookha bomil	Sookha boomla
Butter fish	Bekti	Bekti
Crab	Kakda	Karachla
Carp	Rahu	Rahu
Clam	Tisri	Tisri
Roe	Ghurab	Ghurab
Indian salmon	Ramus	Ramus
Lamprey family		
- dried and salted	Sookha bomil	Sookha boomla
- fresh	Taja boomil	Taja boomla
Lobster	Barra jhinga	Sandh
Mackerel	Bhangra	Bhangra
Mud fish	Laevta	Laevta
Mullet	Boi	Boi
Oyster	Kaloo	Kaloo
Pomfret		
- white	Chamna	Chamno
- black	Halva	Halva
Prawn	Jhinga	Colmi
Sardine	Sardine	Sardine
Shrimp	Jhinga	Colmi
- very small	Chote jhinga	Ambar or Kooto
Shad	Hilsa	Bhing

Fowl	Parinde	
Chicken	Murgh	Murghi
Duck	Buttak	Buttak
Hen	Murgh	Murghi
Partridge	Teetar	Teetar
Peacock	Mor	Mor
Quail	Butaira	Buttur
Rooster	Murga	Murgho
Wild duck	Murghabi	Jungli buttak
Wild fowl	Jungli murgh	Jungli murghi

Fruit	Phul	Ful
Apple	Seb	Saparchan
Apricot	Khurmani	Jurdaloo
Banana	Kela	Kera
Black currant	Kala angur	Kari darak
Cherry	Cherry	Cherry
Custard apple	Sitaphul	Andoos
Date	Khajoor	Khajoor
Fig	Anjeer	Anjeer
Grapes	Angur	Darak
Guava	Amrud	Per
Hog plum	Amla	Amla
Indian plum	Ber	Bor
Ice fruit of		
date palm	Targola	Galeli
Jackfruit	Kathal	Funus
Leechi	Leechi	Leechi
Lemon	Gul gul	Chinai leebu
Lime	Nimbu	Leebu
Mango	Aam	Keri
Marsh melon	Kharbooja	Kharbooj
Orange	Narangi or Suntra	Suntra
Papaya	Papita	Papau
Peach	Aadu	Shaftaloo

Pear	Bagugosho	Bagugosha
Pineapple	Ananus	Ananus
Pomegranate	Anar	Darum
Pomello	Chakotra	Papenus
Plum	Aadu bukhara	Alu
Strawberry	Jharber	Strawberry
Sugarcane	Ganna	Serdi
Sweet lime	Mosumbi	Mosumbi
Water melon	Tarbooj	Kalingar
Wood apple	Bael	Bael
Wood pear	Naspati	Naspati

Game	**Shikar**	**Shikar**
Hare	Khargosh	Sasloo
Rabbit	Khargosh	Sasloo
Vension	Hiran ka gosht	Hurun nu ghost
Wild boar	Jungli soovar	Jungli dukkar

Grain	**Anaj**	**Anaj**
Barley	Jau	Jau
Gram	Channa	Channa
Gram flour	Besan	Channa no atto
Maize	Makki	Makai
Maize flour	Makki ka atta	Makai no atto
Millet	Bajra	Bajra or bajri
Milo	Jowar	Jowar
Rice		
- uncooked	Chawal	Chokha
- cooked	Chawal	Chawal
- flour	Chawal ka atta	Chokha no atto
- pressed	Poha	Pava
- puffed	Murmura	Mumra
Sago	Saboodana	Saboodana
Semolina	Sooji or rava	Sooji or rava
Vermicelli	Sevian	Sev

Wheat		
- whole	Gehun	Ghau
- broken	Dalia	Dalia
- flour	Atta	Ghau no atto
- refined flour	Maida	Maido

Herbs	**Hara masala**	**Leelo masalo**
Aniseed	Saunf	Variali
Basil	Tulsi	Tulsi
Bay leaf	Tej patta	Tamal patta
Coriander leaves	Hara dhania	Kothmir
Curry leaves	Cury patta	Curry patta
Dill	Sua saag	Sau ni bhaji
Fenugreek leaves	Methi saag	Methi ni bhaji
Garlic	Lehsun	Lusun
Ginger		
- dried	Soonth	Soonth
- green	Adrak	Adu
Mint	Pudina	Phudino
Parsley	Ajmod	
Thyme	Ajuan patta	Ajma na patra

Meat	**Gosht**	**Gosht**
Beef	Gai ka Gosht	Gai nu gosht
Bone	Huddi	Hudka
Brain	Bheja	Bheja
Head	Sirr	Mathu
Heart	Dil	Jiggar
Kidney	Gurda	Bukko
Lamb	Med ka gosht	Bakri nu gosht
Liver	Kaleji	Kaleji
Marrow	Ghoor	Goor
Fat of mutton or beef	Churbi	Churbi
Mince	Kheema	Kheemo

Mutton	Bakri ka gosht	Bakri nu gosht
Neck	Gurdan	Gurdan
Pork	Suvar ka gosht	Dukkar nu gosht
Rib	Seena	Seenu
Sweetbread	Gurda kapura	Safed bukko
Tongue	Zabaan	Jeeb
Tripe	Hojri	Hojri
Trotters	Paya	Kharia

Milk Products

Butter	Makhan	Maakhan
-clarified	Ghee	Ghee
Buttermilk	Chhas	Chhas
Cottage cheese	Paneer	Paneer
Cream	Malai	Malai
Curd	Dahi	Dhai
Milk	Doodh	Doodh
-condensed, dry	Khoya	Mavo

Nuts

Almond	Badam	Badam
Cashew	Kajoo	Kajoo
Cheronji	Charoli	Charoli
Groundnut or		
peanut	Mungphali	Singh
Pinenuts	Chilgoza	Chilgoza
Pistachio	Pista	Pasta
Walnut	Akhroat	Akhroat
Water chestnut	Singhara	Singora

Oil

Oil	Tael	Tael
Almond	Badam ka tael	Badam nu tael
Coconut	Nariyal ka tael	Coprel
Gingeli	Til ka tael	Tul nu tel

Groundnut or		
peanut	Mungphali ka tael	Meethu tael
Mustard	Surso ka tael	Rai nu tael
Sesame seed	Til ka teal	Tul nu tael

Pulses	**Dal**	**Dar or kathor**
Bengal gram	Channa dal	Channa ni dar
Black beans	Urad dal	Urad dar
Black eyed beans	Chora	Chora
Chick peas	Kabuli channa	Kabuli channa
Egyptian lentils	Masoor	Masoor
Field beans	Val	Val
Green beans	Moong	Mug
Kidney beans	Rajma	Rajma
Sheet beans	Val	Val
Pigeon peas	Arhar	Toover or toor

Vegetables	**Subji**	**Tarkari**
Arum	Arbi	Arvi
Ash gourd	Petha	Safed koru
Aubergine	Baigan	Vengna
Beetroot	Bhukunder	Beet
Bitter gourd	Karela	Karala
Brinjal	Baigan	Vengna
Cabbage	Band gobi	Kobich
Capsicum	Simla mirch	Mota murch
Carrots	Gajer	Gajer
Cauliflower	Phool gobi	Gobi
Cluster beans	Gwar ki phali	Guvad
Coconut	Nariyal	Nariyal
-Dry	Copra	Copru
Colocasia leaf	Arbi ka putta	Patrel na patra
Courgette	Toori	Tooria
Cucumber	Kheera	Kakri
- ridged	Kakri	Kakri

Drumstick	Surjan ki phali	Sekta ni sing
Elephant foot	Zimikand	Suran
Fenugreek leaves	Methi saag	Methi bhaji
Field or sheet beans	Sem phali	Val papri
French beans	Farash beans	Faraj beans
Gherkin	Kumrukh	Kumrukh
Green peas	Matar	Vatena
Greens	Saag	Bhaji
Horse radish	Sufed mooli	Safed moora
Kohlrabi	Knol-kole	Knol-kole
Ladies fingers	Bhindi	Bheeda
Lettuce	Salit	Salit
Lotus root	Kamal kakri	Kamal kakri
Maize	Makki	Makai
Marrow	Loki or ghia	Dodhi
Mushroom	Gouchi	Dhingri
Mustard leaves	Surson ka sag	Rai ni bhaji
Okra	Bhindi	Bheeda
Onion	Pyaz	Kando
Potato	Alu	Papeta
Pumpkin		
- yellow	Seetaphul, kuddu	Lal koru
- white	Petha	Koru
Red radish	Lal mooli	Lal moora
Ridged gourd	Toori	Tooria
Spinach	Palak	Pala
Sweet potato	Sukerkand	Kan
Tomato	Tamatar	Tamatar
Turnip	Shalgam	Shalgam
Yam	Zimikand	Kand

Miscellaneous

Alum	Phitkari	Fatki
Betel or areca nut	Supari	Sopari
Betel leaf	Paan	Paan

Bread	Double roti	Pau
Chemical lime	Chuna	Chuno
Citric acid	Limbu ka phool	Leeboo na phool
Dough	Goondha	Goodelo atto
Egg	Anda	Eeda
Honey	Shaid	Mudh
Ice	Buraf	Buraf
Isphagula	Isabgul	Isabgul
Jaggery	Gur	Gor
Rose-water	Gulab jhal	Gulab nu pani
Rind	Chhilka	Chhal
Salt	Namak	Meethoo
Saltpetre	Shora	
Seeds of cucumber, water melon, marsh melon, pumpkin	Char magaz	Char magaz
Sugar		
- granulated	Cheeni	Khan
- large crystals	Misri	Saker
Tamarind	Imli	Amli
Toddy	Tari	Tari
Vinegar	Sirka	Surko

Note:

1) Dholi musri: sugar in the form of white batasa
2) Gokkru: the thorny fruit of a herb called gokhru
3) Cocum: garcina indica—Indian black sour plum
4) Pipri mooth na ganth: a dried fruit similar in appearance to cloves
5) Tukhmuri seeds: seeds of a plant belonging to the basil family

Index

(Lime chutney from Navsari)
Meethi Keri ni kair ni chutney   381
(Sweet sliced mango chutney)

CHUTNEYS (FRESH)

Coconut chutney   382
Kopra chutney   383
(Dry sour plum chutney)
Kanda ni chutney   383-80

BEVERAGES

Badam ne magaz ni kanji   115-16
(Kanji of almonds)
Bafloo   118
(Raw mango juice)
Cold coffee   113-14
Egg flip   114-15
Falooda   115
Ghau nu doodh ni kanji   117
Masala ni chai   119-20
(Spiced tea)
Movru (1)   118-19
Movru (2)   119
Ooni ketheli tari   120
(Spiced toddy)
Sooji kanji   116-17
(Kanji of semolina)
Sookha singora ni kanji   116
(Kanji of dried water chestnuts)

Valsad ni kanji   117-18
(Valsad-style kanji)

BREADS (ROTLI)

Bajra na rotla   306
(Millet flour rotla)
Chokha ni rotli   304
(Rice flour rotli)
Dhebra   307
(Thick rotla)
Doodh ma ghau athwa chokha ni rotli   305
(Wheat or rice flour rotli made with milk)
Ghau ni rotli   303-04
(Wheat flour rotli)
Jowar na rotla   307
(Milo flour rotla)
Methi na dhebra   307-08
(Fenugreek leaf rotla)
Poori   305-06
Tari ni rotli   305
(Rotli made with toddy)

CHUTNEYS

Gooseberry chutney   382
Keri ni chutney   380-81
(Mango chutney from Navsari)
Leebu ni chutney   380
(Lime chutney from Navasari)
Meethi keri ni katri ni chutney   381
(Sweet sliced mango chutney)

CHUTNEYS (FRESH)

Coconut chutney   382
Cocum chutney   385
(Dry sour plum chutney)
Kanda ni chutney   385-86

(Onion chutney)
Pooranvati's chutney   383
Sookha boomla ni chutney (1)   383-84
(Bombay duck chutney)
Sookha boomla ni chutney (2)   384
(Bombay duck chutney)
Sookha kooto no powder   384-85
(Dried shrimp powder)

DRY MIXTURES

Dhana dal mixture   391-92
Suva   391

EGGS (EEDA)

Akoori   126-27
(Savoury scrambled eggs)
  - Akoori of hard boiled eggs   130
    (Savoury hard-boiled eggs)
  - Kholi dar ni akoori   128-29
    (Akoori with pigeon peas)
  - Leela lusan ni akoori   128
    (Akoori with green garlic)
  - Meva ni akoori   129
    (Akoori with dry fruits and nuts)
  - Rich Bharuchi akoori   127-28
    (Bharuchi-style scrambled eggs)
Bhaji per eeda   141
(Eggs cooked on fenugreek leaves)
Bheeda per eeda   140
(Eggs cooked on okras)
Bheja per eeda   145
(Eggs cooked on lambs brains)
Charvela eeda   130-32
(Scrambled eggs)
Kanda kothmir per eeda   137-38
(Eggs cooked on onions and coriander)

Kera per eeda   143-44
(Eggs cooked on bananas)
Khari biscot per eeda   149
(Eggs cooked on flaky biscuits)
Kheema per eeda   144
(Eggs cooked on mince meat)
Koota per eeda   146
(Eggs cooked on shrimps)
Omelette(Poro)
  -Bheja no poro   135
    (Brain omelette)
  -Bhoojelo poro   134
    (Baked omelette)
  - Chana no atto no poro   136
    (Gram flour omelette or eggless omelette)
  - Kapela masala no poro   132-33
    (Omelette with chopped vegetables)
  - Kharo poro   132
    (Plain omelette)
  - Lohri per poro   134-35
    (Omelette cooked in a griddle)
  - Peesela masala no poro   133-34
    (Omelette with ground spices)
Papeta per eeda   139-40
(Eggs cooked on potatoes)
Pau per eeda   136-37
(Eggs cooked on bread)
Sekta ni singh na phool per eeda   142
(Eggs cooked on drumstick flowers)
Sookha boomla per eeda   148
(Eggs cooked on Bombay duck)
Tamatar per eeda   138-39
(Eggs cooked on tomatoes)
Tooria ne ambar per eeda   147
(Eggs cooked on courgettes and small shrimps)

FISH (MACHHI)

Bhoojelo Bharuchi bhing   188-89
(Barbequed shad—Bharuch style)
Curries
  - Anna's Goa curry   217
  - Anna's Goa curry without coconut   217-18
  - Devji ni machhi athwa colmi ni curry   211-12
    (Devji's fish or prawn curry)
  - Mr. Fernandes' Goa curry   218
  - Goa curry (1)   213-14
  - Goa curry (2)   215
  - Goa curry (3)   215-16
  - Mother's fish mooli   212-13
  - Philip's Goa curry   216-17
Lamprey (Boomla)
  - Bharuchi tari ma sookha boomla   194-95
    (Bombay duck cooked in toddy—Bharuch style)
  - Devji's Khara boomla   191
    (Savoury lamprey)
  - Devji's masala na boomla   192
    (Devji's spiced lamprey)
  - Lohri per sookha boomla no patio   196
    (Bombay duck patio cooked on a lohri)
  - Mappy's tarela sookha boomla   193-94
    (Fried Bombay duck)
  - Sookha boomla na cutlets   210-11
    (Bombay duck cutlets)
  - Taja boomla no patio   196-97
    (Lamprey patio)
  - Tarapori patio   195
    (Bombay duck patio—Tarapore style)
  - Tarela boomla   189-90
    (Fried lamprey)
  - Tarela masala boomla   190-91
    (Fried spiced lamprey)

- Tarela sookha boomla   193
    (Fried Bombay duck)
Patio
  - Amli ne machhi no patio   199
    (Tamarind and fish patio)
  - Colmi ne bheeda no patio   199-200
    (Prawn and okra patio)
  - Devji's machhi no patio   197-98
    (Devji's fish patio)
  - Gharub ne kora no patio   203-04
    (Fish roe and pumpkin patio)
  - Lohri per sookha boomla no patio   196
    (Bombay duck patio on lohri)
  - Maja's prawn or fish patio   198-99
  - Sandhna no Bharuchi patio   201
    (Jumb prawn patio—Bharuchi style)
  - Sookhi gharab ne govad no patio   202-03
    (Dried fish roe and cluster bean patio)
  - Taaja boomla no patio   196-97
    (Lamprey patio)
  - Taaja kooto athwa ambar no patio   202
    (Small shrimp patio)
  - Tarapori patio   195
    (Bombay duck patio—Tarapore style)
Patra ni machhi   186-87
(Fish in banana leaves)
Prawns (Colmi)
  - Colmi na kabab   210
    (Prawn kababs)
  - Colmi ne bheeda no patio   199-200
    (Prawn and okra patio)
  - Nariel na doodh ma bheeda ne colmi   204-05
    (Prawn and okras cooked in coconut milk)
  - Sandhna no Bharuchi patio   201
    (Jumbo prawn patio—Bharuchi style)

- Taaja kooto athwa ambar no patio   202
  (Small shrimp patio)
Sas
   - Bhoojelo sas   209
   (Baked sweet and sour prawns)
   - Lagan no machhi no sas   208
   (Sweet and sour fish cooked for weddings)
   - Machhi no sas (1)   205-06
   (Sweet and sour fish)
   - Machhi no sas (2)   207
   (Sweet and sour fish)
Tareli machhi   186
(Fried fish)

KITCHEN MEDICINE

An excellent face pack   397
Doodh soda   396
Eye wash to improve eyesight   396
For broken bones and sprains   396
For excellent complexions   396-97
For prickly heat   397
Hot compress of ajwain—Ajma no sek   393
Hot compress of paan—Paan no sek   393-94
Kavo   395-96
Limbu pani   395
Mango Turmeric—Ama hurad   394
Peach stone   394
Pure turmeric powder   394
Rice paste   396
Rock salt   395
Rose petal jam—Goolkand   395
Sago kanji—Sabudana kanji   395
Sandalwood paste   394
To keep sunstroke at bay   395
Wood apple syrup—Baelfruit syrup   394

LENTILS (KATHOR OR DAR)

Channa ni dar   273
(Husked Bengal gram)
Channa ni dar ma gosht   281
(Meat cooked with gram)
Chora   276
(Black eyed beans)
Dhan sakh   282-84
  - Mamaiji's dhan sakh   284-85
Ghambar ni dar   281-82
(Dal cooked for ghambars)
Masoor ma gosht, murghi athwa jeeb   280
(Meat, chicken or tongue cooked with Egyptian lentils)
Mori dar   269-71
(Plain dal)
Mug ni dar   271-72
(Husked green beans)
Sookhi val ni dar   277
(Dried field beans)
Teetori   278-79
(Sprouted field beans)
Toover ni dar (1)   274
(Pigeon peas)
Toover ni dar (2)   275
(Pigeon peas)
Val ni dar   276-77
(Husked field beans)
Valsadi vadu   278
(Sprouted lentils—Valsad style)

MEAT AND POULTRY (GOSHT NE MURGHI)

Aleti paleti   261-62
(Savoury chicken liver and gizzard)
Ambakalia ma gosht   226
(Savoury meat with mangoes)

Annanus ma murghi   226
(Chicken with pineapple)
Badam nu gosht   230-31
(Savoury meat with almonds)
Bafat   240
(Meat cooked in spiced vinegar)
Bafelo rus   238
(Boiled lamb soup or gravy)
Batero   230
(Meat stewed in toddy)
Bhaji dana ma gosht athwa murghi   226
(Savoury meat or chicken with greens and green peas)
Bheeda ma gosht athwa murghi   223
(Savoury meat or chicken with okras)
Bhoojan   244
(Barbecued meat)
Brains (Bheja)
  - Bheja na cutlets   260-61
    (Brain cutlets)
  - Khara bheja   260
    (Savoury brains)
  - Tarela bheja   259-60
    (Fried brains)
Curries
  - Anna's mutton, beef or chicken Goa curry   263-64
  - Bharuchi curry   264-65
  - Gosht ni curry   262-63
    (Lamb curry)
  - Mother's almond and pistachio curry   265-66
  - Mulligatawny   267-68
  - Sau badam ni curry   266-67
    (Hundred almond curry)
Cutlets
  - Chicken cutlets   250-51
  - Frill na cutlets   248
    (Frill cutlets)

- Kheema na cutlets   247-48
  (Mince cutlets)
- Kurkoos   249-50
  (Iranian mince cutlets)
- Tamatar ni gravy ma cutlets   248-49
  (Cutlets in tomato gravy)
Dhai ma gosht athwa murghi   231-32
(Savoury meat or chicken with curd)
Dodhi ma gosht athwa murghi   225
(Savoury meat or chicken with marrow)
Dodhi no dumbo   227-29
(Lamb stuffed in pumpkin)
Doodh ma gosht athwa murghi   225
(Savoury meat or chicken with milk)
Jerdalo ma gosht athwa murghi   223-24
(Savoury meat or chicken with dried apricot)
Kababs
  - Chicken kababs   251
  - Mutton kababs   251
Kanda papeta ma butack, gosht athwa murghi   224
(Savoury duck, meat or chicken with baby onions and potatoes)
Kera ma gosht athwa murghi   224
(Savoury meat or chicken with bananas)
Khara rus chawal   236-37
(Savoury meat or chicken with rice)
Kharu gosht athwa khari murghi   222-23
(Savoury meat or chicken)
Mai vahala murghi   242-43
(Beloved of mother)
Masala roast gosht   241
(Spiced roast leg of lamb)
Meva ma gosht athwa murghi   224
(Savoury meat or chicken. with dry fruits)
Mince(Kheemo)
  - Bafelo kheemo   247
    (Boiled mince)

- Chicken cutlets   250-51
- Chicken kababs   251
- Frill na cutlets   248
  (Frill cutlets)
- Kheema na cutlets   247-48
  (Mince cutlets)
- Kheema na pattis   252-53
  (Mince patties)
- Kheemo   246-47
  (Parsi mince)
- Kurkoos   249-50
  (Iranian mince cutlets)
- Mutton kababs   251
- Tamatar ni gravy ma cutlets   248-49
  (Cutlets in tomato gravy)
Mosumbi na chhal ma gosht athwa murghi   225
(Savoury meat or chicken with sweet lime peel)
Mughlai murghi   241-42
(Mughlai chicken)
Murghi na farcha (1)   254
(Fried chicken)
Murghi na farcha (2)   254-55
(Fried chicken)
Offals
  - Gurchan athwa khurchan   258-59
    (Spiced offals of lamb)
  - Khara kaleji booka   256-57
    (Savoury liver, kidney and sweetbread)
  - Masala ni kaleji   257
    (Spiced fried liver)
  - Mughlai booka   258
    (Mughlai kidneys)
Oomberiu   245-46
(Lamb with sheet beans cooked in an earthen pot buried in
  the ground)
Papeta ma gosht athwa murghi (1)   223

(Savoury meat or chicken with potatoes)
Papeta ma gosht athwa murghi (2)   233-34
(Savoury meat or chicken with potatoes)
Papeta ma kid   234-35
(Baby lamb cooked with potatoes)
Papri ma gosht athwa murghi   223
(Savoury meat or chicken with sheet beans)
Parsi style crumb chops   253
Patties
  - Kheema na pattis   252-53
    (Mince patties)
Sali ma gosht athwa murghi   225
(Savoury meat or chicken with julienned potatoes)
Sekta ni singh ma gosht athwa murghi   224-25
(Savoury meat or chicken with drumsticks)
Surti khatu ghost   232-33
(Savoury meat—Surat style)
Tamatar ma gosht athwa murghi   223
(Savoury meat or chicken with tomatoes)
Tari ma gosht athwa murghi   229-30
(Savoury meat or chicken with toddy)
Trotters (Kharia)
  - Kharia ni jelly   124-25
    (Trotter jelly)
  - Khara kharia   255-56
    (Savoury trotters)
Vagharela chawal ne murghi   237-38
(Savoury rice with chicken)
Valsadi Dodhi ma gosht   226-27
(Savoury meat with marrow—Valsad style)
Vatena ma gosht athwa murghi   223
(Savoury meat or chicken with green peas)
Vengna ma gosht athwa murghi   225
(Savoury meat or chicken with aubergines)
Vengana ni buriani   235-36
(Savoury meat and aubergine stew)

Vindaloo   239
(Meat cooked with spiced vinegar—Goan style)

PICKLES (ACHARS)

Baffena   374-75
(Mango pickle with mustard)
Colmi nu achar   377
(Prawn pickle)
Gajer nu achar   373
(Carrot pickle)
Gharab nu achar   375-76
(Fish roe pickle)
Gor keri nu achar   373-74
(Mango and jaggery pickle)
Gosht nu achar   379
(Lamb pickle)
Lagan athwa meva nu achar   371-72
(Wedding or dry fruit pickle)
Leebu nu achar—Navsari style   370
(Lime pickle from Navsari)
Masala ni sukhi machhi no achar   377-78
(Dried fish pickle)
Methia nu achar   372
(Mango pickle with fenugreek)
Pani nu achar   370-71
(Raw mango pickle in brine)
Sukhi gharub nu achhar   378
(Dry fish roe pickle)
Taji sardine nu achar   376
(Fresh sardine pickle)

PRESERVES (MURAMBAS)

Baelfruit murambo   386
(Woodapple preserve)
Kora no murambo (1)   387-88
(Ash gourd preserve)

Kora no murambo (2)   388
(Ash gourd preserve)
Mango preserve
  - Kachi keri no murambo   388-89
    (Raw mango preserve)
  - Kapeli keri no murambo   386-87
    (Sliced mango preserve)
Naspati no murambo   389
(Naspati pear preserve)
Peach no murambo   390
(Peach preserve)

RICE (CHAWAL)

Bafela chawal   287-88
  (Boiled rice)
Conji   288-89
Khara rus chawal   236-37
  (Savoury meat or chicken gravy with rice)
Khichdi
  - Aek tapeli ma khichdi ne patio   298-99
    (Khichdi and patio cooked in one pan)
  - Bafeli khichdi   290-91
    (Yellow rice with dal—boiled)
  - Bharuchi vaghareli khichi   294-95
    (Savoury khichdi—Bharuch style)
  - Che dar ni khichdi   291-92
    (Khichdi with six dals)
  - Colmi ni khichdi   297
    (Khichdi with prawns)
  - Eeda ne paneer ni khichdi   296-97
    (Khichdi with eggs and cream cheese)
  - Masala ni khichdi   295-96
    (Spiced khichdi)
  - Pochi or Malidar khichdi   291
    (Soft khichdi)
  - Vagharela khichdi   292-93

(Savoury khichdi)
Parsi pulao   299-300
(Savoury rice cooked with meat or chicken)
Pish pash   289
Vagharela chawal   290
(Brown rice)

SHERBETS

Baelfruit sherbet   391
(Woodapple sherbet)
Gulab no sherbet   390
(Rose sherbet)

SPICES (MASALAS)

Basic garam masala   96
Bharuchi curry powder   99-100
Bharuchi garam masala   96-97
Complete curry powder   98-99
Dhan sakh masala   97
Murcha ni bhukhi   96
(Chilli powder)
Sambhar no masala   98
(Sambhar spices)
Traditional Valsad masala (dry)   100
Traditional Valsad masala (green)   100-01

SWEETS (METHAI)

Ariso   352
Audh   359
Barfi
   - Badam ni barfi   354
Chickee
   - Copra ni chickee   358
     (Coconut toffee)
Custer   351

(Parsi baked custard)
Doodh na puff   123-24
(Milk froth)
Doodh pava   347
(Pressed rice pudding)
Ghau nu doodh   94
Goolkund   352
Jalebi   355-56
Kharia ni jelly   124-25
(Trotter Jelly)
Kheer
  - Kheer   353
    (Rice pudding)
  - Santra ni kheer   353
    (Milk pudding with oranges)
Kulfi
  - Kulfi   348
  - Mango kulfi   348-49
Larva   356-57
Malai na khaja   360-61
(Cream filled pastry)
Meethu dhai   346
(Sweet curds)
Mehsoor   357
Pakhs
  - Badam pakh   361-62
  - Copra pakh   358-59
  - Doodh pakh   354
  - Eeda pakh   362-63
  - Pasta pakh   362
  - Soonth   363-64
  - Suva pakh   364-65
Ravo   344-45
(Semolina pudding)
Sev   345-46
(Vermicelli)

Soufflés
- Mango soufflé   349-50
- John's Byculla soufflé   350-51

Sweet poori   360

Vanilla ice cream   347-48

Vasanu   365-66

TABLE OF MEASURES 101-03

TEA-TIME SNACKS

Batata poori   334-35
(Flat poori with potato topping)

Bhajia
- Bhajia   330
  (Batter fried vegetables)
- Kooto athwa colmi na bhajia   331
  (Batter fried small shrimps)
- Tarkari na bhajia   331-32
  (Batter fried vegetables)

Bhakra   315
(Parsi doughnuts)

Bhakra with toddy   315-16
(Parsi doughnuts)

Bhel poori   332-34

Biscuits
- Khara batasa   313-14
- Khari biscot   312-13
  (Savoury puff pastry biscuits)
- Nankhatai   314
  (Shortbread biscuits)
- S rewsbury biscuits   312

Chapat   316-17
(Parsi pancake)

Choora   336-37
(Savoury pressed rice)

Dar ni pori   323-24
(Cakes stuffed with lentils)
Ganthia   337-38
(Savoury gram flour strips)
Hariso   319
Karvai   320-21
(Banana fritters)
Kera na kerkeria   322
(Banana fritters)
Kerkeria   321
(Fritters)
Khajoor ni ghari   324-25
(Date filled pastry)
Khaman na larva   322-23
(Rice dumplings with grated coconut)
Kharo ravo   336
(Savoury semolina)
Kumas   317
(Semolina cake)
Malido
  - Meherbai gorani no malido   325-26
  - Meva no malido   326-27
Paneer
  - Paneer   327-28
   (Cream cheese)
  - Topli na paneer   328
   (Cottage cheese made in small baskets)
Papri   327
Patrel   328-29
Popatji   319-20
(Yeast or toddy batter fried fritters)
Sadhna   318-19
(Steamed cakes made with toddy)
Saria   338-39
(Rice crackers)
Varad vara   339

(Parsi wedding cakes)

VEGETABLES (TARKARI)

Ambakalia
  - Ambakalio (1)   171
    (Fresh mango cooked in syrup)
  - Ambakalio (2)   172
    (Fresh mango cooked in syrup)
  - Bharuchi ambakalio   172
    (Fresh mango cooked in syrup—Bharuchi style)
Aubergines (Vengna)
  - Raveya vengna   164
    (Stuffed aubergines)
  - Tarela papeta ne vengna   156
    (Fried potatoes with aubergines)
  - Tarela vengna   162-63
    (Fried aubergines)
  - Vengana ne dhai ni buriani   164-65
    (Savoury aubergine stew with curd)
  - Vengna ne tooria no patio   168
    (Aubergine and courgette patio)
  - Vengna nu bhurtu   163
    (Dry roasted aubergines)
Banana (Kera)
  - Kera nu raitu   175
    (Banana and curd salad)
  - Tarela kera   169-70
    (Fried bananas)
Bhaji dana   150-51
(Savoury green peas and fenugreek leaves)
Capsicum (Mota murcha)
  - Koru ne mota murcha   160
    (Yellow pumpkin with capsicum)
  - Papeta ne mota murcha   156
    (Savoury potatoes and capsicum)

Chas paialo kan   172-73
   (Sweet potato or yam in syrup)
Courgette (Toori)
   - Khara tooria   166
     (Savoury courgettes)
   - Vengna ne tooria no patio   168
     (Aubergine and courgette patio)
Curries
   - Cocum curry   176-77
   - Guava ni curry   177-78
     (Guava curry)
Custer na cutlets   170-71
(Savoury custard cutlets)
Drumsticks (Sekta ni sing)
   - Nariel na doodh ma papeta ne sekta ni singh   155
     (Potatoes and drumsticks cooked in coconut milk)
   - Tari ma sekta ni singh   165-66
     (Drumsticks cooked in toddy)
Gobi ni salad   174
(Cabbage salad)
Gor amli nu doru   173
(Sweet and sour sauce to serve with khichdi)
Kachumber
   - Dhai kachumber   176
     (Curd kachumber)
   - Gor amli nu kachumber   176
     (Jaggery and tamarind kachumber)
   - Kachumber   175
Kharu dodhi   159
(Savoury marrow)
Khatu meethu estew   166-67
(Sweet and sour stew)
Kudhis
   - Chhas ni kudhi   180-81
     (Buttermilk kadhi)
   - Dhai ni kudhi   179

(Curd kudhi)
- Keri ni rus ni kudhi (1)   181-82
  (Mango juice kudhi)
- Keri ni rus ni kudhi (2)   182-83
  (Mango juice kudhi)
- Tari ni kudhi   181
  (Toddy kudhi)
- Valsadi dhai ni kudhi   179-80
  (Curd kudhi—Valsad style)

Okras (Bheeda)
- Dhai ma bheeda   162
  (Okras cooked with curd)
- Khara bheeda   161-62
  (Savoury okras)
- Tarela bheeda (1)   160
  (Fried okras)
- Tarela bheeda (2)   161
  (Fried okras)

Patio
- Vengna ne tooria no patio   168
  (Aubergine and courgette patio)

Potatoes (Papeta)
- How to make perfect wafers and sali   94
- Khara papeta   152-53
  (Savoury potatoes)
- Nareil na doodh ma papeta ne sekta ni sing   155
  (Potatoes and drumsticks cooked in coconut milk)
- Papeta na pattis   156-57
  (Potato patties)
- Papeta ne mota murcha   156
  (Savoury potatoes and capsicum)
- Papeta ne vatena ni sookhi tarkari   154-55
  (Savoury dry potato and green peas)
- Papeta ni tarkari   151-52
  (Savoury potatoes)
- Papeta nu salnu   154

(Savoury potatoes)
  - Tarela papeta ne vengna   156
  (Fried potatoes with aubergines)
Pumpkin (Koru)
  - Kharu koru   159
  (Savoury pumpkin)
  - Koru ne mota murcha   160
  (Yellow pumpkin with capsicum)
  - Kora nu doru   174
  (Sweet and sour pumpkin sauce)
Raitu
  - Kera nu raitu   175
  (Banana and curd salad)
  - Raitu   175
  (Curd based salad)
Sas
  - Dhai tamatar no sas   169
  (Hot sweet and sour sauce with curd and tomatoes)
Vegetable jalebi   157-58

List of References

1. *Religious Ceremonies and Customs of The Parsees*, Dr Sir J J Mody.
2. *The Parsis*, Pillo Nanavati.
3. *The Parsees in India*, E C K Chand Kalke.
4. *History of The Parsis*, D F Karaka.
5. *Zorastrian Civilization*, M N Dhalla.
6. *History of the Persian Empire*, A T Ohnstead.
7. *The Heritage of Persia*, Richard N Frye.
8. *Vivid Vani*, Mrs Meherbai J N Wadia.